BEN JONSON
AND THE ROMAN FRAME OF MIND

BEN JONSON
AND THE
ROMAN
FRAME OF MIND

Katharine Eisaman Maus

PRINCETON UNIVERSITY PRESS
PRINCETON, NEW JERSEY

Copyright © 1984 by Princeton University Press
Published by Princeton University Press, 41 William Street,
Princeton, New Jersey 08540
In the United Kingdom:
Princeton University Press, Guildford, Surrey

All Rights Reserved

Library of Congress Cataloging in Publication Data will be
found on the last printed page of this book

ISBN 0-691-06629-9

Publication of this book has been aided by a grant from the
Henry A. Laughlin Fund of Princeton University Press

This book has been composed in Linotron Bembo

Clothbound editions of Princeton University Press books
are printed on acid-free paper, and binding materials are
chosen for strength and durability

Printed in the United States of America
by Princeton University Press
Princeton, New Jersey

For
FRED MAUS

CONTENTS

ACKNOWLEDGMENTS

IT IS A PLEASURE to record here my gratitude to many friends and colleagues. Stephen Orgel was an immensely helpful supervisor of the dissertation from which this book evolved. Walter Cohen, Lawrence Danson, Stanley Fish, Seth Lerer, Earl Miner, David Sachs, and Barry Weller read the manuscript in various stages of revision and offered numerous intelligent suggestions. Thomas Roche kindly arranged for me to present a lecture on Jonson before a perceptive audience at the 1983 Modern Language Association convention. Anne Barton allowed me to see parts of her own manuscript-in-progress. Steven Shankman puzzled with me over a difficult passage in Horace. Michael Frede's graduate seminar on *De finibus*, and Fred Maus's forthright, careful comments upon early drafts of the book, gave me some sense of how a trained philosopher would deal with texts I was approaching from a somewhat different angle.

Institutions as well as individuals have been supportive. The Johns Hopkins University, where I began this project, and Princeton University, where I finished it, both provided me with highly congenial intellectual environments. A summer research grant from the Surdna Foundation, and a Fellowship for Independent Study and Research from the National Endowment for the Humanities, have given me the time I needed to complete the book.

BEN JONSON
AND THE ROMAN FRAME OF MIND

I

Introduction: Jonson's Classics

BEN JONSON is a "classical" artist: "not onely a professed Imitator of *Horace*," as Dryden says, "but a learned Plagiary of all the others; you track him every where in their Snow."[1] "All the others" is really an overstatement; for while Jonson's reading in Greek and Latin literature is remarkably varied and wide-ranging, certain texts inevitably attract him more than others. His favorite authors are Latin ones, and a select group of Latin ones at that: Seneca, Horace, Tacitus, Cicero, Juvenal, Quintilian, and a few others. These are the writers he continually quotes and paraphrases, recommends to friends and readers, cites as authorities or precedents, and in a couple of cases portrays on the stage. This book will explore some of the consequences of such preferences—of this particular brand of classicism—upon Jonson's art, and upon his conception of himself as an artist.

Jonson's tastes are not unorthodox. "His" classics are central to Renaissance European humanist culture, and in sixteenth- and seventeenth-century England they form the basis of the curriculum for grammar-school children as well as for university students.[2] From such humanist forebears and contemporaries as Petrarch, Erasmus, Juan Luis Vives, Justus Lipsius, William Camden, Daniel Heinsius, Isaac Casaubon—the learned men Jonson considers his intellectual compeers—he inherits not only a regard for particular Latin texts, but more important, examples of serious lifelong engagement with classical literature. Naturally the way Jonson reads and responds to the classics is conditioned by the way these great editors, commentators, and educators have approached and defined them. He shares that distinctive, complex humanist view of the classics, contradictory in theory but powerful in practice, which acknowledges the historical and cultural remoteness of ancient writers, even while insisting upon their extraordinary relevance for the contemporary world.[3] He boasts, for instance, of his scrupulous adherence to Roman sources in *Poetaster*, *Sejanus*, and *Catiline*; of the care he has taken to avoid anachronism and to depict accurately an alien culture. But this conscious antiquarianism coincides, in *Poetaster*, with a polemic against the enemy playwrights, Thomas Dekker and John Marston; in *Sejanus*, with political commentary pointed enough to get Jonson in trouble with the authorities; in *Catiline*, with what are probably reflections on the Gunpowder Plot. Jonson derives from his humanist intellectual milieu, then, the crucial assumption upon which his classicism depends—the conviction that thorough immersion in a lost culture is a prerequisite for comprehension of, and contribution to, one's own culture.

On the other hand, it would be wrong to suppose that Jonson's literary biases are inevitable ones for an educated person in his time and place. His tastes, though unexceptionable, do not simply duplicate those of his contemporaries. He fails to share, for example, the enthusiasm for Ovid which so marks the work of Edmund Spenser, Christopher Marlowe, William Shakespeare, and John Donne. While his estimation of Virgil is conventionally high, the *Georgics* and the *Aeneid* do not excite his imagination as they excite Spenser's or Milton's. Nor does Jonson's friendship with George Chapman kindle a serious interest in Homer, or in Platonic philosophy.

What are the principles governing Jonson's selectivity? His favorite authors practice a wide variety of literary modes: satire, ode, epistle, history. Stylistically, too, they are very diverse. Cicero, with his flowing periods and smooth transitions, in some ways seems to occupy the opposite end of the prose spectrum from the abrupt, aphoristic Seneca; and certainly in the sixteenth and seventeenth centuries some authorities insisted upon the exclusive propriety of one or the

4

other as models for Latin prose.[4] The humanists Jonson finds most congenial, however—such writers as Erasmus and Vives—polemicize not for "Ciceronianism" or for "Senecanism," but for a catholicity which, they point out, Cicero and Seneca themselves recommended.[5] For in fact, as many of the humanists realize, the dispute over style can obscure the very considerable similarities of doctrinal emphasis among the Latin writers they value most.

The writers that constitute the core of the Jonsonian canon, in other words, share a general philosophical outlook, sometimes elaborately articulated, sometimes only implied. Typically they are, or at least claim to be, ethically serious writers. The virtues they most appreciate are often austere ones: temperance, self-reliance, fortitude, altruistic self-sacrifice. Their commitment to community life is strong, and their sense of Roman history lively and patriotic. These "Roman moralists" are philosophically well-educated, but eclectic on principle. They assimilate what seems true or useful from the major philosophical schools of the day—Stoic, Epicurean, Peripatetic, Skeptic. Meanwhile they ignore, discard, or ridicule the sometimes extreme and improbable conclusions that their more rigorously logical Greek forebears had shown to follow from apparently innocuous premises.

The mainly ethical nature of the Roman moralists' philosophical interests considerably simplifies their synthetic endeavor. Even for writers like Cicero and Seneca, certain important issues seem peripheral—the epistemological quarrels between the Stoics and the skeptical New Academy, for instance, or the metaphysical disagreements between the Peripatetics and the Epicureans. The less deliberately "philosophical" among the Roman moralists, like Horace and Juvenal, ignore such problems altogether. Moreover, even when the Roman moralists deal with the relatively narrow range of philosophical issues they consider significant, they are remarkably undogmatic. The nature of divinity, the immortality of the soul, the value of asceticism, the relation of political expediency to virtuous action, the desirability of popular acclaim—the Roman moralists disagree among themselves about such matters, and the same author may resolve them in different ways at different times.[6] Nonetheless, the Roman moralists' eclecticism follows certain distinctive patterns. They are eager to apply their intellect and sensibility in practical ways, to put the contemplative faculties at the service of the active life. They want to weld philosophy and forensics, literature and pedagogy, integrity and urbanity.

THESE Roman ideals appeal strongly to many Renaissance humanists. The humanists' ethical emphasis, their preference for rhetorical effectiveness and formal beauty over logical rigor, their responsiveness to the educational, literary, and political needs of a secular governing class—all receive reinforcement from the Roman moralist example.[7] Moreover, the circumstances of Jonson's career render him sensitive not merely to Roman ideals in the abstract, but to the ways in which his favorite classical authors have realized those ideals in their own lives. His particular literary preferences are understandable in biographical as well as intellectual terms.

For Jonson as for most of his English and Continental contemporaries, a successful literary career depends upon the generosity of patrons.[8] But Jonson, former bricklayer's apprentice and convicted murderer, has reason to feel particularly keenly the anomalous character of his intimacy with wealth and power. He lives with Lord Aubigny and at Penshurst; he is awarded pensions from King James and the Earl of Pembroke; he becomes friendly with the Countesses of Bedford and Rutland. His social triumphs, however, do not translate into economic security. "Sundry times," William Drummond informs us in the *Conversations*, "he heth devoured his books [and] sold them all for Necessity" (328-329). Unlike Shakespeare, whose prudent investments make him a wealthy gentleman in his own right, or Donne, who eventually accepts ecclesiastical preferment, Jonson never acquires an extraliterary source of income or prestige. "He dissuaded me from Poetrie," Drummond reports, "for that she had beggered him, when he might have been a rich lawyer, Physitian, or Marchant" (615-616). In the *Discoveries*, Jonson bitterly personifies Poetry as

> but a meane *Mistresse*, to such as have wholly addicted themselves to her, or given their names up to her family. They who have but saluted her on the by, and now and then tendred their visits, shee hath done much for, and advanced in the way of their owne professions (both the *Law*, and the *Gospel*) beyond all they could have hoped, or done for themselves, without her favour. Wherein she doth emulate the judicious, but preposterous bounty of the times *Grandes*: who accumulate all they can upon the *Parasite*, or *Fresh-man* in their friendship; but thinke an old Client, or honest servant, bound by his place to write, and starve.[9]

Poetry, with her ambiguous charity to those who "have but saluted her on the by, and now and then tendred their visits," seems a mistress both in the social and the sexual sense, who supports and advances those who know how to satisfy her own dubious inclinations. Given the economic realities of authorship in the Renaissance, the connection between the artist and the servant or client seems a natural one. Elsewhere, too, Jonson associates inventiveness with dependency, and with the subordination of one's own desires to another's. The highly charged economic and psychological intimacy between a creative servant and his patron dominates the action of plays otherwise as diverse as *Every Man in His Humour*, *Cynthia's Revels*, *Poetaster*, *Sejanus*, *Volpone*, and *The Alchemist*. In every case, though the master needs the servant's executive talents, the servant can never obtain real power of his own. Sejanus and Mosca fail when they forget the actual terms of the relationship; Brainworm and Jeremy succeed by remaining aware of its limitations and appealing to their masters' interests.

Not all economic dependency, of course, need seem merely

arbitrary or unfair. In the *Discoveries* Jonson finds it possible to imagine an ideal reciprocity of benefits between the poet or scholar and the wealthy, powerful people who support him.

> Learning needs rest: Soveraignty gives it. Soveraignty needs counsell: Learning affords it. There is such a Consociation of offices, between the *Prince*, and whom his favour breeds, that they may helpe to sustaine his power, as hee their knowledge. (65-69)

Sometimes Jonson seems to have thought of his "consociation" with James I in these terms; and his relations with his less exalted patrons can appear even more rewarding. In "To Penshurst" Jonson celebrates the household of Sir Robert Sidney, brother of the late poet. Sir Robert, himself undistinguished, maintains the Sidney connection with the arts by supporting Ben Jonson, the best poet he can find. What Philip Sidney could do alone—combine in himself the advantages of literary genius and aristocratic status—Robert Sidney and Jonson can achieve together through a version of the alliance Jonson describes between "Soveraignty" and "Learning."

Yet the equality Jonson implies, in the carefully balanced clauses of the *Discoveries* passage, seems unstable even in "To Penshurst." Jonson pictures the centripetal energies of Sidney's estate converging upon the manor house—partridges, fish, fruit, and other delicacies virtually thrust themselves upon their master; farmers laden with agricultural bounty troop in to "salute / [Their] lord, and lady, though they have no sute." Once inside the great house, however, we confront not the aristocratic proprietors, as we expect, but Jonson himself, gorging himself at table "As if thou, then, wert mine, or I raign'd here." It is an ambiguous moment, because Sidney's superlative hospitality constitutes both a favor and a temptation for his dependent. Jonson would be ungrateful if he failed to appreciate Sidney's gracious reversal of social roles. But he would also be ungrateful if he took the reversal at face value, forgetting the derivative and provisional character of those privileges. So while acknowledging the attractions of mastery, Jonson phrases his displacement of his host in carefully conditional form. He usurps the center stage, and then turns his usurpation into a compliment to his patron's generosity. Of course Jonson's motives differ from Mosca's or Jeremy's; but he shares their talent for adroitly managing his own repressed competitiveness, for making gestures that covertly challenge the powerful, even while they gratify them.

Given Jonson's acute consciousness of his peculiar social position, it is surely significant that the Latin authors he translates, adapts, and imitates are men whose careers roughly resemble his own. Formative for all the Roman moralists is a movement in boyhood or young manhood from provincial towns to Rome, where they become intimate with members of powerful elites. Seneca and Quintilian hail from Spain, Cicero from Arpinum, Juvenal from Aquinum, Horace from Venusia. In some cases social disabilities compound the original geographical marginality; Horace is the son of a former slave, and Cicero is the first of his family to achieve consular rank.

> You will say of me that, born of a freedman father and
> in mean circumstances,
> I extended wings greater than the nest
> . . . .
> That I pleased the most important people in the state
> Both in war and in peace.[10]

Horace, describing his flight from narrow circumstances into privileged eminence, charts the typical Roman moralist trajectory. At some point in their lives almost all these Latin writers are among the foremost men of their age. In the course of a brilliant career as a lawyer and politician, Cicero is elected to the consulship, the highest republican office. Horace becomes the protégé of the emperor Augustus and Augustus' minister Maecenas. Quintilian, the head of Rome's principal school of oratory, is granted pensions by the emperors Galba and Vespasian, and instructs Domitian's nephews. Seneca, an eminent lawyer, becomes tutor of the young Nero, and during his pupil's minority one of the two most powerful administrators in the empire. Tacitus, another highly successful lawyer, holds numerous important political offices.

This shared experience stamps the Roman moralists' work indelibly even when they suffer reverses later in life. Though they by no means subscribe to identical political, social, or artistic principles, and though the actual circumstances under which they compose their works are often inauspicious, their hard-won success uniquely qualifies them in their own eyes as spokesmen for the best aspects of Roman culture. Cicero makes the analogy between his political role and his cultural role explicit in *De finibus*: "Just as I do not seem to myself to have shirked labors, dangers, or public service in the position in which I was placed by the Roman people, so I surely ought to strive as zealously as I can to make my fellow-citizens more learned."[11] This distinctive self-conception separates the Roman writers Jonson favors from those who, like Ovid, cultivate the sensibilities of exile, the voice of exclusion.

For Renaissance men of letters, and particularly for those of undistinguished birth, the Roman moralists' upward mobility and politico-cultural centrality seem potently attractive precedents. "Neither are the truly valorous or any way virtuous ashamed of their so mean parentage," writes Henry Peacham, Jonson's contemporary,

> but rather glory in themselves that their merit hath advanced them above so many thousands far better descended. . . . Cicero was born and brought up at Arpinum, a poor and obscure village; Virgil, the son of a potter; Horace, of a trumpeter; Theophrastus, of a botcher; with infinite others I might allege as well of ancient as of modern times.[12]

Horace and Cicero, in their autobiographical remarks, cast themselves as the heroes of a perennially appealing kind of story, which by Roman times already had a long history of apocryphal application to various Greek sculptors and painters: the story of a gifted youth of undistinguished origins, whose astounding talent brings him to the attention of appreciative, powerful men, and translates him eventually into a far higher social sphere.[13] In the Renaissance, Giorgio Vasari tells such tales of Giotto, Caravaggio, and others; Justus Lipsius, in his biographies of Seneca and Tacitus, plays down his subjects' inherited wealth and status presumably in order to make their success seem more astonishing.[14] Jonson makes both the lowborn Horace and the "upstart" Cicero dramatic heroes, and displays them in *Poetaster* and *Catiline* at the pinnacles of their respective careers. His detractors—like Thomas Dekker, who mocks his Horatian pretensions in *Satiro-Mastix*—were very likely right to perceive a strong personal investment in his choice of protagonists.

THE fact that the Roman moralists are self-made men, or at least like to think of themselves as self-made men, affects their outlook in important ways. They are naturally interested in methods of obtaining position and prestige, in the means by which an outsider prepares himself to excel as an insider. Cicero's oratorical treatises and Quintilian's *Institutiones* describe the education of individuals headed for powerful or influential positions. To all the Roman moralists, proper schooling seems absolutely crucial: living well, speaking well, and writing well require the acquisition and deployment of certain kinds of knowledge. They typically minimize the distinction between learned skills and natural faculties—not for them the untutored genius or the naive saint. Even virtue itself, claims Quintilian, "although it originates in a natural impulse, must be perfected by instruction."[15] Cicero and Quintilian give young rhetoricians, and Seneca provides aspiring philosophers, the same advice Horace dispenses to poets in the *Ars poetica*:

11

Neither study without abundant talent,
nor genius without education seems much use to me;
each
demands the aid of the other, and they join together as
friends.
The man who, running a race, strives to reach the
desired goal,
has endured and performed much as a boy: has
sweated and shivered,
and abstained from wine and sex. The man at the
Pythian games who plays
the flute learned it beforehand, and once stood in awe
of a teacher.[16]

Like the other Roman moralists, Horace conceives of creative virtuosity as the result of sustained practice, a period of preparation that could well take years. It is a conception that inevitably places less emphasis upon the performance or created object itself, formally considered, than upon artistry as the testimony of a rigorous apprenticeship.

Jonson, who uses the word "labored" as a term of praise and risks the derision of his contemporaries for calling his plays "works," subscribes with enthusiasm to the Roman moralists' notion of the creative enterprise. He shares their interest in development and preparation: "*A Poeme*," he writes, defining the term in *Discoveries*, "is the worke of the Poet; the end, and fruit of his labour, and studye" (2375-2376). The prologues and prefaces to his plays do not so much entice audiences with accounts of what is to follow, as they inform us of what has preceded the performance. We learn of the author's plans and intentions, the rules to which he has adhered, the kinds of spectators he has imagined himself addressing in his play, and the length of time he has spent writing it.

Jonson's aesthetic is thus, in a sense, profoundly antiformalist. His favored word "work" itself ambiguously suggests both product and process—or rather a product that can be understood only in terms of the way it has been made. His elaborate compositional histories often necessarily verge on autobiography, and Jonson seems even more eager than his Roman predecessors to stress the intimacy between self and work.

> Who casts to write a living line, must sweat,
> (Such as thine are) and strike the second heat
> Upon the *Muses* anvile: turne the same,
> (And himselfe with it) that he thinkes to frame.
> ("To the Memory of My Beloved, the Author,
> Mr. William Shakespeare . . . ," 59-62)

Jonson purposely obscures the difference between the living line and the live poet, who "frames" himself and his poetry on the same anvil, with the same artful blows.

Jonson likewise takes the Roman appreciation of creative labor to new lengths in this passage. The impression of extraordinary strenuousness here is partly a result of the slightly skewed word order and the retrospective pun on "casts," which forces the reader to double back, to perform himself some counterpart to authorial revision. But Jonson's very rigorous construal of the poetic process also contributes to the sense of difficulty and effort. The sweat of Horace's athlete, the timidity of his young musician, are phenomena the aristocratic recipients of the *Ars poetica* would have recalled from their own boyhood. The wellborn artist does not compromise his class identity when he engages in these forms of exercise. The efforts of Jonson's blacksmith have a different social resonance.[17] The objects he makes may be beautiful and useful, but his labor is devoid of glamor. The relationship between that labor and the finished work of art differ, too, in Horace and Jonson. Horace envisions a period of self-denial and subjugation eventually culminating in effortless virtuosity. By the time his performers distinguish themselves in public their years of trial are behind them, and Horace refers to their mortifications in the past tense: "sweated," "shivered," "abstained." Jonson's blacksmith, by contrast,

13

labors not only in youth but for a lifetime. Casting, striking, and sweating are present-tense verbs in "To Shakespeare." Art never becomes easy, and the artist looks forward to no gratifying moment of self-display or applause. Toil is not merely a preparation for the creative process, but its true essence.

JONSON and many of his contemporaries admire the way the Roman moralists acquire political and cultural authority, and they desire to emulate them; they share the Roman desire to be of service to a secular power.[18] Intimacy with the mighty, however, is no less perilous in Renaissance England than in late republican or imperial Rome. The recoil of such poets as Thomas Wyatt, George Gascoigne, and Walter Raleigh against the transience and superficiality of life at court derives not merely from the availability of various traditional *topoi*, but also from personal experience with instability and injustice.

The natural impulse under such circumstances is to find some locus of refuge, some factor immune to destructive flux. As Cicero, no stranger to sudden reversals of fortune, writes in the *Tusculan Disputations*: "None of the things upon which a happy life depends ought to dry up, die out, or decay. For he who fears the destruction of such things cannot be happy."[19] Socially and geographically uprooted, the Roman moralists cannot find the stability they seek in local rituals, or in familial connections or prerogatives, or even in the reassuring presence of a native landscape. Nor would the Christian method of coping with frightening mutability—a faith in otherworldly permanence—seem plausible to the Romans even if it were available to them.

Instead, the Roman moralists tend to seize upon the self as the factor that persists through changing circumstances. In an unpredictable world, personal identity seems comfortingly continuous and inalienable. One of Jonson's poetic personae, paraphrasing Seneca and Horace, suggests some of the relief of this discovery.

14

Nor for my peace will I goe farre,
  As wandrers doe, that still doe roame,
But make my strengths, such as they are,
  Here in my bosome, and at home.[20]

The Roman moralists are clearly well situated to appreciate
a philosophy like Stoicism, which claims that all one's inalienable resources lie within oneself and that, properly understood, those resources are sufficient to sustain the genuinely
happy life. Indeed, one of the most striking similarities among
Jonson's favorite authors is their willingness to subscribe, if
not to the rigors of the orthodox Greek school, at least to
some dilute and worldly-wise version of the same doctrine.[21]
By contrast the Epicureans, who associate happiness with
pleasure, seem to most of the Roman moralists to rely dan-
gerously upon forms of gratification that can only be provided from without. So, to a lesser extent, do the Peripatetic
followers of Aristotle, who maintain that even a virtuous
man needs certain gifts of fortune—good birth, health, progeny, financial security—to be entirely happy.

The Roman moralists are not so naive as to think that the
self is *automatically* a source of stability. It must be cultivated,
fortified, weaned from external things, and convinced of its
actual self-sufficiency. The Roman moralists are following
the Stoics when they maintain that a desire for the benefits
conferred by fortune is ultimately based upon a mistaken sense
of personal identity, a false idea that the value of the self is
somehow dependent upon external goods. "You're no divinity," as Juvenal tells Fortune. "It's we who make you a god-
dess, and put you in the sky."[22] Quite foolishly, people esteem themselves not for strength of character, or for their
capacity for virtuous action, but for contingent things like
wealth or political success. Then if for some reason circumstances work against them—the wealth vanishes or a political
reversal puts them out of office—their sense of self crumbles,
and they feel personally annihilated. Even if nothing of the
kind ever comes to pass, the unstable foundation of their

15

lives keeps them in a state of constant anxiety and uncertainty. "To wonder at nothing is practically the one and only thing . . . that can make and keep one happy," writes Horace to his friend Numicius.[23] This does not mean that the Greek Stoics, or the Roman moralists, reject wealth, health, or other advantages if they come their way. They employ the gifts of fortune in the service of virtue when they have them, but they do not regret the lack of such advantages either. "A man, therefore, who is temperate, stable, without fear, without sorrow, without any kind of eagerness, without desire, is he not happy?" asks Cicero.[24] Once one realizes that happiness is to be found in the exercise of virtue, and that pleasure is not only irrelevant but positively militates against a happy life, nothing need disturb one's self-contained tranquillity of mind.

Without requiring a prior belief in any elaborate supernatural system, the Stoics are able to make happiness wholly dependent upon the moral status of the individual, and entirely separate from circumstances over which he can have no control. The accidental afflictions borne by good men, and the undeserved success enjoyed by bad men, no longer seem unjust, for the rewards of fortune are deceptive and inadequate. "By no greater means can God disgrace coveted objects," writes Seneca, "than by granting them to the worst people, and withholding them from the best."[25] Everyone gets his just deserts, once those deserts are correctly understood.

Thus the Roman moralists' attitude toward their own careers is complex, even contradictory at times. Their very ambitiousness makes them aware of the limits of that ambition, the ultimately ungratifying nature of financial and social advancement pursued as ends in themselves. Many talented Renaissance writers both in England and on the Continent, finding their own lives blighted and whole societies thrown into turmoil by civil wars, religious revolutions, plagues, and other calamities, exhibit the same apparently paradoxical attraction to and repulsion from the possibility of worldly success. If they are at all alert to their surroundings they recognize the precariousness of even the apparently most stable prosperity; if their desire for advancement is frustrated they have all the more reason to turn inward, to achieve mastery and freedom where they can by cultivating the resources of the self. In the first book of *De constantia*, the influential neo-Stoic Lipsius claims to have been driven to philosophy as a way of coping with the devastation of his native Flanders. Guillaume du Vair, in the *Traité de la Constance*, represents himself discovering the comforts of Stoicism while suffering through the siege of Paris.

Jonson, too, inherits the Roman moralists' esteem for Stoic ethics, and in fact emphasizes the Stoic aspects of authors he admires. Martial, in the preface to his witty, often scurrilous epigrams, jocularly warns the severe Cato away in advance. But when Jonson adapts Martial's poetic techniques to English subjects, he pointedly welcomes the Stoics among his readers: "In my *Theater* . . . CATO, if he liv'd, might enter without scandall."[26] Jonson takes Horace as a personal and artistic model; but during the first two-thirds of his career, the period of his most significant accomplishment, he imitates Horace the moral satirist and not the wanton, self-deprecatory Horace of the *Odes*. Like Lipsius and du Vair, Jonson recoils, in some moods, from what seems the overwhelming viciousness and confusion of the external world:

> I'le bid thee looke no more, but flee, flee friend,
> This *Praecipice*, and Rocks that have no end,
> Or side, but threatens Ruine.
>> ("An Epistle to a Friend, to Persuade
>> Him to the Wars," 129-131)

Under these circumstances the Stoic impulse takes a paranoid form, a defense of the self against constant threats of incursion or disruption.[27] In happier situations, however, what Jonson calls "the gathered self," in his epigram to Thomas Roe, can become an ideal of balance and sureness in one's relations with one's environment, a prerequisite for, rather than an alternative to, sociability. In bad times Stoicism provides a necessary consolation; in good times it allows one to retain some sense of proportion, some means of distinguishing between what is important and what is superfluous.

THE STOIC position appeals to the Roman moralists not least because it stresses values they believe to have been characteristic of Romans in earlier, purer days: physical and emotional fortitude, civic self-sacrifice, absolute integrity, contempt for sensual indulgences. Cicero's observation at the beginning of *Tusculan Disputations* is typical: "In whom was there ever such severity, such constancy, greatness of spirit, honesty, loyalty—such excellence in every species of virtue—that might be compared with our ancestors?"[28] Cultivated Latin authors from Cicero's time to Quintilian's wish to combine Greek intellectual sophistication with Roman vigor and statesmanship. Just as Renaissance writers are educated in Latin, so Latin writers are educated in Greek, and learn to draw upon a foreign tradition not to weaken but to reinforce their own patriotism. In an important passage, Jonson declares:

> I know *Nothing* can conduce more to letters, then to examine the writings of the *Ancients*, and not to rest in their sole Authority, or take all upon trust from them. . . . For to all the observations of the *Ancients*, wee have our owne experience: which, if wee will use, and apply, wee have better meanes to pronounce. It is true they open'd the gates, and made the way, that went before us; but as Guides, not Commanders. (*Discoveries*, 129-139)

This declaration of artistic and critical independence is in fact translated from Vives, who adapts it from Quintilian and Seneca, who in turn derive it from Cicero.[29] This does not mean that Jonson is hypocritical or obtuse here—just that the retesting of traditional values in the light of contemporary experience is itself a very traditional occupation.

It is wrong, therefore, to construe the native and the classical past as inevitably competitors for Jonson's attention.[30] Indeed, the Roman moralists show him how to employ and refine the best elements in the vernacular tradition. Jonson plans an epic on the English worthies, commemorates the significant features of British national history in his masques, and imports the methods of the indigenous morality play into his own drama. In *Discoveries*, 899–920, he praises the eloquence and intelligence of great English statesmen: "*Cicero* is said to bee the only wit, that the people of *Rome* had equall'd to their *Empire*. *Ingenium par imperio*. We have had many, and in their severall Ages." Jonson singles out for praise such famous writers and speakers as Thomas More, Thomas Wyatt, Thomas Elyot, Philip Sidney, Richard Hooker, Walter Raleigh, and above all Francis Bacon, "who hath fill'd up all numbers; and perform'd that in our tongue, which may be compar'd, or preferr'd, either to insolent *Greece*, or haughty *Rome*." On one hand, a sturdy independence from the classical past seems implied by the contemptuous locution "insolent Greece, or haughty Rome." On the other hand, Cicero still looms as the obvious model against which the English must be judged; and even more tellingly Jonson adapts his description of Bacon from the Elder Seneca, who compares the talented speakers of the Ciceronian era to "insolenti Graeciae."[31] "Emulous rivalry," the phrase Richard Peterson uses to describe Jonsonian imitation of Greek and Latin authors,[32] captures nicely the combination of assimilation and competitiveness typical not only of Jonson's compositional practice but also more generally of his sense of the relation between the classics and his own art.

THE following chapters will trace the effects of the Roman moralist sensibility upon Jonson's work. They lay particular emphasis on the plays, which arguably present Jonson with his greatest intellectual and artistic challenges, but they also try to coordinate his development as a playwright with his achievement as a poet and masque author. The ambitiousness and pertinence of Roman moralist ideals clearly constitute a large part of their appeal for Jonson and for many of his contemporaries. But the same admirable qualities result as well in certain characteristic kinds of strain. When Christian philosophers boldly claim God to be all-powerful as well as all-knowing, they solve important metaphysical problems but simultaneously create others. In the same way, the Roman moralists' moments of greatest philosophical audacity often become the points at which they confront their most obvious difficulties. Thus an investigation into Jonson's literary and intellectual heritage will not necessarily abolish or resolve the traditional problems with which his readers and critics grapple. It will suggest, however, why these particular considerations should loom so large in the first place—why problems of authority and subversion, self-control and saturnalia, independence and social responsibility should fascinate Jonson so much more than, say, the emotional dynamics of unrequited love, which interest many of his contemporaries.

Together the Roman moralists pass down to Jonson a set of moral and psychological assumptions that condition the way he construes ethical, social, and artistic issues. He acquires not merely rules of conduct—"this kind of action is virtuous, that kind of action is base"—but something that underlies those rules, a special understanding of human nature and the way that nature expresses itself. He learns from the Roman moralists not only what characterizes the best forms of social intercourse, but also what makes people sociable, and how their institutions reflect their social impulses. In other words, he inherits not just a set of precepts, or a warehouse of convenient tropes, but a frame of mind that renders him especially sensitive to certain issues and dulls his awareness of others.

This book, therefore, is organized as a discussion of broad topical concerns rather than as close readings of particular works. It attempts to describe the progress of Jonson's career in terms of his changing response to certain crucial concepts. Once the nature and extent of the Roman moralist influence

is understood, various Jonsonian idiosyncrasies—his techniques of characterization, his critical stance, his bias toward
certain dramatic and poetic genres, his preference for certain
kinds of plot, his unusual relationship with his theatrical and
literary audience—all begin to seem the inseparable consequences of an inherited frame of mind.

II

Virtue and Vice:
Characterization in the Early Plays

SOME TIME before Jonson gained his reputation as the most "classical" of English dramatists, his contemporaries had already remarked upon his distinctive methods of dramatic characterization. "Monsieur Humourist," John Weever calls him in *The Whipping of the Satyre*. In *Satiro-Mastix*, Thomas Dekker imagines members of the theater audience pointing Jonson out to their friends—"That's he, that's he, that pennes and purges Humours and diseases."[1] Restoration critics and dramatists are likewise struck by Jonson's characterization. John Oldham marvels at Jonson's "universal vast Idea of Mankind," and Thomas Shadwell praises him as "the onely person that appears to me to have made perfect Representations of humane life" in the drama.[2]

For later critics, too, an assessment of Jonson's methods of characterization often proves basic to a more general evaluation of his work. The verdict, though, is usually flatly opposed to Shadwell's or Oldham's. Instead of celebrating Jonson's breadth of vision and depth of insight, eighteenth- and nineteenth-century readers ordinarily find him a narrow and superficial observer of human nature. And while modern academic critics rarely attack Jonson's notion of character with the vehemence of an Edmond Malone or a William Hazlitt, many at least implicitly accept Harry Levin's judgment that in a Jonsonian play

> its cast of characters is not its outstanding feature. Each has only his characteristic move, as in chess, and the object of the game is to see what new combinations have

been brought about. Between the abstract idea of the plot and the concrete detail of the language, there is a hiatus.[3]

Most recent critics have made the case for Jonson's greatness on the basis of other merits—the virtuosity of his dramatic and poetic idiom, the thematic appropriateness of his imagery, the incisiveness of his satire.[4] Perhaps, however, it is possible to approach Jonson's characters in some way conducive to appreciation—and if not to regain the seventeenth-century excitement in this regard, at least to recognize the grounds for that excitement. Two lines of inquiry need pursuing. First of all, what psychological and moral considerations inform Jonson's conception of character? Second, how does this understanding of human nature relate to his practice as a dramatist? Jonson's innovative "humours" characterization makes sense in terms of Roman psychological assumptions, and his experimentation during the years of the comical satires may be seen as a series of attempts to make Roman moral psychology theatrically viable. Eventually, Jonson's experience in the theater leads him to rethink not only his dramatic methods, but also the assumptions about moral thought and action which had informed those methods.

PERHAPS Jonson signals his indebtedness to the Roman moral tradition most obviously and persistently when he portrays fools and villains in the plays, masques, and poems. Many critics claim quite correctly that Jonson's conception of "humour" is far less schematic and rigorous than the Galenic psychology which was received medical wisdom in the Renaissance. Jonson exploits, rather, the popular psychological clichés of his period.[5] At the same time, however, his apparently haphazard, opportunistic use of humours psychology is perfectly consistent with the Roman moralists' approach, and even after he abandons the explicit methods of the early humours comedies, he retains the imagery they associate with folly and vice.

Cicero and Seneca, who predate Galen, derive their psychological terminology from a much less highly wrought Hippocratean theory of humours. Moreover, the general premises of this kind of psychology interest them more than its details. They are particularly intrigued by the notion that body and spirit operate according to the same principles. Seneca writes that mental disorders are produced by an imbalance among the elements in the human body; anger, for example, is caused by an oversupply of heat.[6] The Greek Stoics had believed that mental processes were in fact ultimately material ones; Cicero and Jonson more cautiously insist only that "the name of Humours . . . may, by *Metaphore*, apply it selfe / Unto the generall disposition."[7]

Whether as simple fact or as illuminating analogy, bodily dysfunction provides the Romans—and Jonson—with a vocabulary for moral and intellectual defects. The Greeks call irrational impulse *pathos*, the same word used for physical disease; the Romans use *morbus* (disease), *aegrotatio* (sickness), *vitium* (defect), *perturbatio* (disorder). And the analogy between body and soul can be extended further; philosophy, or responsible poetry, since it corrects errors and amends vices, becomes a kind of cure—"the physicke of the minde," as Asper in *Every Man Out of His Humour* translates Cicero's "animi medicina."[8] In *Cynthia's Revels*, Crites recalls one of Seneca's maxims when he is scorned by fools:

> And who'ld be angry with this race of creatures?
> What wise physician have we ever seene
> Moov'd with a franticke man? the same affects
> That he doth beare to his sicke patient,
> Should a right minde carrie to such as these.[9]

The opposite of the philosopher's "right mind" can be stupidity, ignorance, or vice—all of which are for the Roman moralists, as for many other classical philosophers, forms of diseased judgment. "What then is good?" asks Seneca. "The knowledge of things. What is bad? The ignorance of things."[10] The difference between folly and wickedness is one of degree, not of kind. Jonson may sometimes claim that comedy "sport[s] with humane follies, not with crimes,"[11] but the comical satires, the tragedies, and the great comedies of mid-career—*Volpone, Epicene, The Alchemist,* and *Bartholomew Fair*—transgress or eliminate the boundaries between silliness and pathology, folly and vice.

Other associations yield a distinct but equally apposite cluster of descriptive metaphors. "Humour" is originally a fluid bodily substance; the image of irrational impulse as a liquid appeals greatly to the Roman moralists. *Permadescere* (to render sodden) is one of Seneca's more expressive words for the effect of pleasure on the mind.[12] *Fluere* (to flow) is a verb that all the Roman moralists associate with vice. "They float with the current; they do not proceed, but are carried away," writes Seneca of men who have not yet attained to virtuous philosophical stability.[13] The soul succumbs to "streams of humour," a passive victim of its own excesses, like a body swept into a fast-moving river or tossed on a stormy sea. In *Catiline* Jonson's Cicero, learning of Catiline's nefarious plots, reflects that "ambition, like a torrent, ne're lookes back"; the loyal general Petreius combines metaphors of flood and disease when he calls the rebel army "all the sinke, / And plague of *Italie*, met in one torrent."[14] The subversives, far from rejecting this kind of description, positively glory in it. The perverse energy of Catiline's rhetoric largely derives from his sense of himself and his confederates as an overwhelming and disruptive elemental force:

> In your violent acts,
> The fall of torrents, and the noyse of tempests,
> The boyling of *Charybdis*, the seas wildnesse,
> The eating force of flames, and wings of winds
> Be all out-wrought, by your transcendent furies.
> (III.651–655)

Not only the violence of these floods, torrents, and tempests, but also their frightening unpredictability, makes them apt metaphors for vice. For the Roman moralists, vice is radi-

cally unstable. As Quintilian writes, "Nothing is so multi-
form, so cut up and mangled by so many emotions as is a
vicious mind."[15] Seneca classes with the single-mindedly avaricious, ambitious, or lustful those who "following nothing
certain, unsteady and inconstant and displeased with themselves, capriciousness tosses into fresh courses."[16] Jonson is
drawing on standard Roman conceptions when he describes
as obsessive not only those characters who repeat one narrow
ritual, like Fungoso in *Every Man Out* or Trouble-All in *Bartholomew Fair*, but those like Amorphus and Fantaste in *Cynthia's Revels*, Lady Would-be in *Volpone*, or Sir Amorous La
Foole in *Epicene*, who devote themselves to frivolous variety.

THE Roman moralists, in other words, provide Jonson with
a potent way of construing and representing psychological
and moral phenomena. Mercury's commentary upon Asotus
in *Cynthia's Revels* suggests some of the dramatic consequences of Jonson's humours psychology:

> He doth learne to make strange sauces, to eat *aenchovies*,
> *maccaroni*, *bovoli*, *fagioli*, and *caviare* . . . he buyes a fresh
> acquaintance at any rate. His eye and his raiment confer
> much together as he goes in the street. He treades nicely,
> like the fellow that walkes upon ropes; especially in the
> first *sunday* of his silke-stockings: and when he is most
> neat, and new, you shall strip him with commenda-
> tions. (II.iii.105-115)

Each outlandish trait upon which Mercury remarks seems
unrelated to the last, and yet so entirely predictable that a
comically accurate account, or rather summary, of Asotus
can enter into minute particulars. His body is morally expressive; the stupidity to which his name refers inevitably
takes the external form of gesture, affectation, habit. Jonson
conceives a materialist psychology to entail a complete availability of a self to observers—obviously an advantage in the
theater, where mental processes need to be rendered in some
active or visible form. The apparent "flatness" of the Jonson-

26

ian humours character, on the other hand, may be due to this impossibility of his possessing hidden depths, some implied level of experience from which the audience is excluded. A character like Asotus cannot have "that within which passeth show."

So the very advantages of Jonson's methods involve certain limitations—and they are limitations that Jonson confronts early in his career. Moreover, the metaphysics of the "humours psychology" he inherits is more complicated than it might appear. Since humours psychology is fundamentally materialist, the Roman moralists should logically insist just as vigorously upon the physical nature of virtue as they do upon the physical nature of vice. But though generations of athletically minded educators have taken Juvenal's "mens sana in corpore sano" to imply some connection between fit bodies and clear minds, the Roman moralists waver on this issue. They are influenced not only by orthodox, materialist Stoicism but also by the Greek philosopher Posidonius' revisionist doctrine, which imports metaphysical dualism into a basically Stoic framework.[17] In *Tusculan Disputations*, Cicero invokes humours psychology when he discusses passion, but abandons it when he argues for the immortality of the soul:

> No origin of souls can be found on earth, for in the soul nothing seems to be combined or congealed, nor anything born from or shaped out of the earth, nothing even watery or gaseous or fiery. . . . The nature and power of the soul is therefore unique, distinct from these familiar and well-known elements.[18]

In *Epistulae morales* CVI, Seneca adheres to the materialist Stoic position—since virtuous action is physical, he argues, it requires a physical cause; therefore virtuous intentions must be corporeal. Elsewhere he asks, "What then is the soul except air constituted in a certain manner?"[19] Nonetheless, he often depicts the body's inevitable demands for maintenance, and its ineradicable instinct for pleasure, as hindrances with which he would be glad to dispense. And when he praises the virtuous mind of the feeble Claranus in another letter, he sounds like an outright dualist:

> A great man can issue from a cottage, and out of an ugly little body a beautiful, great soul. . . . Claranus seems to me to be given as an example, so that we can know that the soul is not defiled by the ugliness of the body, but the body adorned by the beauty of the soul.[20]

Here Seneca classes the body in the morally irrelevant category of the accidental, the trivial, the excrescent; like one's birthplace or financial condition, it is an aspect of fortune, something the virtuous man will ignore as completely as possible. In another letter Seneca tells Lucilius that "when you wish to know and understand the true estimate of a person—what kind he might be—examine him naked; he should put aside his patrimony, put aside honors and other lies of fortune; he should leave even the body itself."[21] So the Roman moralists' materialism seems to be a selective phenomenon. When virtue rather than vice is under consideration, they tend to conceive of the body not as the mind's expressive vehicle, but as its antagonist.

The Roman moralists avoid confronting directly this tension in their psychological doctrine. Their ambivalence toward the body, however, affects their characteristic modes of discourse. They invoke physical causes and explanations when they discuss vice; when they talk about virtue, though— even when they claim that the virtuous mind is corporeal— they ignore or exclude explicitly physical descriptions. Jonson inherits this asymmetry. In *Cynthia's Revels*, Mercury praises the paragon Crites as

> One, in whom the humours and elements are peaceably met, without emulation of precedencie . . . in all, so composde and order'd, as it is cleare, *Nature* went about some ful worke, she did more then make a man, when she made him. His discourse is like his behaviour, un-

28

common, but not unpleasing; he is prodigall of neither.
Hee strives rather to bee that which men call judicious,
then to bee thought so: and is so truly learned, that he
affects not to shew it. . . . For his valour, tis such, that
he dares as little to offer an injurie, as receive one.
(II.iii.124–137)

The list of quirks and mannerisms that constitute a full and
sufficient account of Asotus is inadequate here. On one hand,
Mercury suggests a physical basis for Crites' virtues: "the
humours and elements are peaceably met" in him. On the
other hand, Crites seems to transcend the limitations of the
humours entirely: "*Nature* . . . did more then make a man,
when she made him." Most important for his stage presence,
his virtue consists not in exuberant display but in the avoidance of display; he is "prodigall" of neither speech nor gesture, "and is so truly learned, that he affects not to shew it."
The virtuous man's external appearance may not constitute
any guide at all to his moral condition, and even if his de-
meanor and speech do suggest an essential goodness, his self-
restraint and lack of ostentation threaten to render his distinguishing characteristics invisible.

It is not surprising, therefore, that Jonson's plays should exhibit an increasingly erratic and peculiar relation to Roman
moral ideals. In the comical satires, he presents those ideals
in a straightforward, even heavy-handed fashion. In the
comedies after *Sejanus*, however, the virtuous protagonist is
more and more thoroughly eclipsed. The moral obliquity of
Volpone, Epicene, The Alchemist, and *Bartholomew Fair*—the
work that is generally considered Jonson's finest—has led some
critics to discount the effect of Roman moral writing upon
Jonson's mature drama. As Jonson grows older and wiser in
the ways of the world, they assume, he learns to discard the
cut-and-dried prescriptions of the Roman moralists.[22] In fact,
though, Jonson has not renounced the Roman moral tradition. His relation to its conception of virtue has merely grown

more interesting and more complex—and his changing attitude profoundly affects the evolution of his drama during the first half of his career.

If Jonson really finds the Roman moral outlook attractive, it is reasonable for him to try to develop a protagonist who embodies virtues the Romans obviously admire. This is exactly what happens. In *Every Man Out of His Humour*, the first play Jonson admits into his folio without massive revision, he abandons the Plautine conventions he had successfully handled in *The Case Is Altered* and *Every Man in His Humour*. He invents a new genre, comical satire: something "strange, and of a particular kind by it selfe."[23] Simultaneously, he informs his drama with a new and more severe moral vision.

Cordatus, the perfect spectator, is quite correct when he claims that *Every Man Out* is boldly innovative. Its unusual plot structure, its satiric aggressiveness, and its patent didacticism distinguish it from "humours comedies" like Chapman's *Humourous Day's Mirth* or Jonson's own *Every Man in His Humour*. In the kind of satiric spokesman it features, it departs significantly as well from the nondramatic satiric modes that had flourished in the 1590s. Late Elizabethan verse satirists, such as John Marston and Joseph Hall, favor "malcontents" as their satiric spokesmen—talented, obsessive, and embittered. They assume that the envious sensibility is fundamental to satire, that its very perverseness and narrowly focused energy are valuable literary resources. Jonson, however, explicitly rejects discontent and malice as satiric motives, playing down the ferocity of his personae.[24]

Jonson's satirists are wise and virtuous men: wise and virtuous as the Roman moralists understand those terms. He need not read far in the *Epistulae morales*, the *Tusculan Disputations*, the *Sermones*, or the *Institutiones* to find passages that would (and do) sound appropriate in the mouths of Asper, Cordatus, Crites, Arete, Horace, or Augustus. In *Cynthia's Revels*, Mercury praises Crites in terms taken from Seneca's *De vita beata*, invoking the superiority to passion, independence of mind, and wholehearted dedication to virtuous living which together comprise the Stoic ideal:

> *Fortune* could never breake him, nor make him lesse. He counts it his pleasure, to despise pleasures, and is more delighted with good deeds, then goods. It is a competencie to him that hee can bee vertuous. He doth neither covet, nor feare; he hath too much reason to doe either: and that commends all things to him. (II.iii.139-145)

Since the Roman moralists believe that discernment is inseparable from virtue, they cannot concede that the unbalanced mind enjoys privileged access to certain kinds of truth. If Jonson's satire is to be at all authoritative, it must issue from reliable characters, people like Crites or Horace rather than the venomous Carlo Buffone. Jonson's moral categories discredit the malcontent.

Jonson's attraction to Roman moral paradigms in the comical satires is one reason for their generic unorthodoxy. The wise man, as the Roman moralists imagine him, is not at all a tragic figure. It is rather the stupid and the vicious who are tragic—in their hopeless and unending effort to close the gap between excessive desire and inadequate gratification, in their grotesque susceptibility to the ravages of fortune and time. (Thus Jonson's tragic characters, Sejanus and Catiline, are both villains.) The Stoic wise man, in contrast to his foolish neighbors, achieves tranquillity and happiness by wholeheartedly accepting his fate. "What is appropriate for the good man?" Seneca asks. "To yield himself up to fate. It is a great relief to be carried along with the universe."[25] This emphasis upon adapting oneself to circumstances, rather than struggling against the limitations of the human condition, is one of the fundamental emphases of comedy.

The Stoic sage is not comic either, though, in the conventional sense. Ordinarily, comic submission to limitation is understood as an admission of something like universal erotic susceptibility. One renounces the grand possibilities of tragic isolation and admits one's vulnerability and ridicu-

31

lousness, one's participation in the general human plight. Having made that admission, one obtains certain benefits— the pleasures of community life in general and of marital bliss in particular. The Roman moralist's acceptance of life's vicissitudes, however, is based upon an assumption not of vulnerability but of invulnerability. The good man achieves his goal not by indulging but by suppressing desire, not by joining the multitude but by rising above its vulgar errors.

So although Jonson's new kind of protagonist is not a completely improbable comic hero, he is far from the impulsive, silly, endearingly romantic male lead one comes to expect in Elizabethan comedy. The intuition that Jonson is deeply—perhaps too deeply—involved in characters like Crites and Horace is probably well founded. He is not merely delineating an intriguing or dramatically useful kind of protagonist in the comical satires, but trying to convey to his public the values he takes most seriously. Certainly *Poetaster*'s "apologetical dialogue" suggests that Jonson's ideal self would share the superior invulnerability of his Stoic heroes:

> The *Fates* have not spun him the coursest thred
> That (free from knots of perturbation)
> Doth yet so live, although but to himselfe,
> As he can safely scorne the tongues of slaves;
> And neglect *Fortune*, more than she can him.
> (24-27)

The author's argument—that it is impossible for the truly wise man to receive an injury—is taken from Seneca's *De constantia*.

In fact, however, the injury is delivered in the very next play. *Sejanus* is full of good and wise men: Arruntius, Silius, Cordus, Sabinus, Lepidus. But this proliferation is not a sign of their increasing control over their environment; they are every one of them politically impotent. After *Sejanus*, the Roman moralist paragon vanishes altogether, then reappears in *Catiline*, then degenerates into burlesque in *Bartholomew Fair*.

32

SURELY the Roman moralist ambivalence toward the body, which makes their conception of virtue difficult to character-ize onstage, contributes to the eclipse of the Stoic protago-nist. But the problem is not merely a certain colorlessness in the Roman moral ideas Jonson adopts. The peculiar decorum of his medium works against him. The figures that develop into generic types on the Renaissance stage are those that shatter norms and threaten social conventions—weak kings, Herculean heroes, usurers, misers, malcontents, fools, shrews, fops, whores, transvestites, tricksters, revengers, straying wives, wastrel knights. Our sense of the genre of a particular play usually derives not from whether it deals in misfits, but from which ones it chooses and how it treats them. The Stoic is more uncomfortable here than he might be in an epic or an essay. The dramatists that use him to good effect (Chapman in *Bussy d'Ambois* and *An Humourous Day's Mirth*, Marston in his *Antonio* plays) portray not his triumph, but the disintegration of his philosophical pretensions under the pressure of various passions: love, ambition, greed, desire for revenge.

Yet more troublesome for the dramatist is the Stoic's lack of emotional engagement with the world around him—the very invulnerability Jonson admires. The Roman moralists like to depict themselves not as characters in a play but as artists, particularly as orators, or as spectators "viewing mankind from a higher place."[26] In *Discoveries* Jonson writes,

> *I have* considered, our whole life is like a *Play*: wherein every man, forgetfull of himselfe, is in travaile with expression of another. . . . But [good men], plac'd high on the top of all vertue, look'd downe on the Stage of the world, and contemned the Play of *Fortune*. For though the most be Players, some must be *Spectators*. (1093-1109)[27]

The prejudice against the Stoic as a dramatic character thus arises not only from the demands of the theater, but from the Stoic personality itself. In *Every Man Out of His Humour*,

Jonson surmounts this difficulty by making the virtuous characters the artist and his audience; when the Stoic playwright Asper enters the world of the play proper he becomes the morally inferior, but theatrically effective, Macilente. In the original ending to the play, Macilente needs the sight of Queen Elizabeth in the audience to knock him out of his humour and convert him into Asper again; in the revised ending the transformation can take place only after the possibilities for new developments in the plot have completely exhausted themselves. Either way, virtue is segregated from the evolution of the dramatic action.

In *Cynthia's Revels* and *Poetaster*, both sovereign and Stoic hero get imported into the world of the play, and manage to constitute around themselves an ideal society to which they can comfortably belong. But Jonson still has trouble involving his Stoic heroes in a plot. Ultimately, in fact, the sense that fortune is irrelevant to Stoic virtue makes plot beside the point. "Words, above action: matter, above words," Jonson promises his audience in the prologue to *Cynthia's Revels*.[28] Like the Roman moralists, and like the hero Crites in his masque at the end of the play, Jonson would like simply to present his virtuous and vicious exempla, and let the audience perceive the difference.

Jonson's career as a dramatist reveals the difficulties he experiences combining shapely plots with straightforward portrayal of moral ideals. *The Case Is Altered* and *Every Man in His Humour*, two meticulously well-plotted comedies with very slight moral pretensions, are followed by several plays in which Jonson's plot-making capacity seems to have disappeared. Then, as the moral ideal recedes, in *Sejanus*, *Volpone*, *Epicene*, and *The Alchemist*, the importance of plot reasserts itself. Critics arguing for their view of Jonson as a didactic artist ordinarily claim that the logical construction of his plots proves that he thought the world was rationally intelligible; critics arguing the reverse position point to the chaotic aspects of the plots in many of his plays.[29] But in fact until Jonson writes *Catiline* in 1611, the equivalence works just the other way. The meandering action of *Every Man Out* or *Cynthia's Revels*, the dilatory plot of *Poetaster*, yield perspicuous morals, while the more elegantly organized *Epicene* or *Alchemist* are ethically problematic.

Perhaps *Volpone* provides the clearest evidence of the antagonism between plot and moral. Critics since Dryden have argued back and forth over the question of its unity of action.[30] Volpone, safe after the investigation of the Venetian court, unexpectedly attempts yet another elaborate deception—the failure of which finally brings about another hearing and the downfall of all the knaves. Volpone himself calls attention to the discontinuity of these final proceedings:

> To make a snare, for mine own necke! And run
> My head into it, wilfully! with laughter!
> When I had newly scap't, was free, and cleare!
> (V.xi.1-3)

To some critics, Volpone's sudden, uncalled-for departure from his wonted cunning breaches probability. Others argue that such self-destructive rashness has been implicit in Volpone's actions all along.[31] The real issue, though, is not whether the fifth act is possible or even probable, but whether it is necessitated by what has come before. Even if one grants the ultimate unity of *Volpone*'s plot, surely the pause in the action at the close of the fourth act is unsettling. "Well, I am here; and all this brunt is past," says Volpone, still shaken by his risky but successful trickery in court. We realize, with a certain horror, that this would make a perfectly plausible conclusion. There is nothing in the nature of events to guarantee the vindication of Celia and Bonario; in this Venice, truth very likely will not out. We are eventually given justice in *Volpone*, justice of a particularly harsh kind. But although the First Avocatore moralizes that "Mischiefes feed / Like beasts, till they be fat, and then they bleed," the audience knows by now that the relation between desert and destiny is hardly so inevitable as he makes it sound.

So Jonson from the beginning encounters problems with the fundamentally undramatic, indeed antidramatic, character of Stoic virtue. But what makes him abandon this kind of hero when he does? One possibility is that the War of the Theaters renders Jonson acutely conscious of the vulnerability of his ideals to dramatic travesty. A more important reason for Jonson's abandonment of the Roman moralist paragon, however, may have been the experience of writing *Sejanus*. Jonson's Roman tragedies differ markedly from Shakespeare's, which tend to focus upon situations in which two contradictory but intelligible moral evaluations are possible—the assassination of Julius Caesar, the relation between Antony and Cleopatra, the career of Coriolanus. Jonson follows instead the precedent of the Roman moralists, concentrating upon the fate of a vice-ridden society. There is never any difficulty identifying the evil men; the problem is, what are the virtuous men to do?

Sejanus, unlike the comical satires, has a vigorous and carefully integrated plot, but the morally exemplary characters have nothing to do with it. The play's real tragedy is that Roman society under Tiberius is so completely corrupt that no moral course of action is possible. There are plenty of good men, but no good statesmen. Unlike the heroes of the comical satires, all of whom are artists, the Stoics in *Sejanus* are fundamentally uncreative. History is the only kind of writing at which they excel, for the moral exempla they invoke—Brutus, Cassius, Cato, Germanicus—are all dead, and the society that produced such paragons is irrecoverable. Most of the good characters are eventually annihilated, and the destruction of one bad man in no way constitutes the return of a tolerable order. Tiberius remains on the throne; Macro, Sejanus' successor, is even more brutal than Sejanus himself. It is no wonder that the play got Jonson in trouble with the authorities, who believed it a dangerous indictment of monarchy. Nor is it any wonder that *Sejanus*, relentlessly pessimistic to the end, has never been a popular play.

The clear but depressing moral vision of this tragedy must

36

owe something to the perspective of Tacitus in his *Annals*, Jonson's primary source for much of *Sejanus*. Unlike the biographer Suetonius, who relays information about imperial sexual deviation with gossipy explicitness, Tacitus takes the moral obligation of a historian seriously: "The most important function of histories, I think, is to ensure that virtue may not be left unmentioned, and that wicked words and deeds might fear disgrace and the opinion of posterity."[32] But though his moral vision is steady and keen, and though he never shrinks from passing judgment on the historical figures he treats, Tacitus has no complacency about the worldly rewards in store for the good man. The Roman moralists, of course, never guaranteed that the truly happy life would be in any ordinary sense of the word *pleasant*. Happiness comes entirely from within. Yet if virtue is its own reward, Tacitus suggests that the good man had better not expect any additional compensation. Though he grants that the evil man suffers incessant moral torment, he also shows how the scheming, the sycophantic, and the unscrupulous score political triumphs time and time again over the noble, the ingenuous, and the wise. He admires (with some reservations) the Stoic pantheon—Cassius, Brutus, Germanicus, Lucius Arruntius, Thrasea Paetus, Seneca. But he does not spare his reader the description of Germanicus' slow death by poison, or Arruntius' political frustration, or Seneca's prolonged and painful suicide at his pupil Nero's command, a death made more difficult by the hardihood of a body accustomed to Stoic austerity.

Tacitus, in other words, separates entirely the rewards of fortune from the rewards of virtue. Success fails to correlate with goodness, and the outcome of events thus becomes morally irrelevant. This is perfectly orthodox Stoicism, but it must have shattered Jonson's hopes of accommodating a portrait of Stoic virtue in a conventional comic framework. For comedy—and indeed tragedy too, in a different way— demands that its audience recognize the appropriateness of the characters' fates. Their fortunes must matter to them and to us.

Tacitus' role in Jonson's development is not merely negative, however; he also most likely suggests the path the comedies after *Sejanus* eventually take. In *Every Man Out*, Macilente had reached beyond the imaginary world onstage to the actual monarch in the audience, who alone possessed the power to end the play. In *Cynthia's Revels* and *Poetaster*, the monarch became a character in his or her own right; in fictional terms the audience saw an allegorical Elizabeth or an Augustus, but it knew that actually it was seeing an actor play the role of queen or emperor. The process of integrating the monarch into the world of the theater goes one step further in *Sejanus*—Tiberius *knows* he is playing a role. Dissimulation is now fundamental to the royal personality. It is not surprising that Jonson should be drawn to Tacitus' depiction of imperial politics at this point in his career; as Justus Lipsius points out, the *Annals* and the *Histories* provide Renaissance readers with masterful descriptions of the relationship between pretense and power.

> You will discover under a tyranny sycophants and informers, evils not unknown in our own age; nothing sincere, nothing straightforward, no genuine trust even among friends; frequent accusations of treason, the only crime of those who were innocent of crime; profuse slaughters of illustrious men, and a peace more savage than any war.[33]

Tacitus is especially aware that Stoic detachment can become a pose. In the *Agricola* he criticizes those who, in order to appear philosophical, display no grief for their children's deaths; in the *Annals* he describes with loathing an informer who "pretended the opinions of the Stoic sect, by dress and countenance imitating the appearance of virtue, but faithless and false in his soul, hiding avarice and lust."[34] In the following sentences he makes it clear that he disapproves of "the false appearance of good practices," not of Stoicism per se.[35]

It is in fact the rectitude of real Stoicism which makes the counterfeit variety particularly revolting. In *Sejanus* Jonson is concerned for the first time with hypocritical Stoic rhetoric; he enlarges upon his sources and puts it constantly in Tiberius' mouth. Nor is the talent for deceit an imperial prerogative; Jonson's informer fools not only the real Stoics in the play, but the audience as well, when he professes philosophical independence of mind.

After *Sejanus*, the drama of hypocrisy holds the Jonsonian stage until *Catiline*. *Volpone*, *Epicene*, and *The Alchemist* are each founded upon a single deceptive project. This change in emphasis produces several significant alterations in Jonson's character types. The Stoic hero has disappeared, but no effective, morally sound alternative comes to the fore. In the comical satires, personal integrity and the ability to act effectively in society had gone hand in hand—an important ideal for the Roman moralists.[36] With the loss of the ideal plane from Jonsonian comedy, the separation between virtue and other kinds of talent, particularly linguistic facility, gapes wide for the first time. In *Volpone* rhetoric is controlled by the unscrupulously intelligent, a new Jonsonian category, while Celia and Bonario are naive and inarticulate. In *Epicene*, *The Alchemist*, and *Bartholomew Fair* the ideal disappears completely; the superior intelligence of the tricksters does not save them from moral obtuseness. In *The Alchemist* the impostors are as avaricious as their dupes. In *Bartholomew Fair* the middle-class fairgoers, despite their apparent propriety, share all the vices of the Bartholomew-birds. In *Epicene* Morose's crazy desire for absolute silence is only an exaggerated version of the general fear of intimacy which characterizes this society as a whole; Dauphine does not confide fully in his closest friends, and Truewit's idea of female beauty, an elaborately embellished surface, requires even lovers to refrain from overclose scrutiny.[37]

Even as Jonson's comic art moves in this new direction, however, the banishment of vice and the triumph of virtue, which had been the main action of the comical satire, begins to be central to the Jonsonian masque. *The Masque of Queens*, the first with a real antimasque, is written in 1608, the same year as *Epicene*. Why does the sense that virtue can become invisible in a bad world never penetrate to the masque? Perhaps it has something to do with the unique focus on the sovereign, an emphasis that solves some of Jonson's problems with the dramatic portrayal of virtue triumphant. The ordinary man can at most aspire to be master of himself; external circumstances, the events of which drama can treat, are out of his control and in general work against the few halfway decent characters in Jonson's middle comedies. But the virtuous king is, by the nature of his position, master not only of himself but also of his circumstances, and the masque is consequently a celebration not merely of his goodness but of his power. In *Every Man Out of His Humour*, *Cynthia's Revels*, and *Poetaster*, an alliance between the satirist and the sovereign is required to bring about the comic denouement; but the presence of Elizabeth, Cynthia, and Augustus is bound to seem somewhat fortuitous here, a *dux ex machina*. If the king becomes the protagonist, though, this particular problem can be overcome. James conveniently combines artist and prince in a single person.

> How, best of Kings, do'st thou a scepter beare!
> How, best of *Poets*, do'st thou laurell weare!
> ("To King James," 1-2)

There is in his case, and in his case alone, nothing accidental or mysterious about the cooperation between virtue and fortune.[38] In the masques, Jonson may remain more or less faithful to the moral intuitions that inform the comical satires.

IN comedy, on the other hand, Jonson eventually needs a different model; and he derives it, once again, from his favorite writers. Ordinarily the Roman moralists identify personal integrity with the consistency of actions and beliefs guided by infallibly correct judgment. "The virtuous mind never changes," Seneca writes, "nor hates itself, nor varies in any way from the best life."[39] Evil and folly, on the other hand, are characteristically inconstant, inharmonious, and unpredictable: "In this way an ignorant spirit especially demonstrates itself: it proceeds one way, then another, and most shameful of all, I think, it is always unlike itself."[40] This simple polarity of virtuous constancy and vicious instability, however, is not entirely adequate to any of these writers' experience. Complications are particularly easy to spot when the Roman moralists write about themselves, for while they certainly do not conceive themselves as wicked, they do not portray themselves as Stoic sages either. Sometimes this sense of distance from the supposed ideal becomes a kind of self-irony, a measure of how far the writer is from true philosophic wisdom. Seneca begins a discussion of old age with an anecdote illustrating his own irascibility.[41] Horace frequently makes a butt of himself in the *Satires*. At one point his slave tells him frankly:

> You praise
> The circumstances and habits of the people of olden
> times, but if
> Some god would take you back there, you would
> refuse every time
> —Either because you don't (genuinely) feel what you
> declare to be the more virtuous,
> Or because you do not steadfastly uphold virtue; you
> stick fast
> In the mire, desiring to pull out your feet.
> In Rome you yearn for the country, in the country,
> capricious,
> You exalt the city to the stars.[42]

Similarly, after favoring his friend Albius with a pearl of Stoic wisdom: "When you want to laugh," he writes, "you will see me fat and sleek, pampering myself, a pig from Epicurus' herd."[43]

This variety of self-irony does not necessarily constitute an attack on Stoicism; in fact it can, as in *De vita beata*, pro-

tect Stoic ideals from critics who think they can use *ad ho-
minem* arguments against them. "I am not a wise man and—
to gratify your malevolence—I will never be one," Seneca
protests. "I speak of virtue, not of myself."[44] Sometimes,
too, self-irony seems to be an attempt to forestall a personal
attack that exploits the discrepancy between the ideal and the
reality. The extraordinary ambitiousness of the Stoic ideal
makes deficiencies inevitable; if one does not appear to be
aware of the discrepancies oneself, one's inadequacies as a
sapiens are sure to attract hostile comment. Moreover, many
of the most eloquent defenders of a Stoically tinged ethic are
those who feel they need some kind of ballast for the perilous
instability they perceive in their own natures. The mercurial
Cicero, the temporizing Seneca, and the vacillating Lipsius
notoriously violate their own precepts.[45] Jonson, "passionately kinde and angry," is similarly vulnerable to the charge
that he fails to practice what he preaches. Dekker, who pil-
lories him under the name "Horace," claims that "if his *Cri-
ticall Lynx* had with as narrow eyes, observ'd in himselfe, as
it did the little spots upon others: without all disputation,
Horace would not have left *Horace* out of *Every Man In's Humour.*" And modern critics remark upon "the obvious conflict between the real-life Jonson and some of his dignified
artistic posturings."[46]

It would be wrong to suppose, however, that the Roman
moralists always perceive this inevitable discrepancy merely
as an unfortunate human weakness. The provisional, adaptable personality which the Roman moralists ascribe to themselves sometimes has an appeal of its own, wholly irreconcilable with orthodox Stoic values. Far from obscuring this
irreconcilability, the Latin writers habitually take care to make
it obvious. In a striking passage in *Tusculan Disputations*, Cicero accuses Epicurus of inconsistency, the philosopher's most
grievous sin: "Philosophers are tested not by single utterances, but by continuity and consistency." "But see that you
also do not lack consistency," the interlocutor retorts. He
points out that Cicero has just contradicted what had been

his main argument in *De finibus*, his most recent publication. "Argue that way with others, who dispute by set laws," Cicero replies grandly. "I live in the present. What strikes my mind as plausible, I say, and thus I alone am free."[47]

Cicero is not the only Roman moralist to take this kind of principled unpredictability as a sort of special grace, a proof of cosmopolitan sophistication. Horace's *Epodes* ii, translated by Jonson and published as *The Underwood* 85, eloquently praises a simple, natural life spent in a fertile countryside, far away from ostentation and luxury.

> *Happie* is he, that from all Businesse cleere,
>   As the old race of Mankind were,
> With his owne Oxen tills his Sires left lands,
>   And is not in the Usurers bands.[48]

The source of this panegyric is not revealed until the last lines of the poem:

> These thoughts when Usurer *Alphius*, now about
>   To turne mere farmer, had spoke out,
> Gainst th'Ides, his moneys he gets in with paine,
>   At th'Calends, puts all out againe.[49]

Alfius, of course, prospers precisely from those who do *not* live simple, natural lives "from all Businesse cleere." Pastoral nostalgia becomes merely a pretext for the prompt collection of debts; dreams of rural contentment, however minutely realized, seem insubstantial beside the possibility of further usurious profits. Our new knowledge does not, however, wholly undercut the panegyric; we responded to it too wholeheartedly before we suspected a trap. Readjustment is possible at this stage, but not denial. The praise of the countryside is "distanced" without being negated; a complex, "urbane" truth, which takes into account human fallibility, irrationality, and attachment to luxury, replaces the simple, "rustic" truth of the first sixty-five lines.

An awareness of this sort of ironic possibility is in fact typical of Roman moral writing. The skeptics of the New

Academy, while their own tactics were too purely negative to suit the Roman moralists, taught them to view the orthodox Greek philosophical schools as restrictive and impractical. It becomes *de rigeur* for Latin authors to assert their philosophical independence. Quintilian believes that the orator should be thoroughly trained in philosophical method, but that he need not ally himself to any particular school. Of himself he boasts, "I have not dedicated myself to any particular sect, as if it were some superstitious belief."[50] Horace maintains, immediately before launching into an exposition of fairly orthodox Stoic doctrine: "I am sworn to heed the word of no master / I am thrown off course, a stranger, / wherever and whenever the storm bears me away."[51] Juvenal describes himself as one who "reads neither the Cynics nor the Stoic doctrines, / which differ by a shirt from the Cynics', nor does he believe Epicurus, / who is happy with a small vegetable garden."[52] Nonetheless, in the lines that follow, Juvenal recommends the kind of indifference to fortune admired by all three schools. Seneca, though he is staunchly anti-Epicurean, quotes Epicurus with approval at the end of one of his letters, telling Lucilius, "I am accustomed to go across into the enemy camp, not however as a deserter, but as a scout."[53] The exploring mind refuses to commit itself too firmly even to a system it finds congenial, for fear of restricting its own openness and flexibility.

Seneca's attitude commends itself to Jonson, who borrows as a motto the words *tanquam explorator*—"but as a scout"— and boasts that he is "neither *Author*, or *Fautor* of any sect."[54] Like Seneca, too, Jonson seems to connect philosophical eclecticism with the uncommitted, incomplete self. Under his device, a broken compass, he puts the words "Deest quod duceret orbem": the unfinished circle constitutes both an opportunity—a locus of creative opportunity—and a reminder of deficiency as well. But the natural environment for the flexible, provisional personality is comedy, and Jonson realizes this very early in his career. The ingeniously protean Musco-Brainworm, in *Every Man in His Humour*, is the master-engineer of comic entertainment. The morally more severe comical satires are less able to accommodate opportunism for its own sake. Even so, the provisional self soon reappears; and like his Roman predecessors, Jonson juxtaposes this sense of personality with the more orthodox Stoic ideal in a particularly abrupt way. The first scene of *Cynthia's Revels*, modeled after Lucian's irreverent *Dialogues of the Gods*, has the impudent Cupid teasing Mercury for the "peculiar virtue you possesse, in lifting, or *lieger-du-maine*":

> You did never steale MARS his sword out of the sheath,
> you? nor NEPTUNES trident? Nor APOLLOES bow? no, not
> you? . . . my mother VENUS . . . but stoopt to imbrace
> you, and (to speake by *metaphore*) you borrowed a girdle
> of hers, as you did IOVES scepter (while he was laugh-
> ing). (I.i.14-16, 61-64)

Mercury cannot deny the charges; he is a god willing to sacrifice strict moral rectitude for the comic advantage of the moment. But this footloose tendency disappears when Mercury enters Cynthia's court. Here he becomes the patron of Stoic virtue—responsible, infallible, morally penetrating. Mercury the witty, courtly *poseur* is never reconciled with Mercury the Stoic's muse, god of moral rhetoric. In *Cynthia's Revels*, however, the inconsistency is not dramatically important; intelligence of any kind is so exclusively the property of the good characters that Mercury's odd double identity remains unproblematic for the comic plot.

As Jonson's sense of the gap between the morally desirable and the comically possible becomes more acute, he is unable to allow the contradiction between these two aspects of personality to remain latent. Like the Roman moralists, Jonson finds the improvisatory, opportunistic personality attractive; it is clever, knowing, supremely adaptable, at home in the bustling cities where all his comedies between *Cynthia's Revels* and *The New Inn* are set. But like the Romans, too, he retains a sense that these attractions are frivolous and superficial ones—that they are detachable from, or even militate against, serious claims to moral integrity. The idea should not be strange to us—we have words like "facile" to describe someone who is socially adept but nothing more, someone whose superficial charm makes us suspect a basic weakness or corruption of character. What makes Jonson distinctive, and what betrays his adherence to the Roman moral tradition, is his insistence upon showing this adaptability in a light which makes both its attractions and its dubiousness strikingly clear. Even after he abandons the Stoic protagonist in comedy, Jonson never returns to the portrayal of amoral opportunism for its own sake. For the mature Jonson, "facility" is not a trivial failing, though it may be an enjoyable one.

Nor is it an accident that Jonson creates his *improvisateurs* in drama, and in drama alone. The virtues of a Volpone, a Face, a Truewit are *theatrical* virtues; Jonson does not construct such characters in his nondramatic work or, by and large, in his masques. And his Roman sense that this sort of virtue does not accompany philosophical virtue leads him into what Jonas Barish describes as an increasingly marked antitheatricalism, even as his theatrical art reaches its high-water mark.[55] Like his literary ancestors, Jonson never allows the improvisatory personality anything remotely like a moral justification. The Roman separation of the two kinds of attraction makes it impossible for someone who works within their ethical framework to conceive of a simultaneously virtuous *and* theatrical character, like Shakespeare's Rosalind or Viola.

On the other hand, the frank willingness of the Romans to admire the adaptable personality suggests that it is wrong to suppose that Jonson's delight in improvisatory genius need be anything covert or unwilling. It *is* contradictory, but it is not covert; the whole tradition is blatant about its paradoxes. In fact, the course of Jonson's early career seems to indicate that he becomes more and more lucidly aware of irreconcilable Roman values; eventually imagining, in *Epicene*, a sort of showdown between rigidity and opportunism in which nobody wins.

Profit, Delight, and Imitation: Theory and Practice in the Middle Comedies

WHEN Mitis, in *Every Man Out of His Humour*, suggests that some members of the audience might have preferred a romantic comedy to a satiric one, Cordatus replies,

> I would faine heare one of these *autumne*-judgements define once, *Quid sit Comoedia?*   if he cannot, let him content himselfe with CICEROS definition . . . who would have a *Comoedie* to be *Imitatio vitae, Speculum consuetudinis, Imago veritatis*; a thing throughout pleasant, and ridiculous, and accommodated to the correction of manners. (III.vi.202-209)[1]

The identical formula will echo through Jonson's prefaces, prologues, and critical remarks for the rest of his life; comedy—and poetry in general—should be mimetic, delightful, and morally persuasive.

The traditional character of the definition appeals both to Cordatus and to Jonson. It was already time-honored when Horace wrote in the *Ars poetica*:

> Poets want either to be profitable, or to delight—
> Or at the same time to say things both pleasant and
>   helpful for life
> . . . .
> Let things imagined for pleasure's sake be close to the
>   truth
> For the story may not demand belief in anything it
>   pleases.[2]

Donatus, writing in the fourth century, expands upon the

Horatian-Ciceronian position in his commentary on Terence, which in turn became the fountainhead for critical writing about comedy during the Renaissance.[3] Then, after Aristotle's *Poetics* became available in the mid-sixteenth century, literary theorists made strenuous attempts to reconcile Horace and Cicero with the new text; Jonson had a long and respectable intellectual tradition behind him when he undertook a commentary on the *Ars poetica* "lighted by the *Stagirite*."[4]

Jonson is familiar with Renaissance Horatians like Antonio Minturno—in fact, Minturno's *De poeta* is the immediate source for Cordatus' remark;[5] but he would have found his favorite formula repeated even by writers whose primary intellectual loyalties lie elsewhere. Philip Sidney, a favorite Jonsonian writer who owes more to neo-Platonism than to Horace or Aristotle, nonetheless adapts the ubiquitous definition for his *Defense of Poetry*: "Poesie therefore is an art of imitation, for so Aristotle termeth it in his word *mimesis*, that is to say, a representing, counterfeiting, or figuring forth . . . with this end, to teach and delight."[6] It is the sort of situation Jonson dearly loves, in which all "the wisest and best learned"[7] seem to be saying exactly the same thing. In fact, the unoriginality of the Horatian formula, and Jonson's almost ritual invocation of it in all sorts of contexts, leads readers to wonder how much this theory has to do with his artistic practice.[8]

It is only charitable, though, to begin by assuming that Jonson knows what he is talking about, and to attempt to discover the sources and consequences of his fascination with the Horatian definition. Recent critics, who tend to dismiss Jonson's remarks wholesale as rigid, moralistic, and dogmatic, seriously underestimate his acuity and self-consciousness; Jonson's critical and creative faculties are actually intimately bound up with one another. This chapter will deal first with the ways Jonson's critical emphases change to accommodate his evolving dramatic and poetic technique, and then with the ways his new critical position in turn engenders a new notion of dramatic situation in *Epicene*, *The Alchemist*, and *Catiline*. An awareness of the terms in which Jonson sees his own art can help clarify, if not resolve, some issues that trouble modern critics of Jonson's work.

AT LEAST three kinds of questions spring to mind regarding Jonson's appropriation of Horatian poetic theory. First, what does he mean by "profit," "delight," and "imitation"? Second, how does his sense of these terms develop over the course of his career? Third, how are the three factors supposed to be related?

The issue of "profit," or moral improvement, in the middle comedies is particularly vexed, since they differ so markedly from Jonson's earlier drama. In the comical satires Jonson presents clear-cut moral choices: the audience is to avoid the stupidity of Asotus, Amorphus, and Fantaste, and to emulate the virtue of Crites and Arete. But as we have already seen, the explicit theatrical presentation of Roman moral ideals presents problems for Jonson. Virtuous characters play a less significant role in Jonson's drama after *Poetaster*, and eventually they disappear entirely. Jonson becomes increasingly fascinated with a kind of protagonist who proves supremely stageworthy, but for whom he is unable to provide a moral justification.

What happens to the element of "profit," the requirement that comedy be "accommodated to the correction of manners," when no virtuous characters remain to illustrate the desirable norm? Certainly artistic pedagogy becomes a more problematic and subtle affair. In his middle plays Jonson generally tries to assert moral criteria obliquely, in ways that make them available to the audience even when they are beyond the grasp of his characters. He depicts not merely the violation of norms but their caricature; the parodic structure implies a positive standard. There is no woman in *Epicene* who embodies Jonson's feminine ideal, but it is not difficult to infer that ideal from the evidence we are given. We know that Jonson does not expect us either to sympathize with

Morose's misogyny or to evaluate the Ladies' College from a modern feminist perspective. To depict social decadence in *Volpone*, Jonson systematically invokes in perverted form those relationships upon which the Roman moralists believe communal life depends: Volpone and Mosca travesty the relationship between master and servant; Voltore assaults the integrity of the law; Corbaccio violates his paternal responsibilities, and Corvino his marital ones.[9]

Parody achieves precision in its description of vice and folly by its constant reference to a higher standard. It presents problems, however, as well as opportunities for the didactic artist. The relationship of the parody to the thing parodied tends to be slippery. On one hand, the availability of moral standards to burlesque can undermine their stability. On the other hand, some of the glamor of the invoked ideal can rub off on the caricature. When the satirized behavior is sufficiently disgusting, interpretive difficulties are not likely to arise; it occurs to no one to admire Corbaccio. But travesty becomes more problematic in the case of protagonists like Volpone or Mosca, who inherit the intelligence, power, rhetorical skill, and pride in their elite status previously reserved for the likes of Crites and Horace. Like Cicero outlining the honorable occupations in *De officiis*, Volpone distinguishes *captatio* from basely mercantile and usurious modes of acquisition.[10] When Mosca exclaims,

> O! Your Parasite
> Is a most precious thing, dropt from above,
> Not bred 'mong'st clods, and clot-poules, here on earth,

he is adapting for his own uses the kind of rhetoric Seneca and Cicero employ to describe virtuous men. "Can this kind of trait, so great and so high, be believed to resemble that body which it inhabits? A divine power has descended upon this man."[11] When Volpone in the guise of a mountebank indignantly repudiates "ground *Ciarlitani*" like Alessandro Buttoni, "that impudent detractor, and shame to our profession,"[12] he exploits the same self-justifying strategies Jonson himself uses quite seriously in his prefatory epistle.

We laugh at Mosca's speech on the celestial origin of parasites because it incongruously applies an exalted rhetoric to an unworthy end, but we also laugh because it insinuates that Seneca's paragon likewise possesses only a tenuous claim to divine power or origin. The interpretive problems for *Volpone*'s critics almost invariably derive from the moral uncertainty its parodies create. It is generally granted, for example, that Volpone's language resembles the language of Marlowe's heroes, but critics seem irreconcilably divided upon the significance of this fact.[13] We might suppose that Jonson demonstrates here the emptiness of this kind of rhetoric and this kind of aspiration. In this case Jonson is indicting both Volpone and Marlovian rhetoric. Or the point might be that Volpone convicts himself by using grand rhetoric in inappropriate situations; in this case we observe the difference between a false, debased use of language and its correct use. We disapprove of Volpone, but we approve of Marlovian rhetoric, provided it is adequately motivated. The third possibility: Volpone's apparently debased aspirations attain to a certain grandeur, because of his eloquent expression of them; in this case one suspects that Jonson has some sympathy for his character. And the same kind of problem arises persistently in later plays as well. Richard Levin complains of the variety of interpretations evoked by Face's final triumph in *The Alchemist*.[14] When Justice Overdo quotes Cicero in *Bartholomew Fair*, are we to conclude that Jonson has gotten fed up with the Cicero of *Catiline*?[15] Or is the crucial point rather the distance between Cicero's genuine civic humanism and Overdo's silly imitation?

If a play like *Volpone* or *The Alchemist* is supposed to reform the manners of its audience, in other words, what shape will that reformation take? One might try to save the situation by claiming that a play like *Volpone*, simply because it is morally difficult and presents interpretive dilemmas, is more truly ethical than the simpler comical satires. Perhaps the moral

process, not the actual decision, constitutes the truly important factor for Jonson.[16] The possibility of contradictory responses to an ambiguous moral situation need not seem
threatening to an ethically inclined artist if he aims to en-
lighten his audience rather than to persuade it.

It is doubtful, though, that Jonson would regard as sufficient the artistic encouragement of fine moral discriminations
in and for themselves. In *Discoveries* Jonson praises poetry
not because it refines the sensibilities, but because it "leades
on, and guides us by the hand to Action" (line 2399). And
what does subtlety have to do with this kind of moral sua-
sion? Seneca writes to Lucilius:

> Our words [the language of philosophers] should not be
> pleasurable, they should be profitable. . . . Why do you
> tickle my ears? Why do you amuse me? Something else
> is at stake; I am to be burned, cut, made to fast.[17]

As Jonson's comedy becomes more oblique and subtle, it
inevitably loses some of the hortatory potential of an art whose
primary emphasis is explicitly ethical. The audience is liable
to misconstrue, or even entirely overlook, the moral lesson.

THERE is something perverse about an analysis that seems to
present the great middle comedies as a falling-off from the
morally obvious comical satires. In fact, Jonson never conceives his plays, masques, or poems exclusively as moral ve-
hicles; instead, following Horace, he claims that his art is
delightful and mimetic, as well as profitable. Problems arise,
however, when one attempts to estimate the relative importance of Jonson's various artistic *desiderata*. Perhaps the most
significant area of dispute among Jonson's audiences and
readers has always been over the relative importance of morality and pleasure in his art.[18] And it is interesting that critics
who focus on the moral aspects of Jonson's middle comedies
almost always tend to downplay the "delights" of these plays,
and that those who emphasize their pleasures tend to downplay their moral seriousness.

Why should "profit" and "delight" be so difficult to discuss in the same breath? The differences between moralistic and nonmoralistic (or antimoralistic) critics of Jonson probably originate in the intuition that, for Jonson, pleasure and profit simply do not automatically come as a pair. The Horatian doctrine upon which Jonson relies depends itself upon an earlier Peripatetic synthesis of two distinct Greek positions—one claiming that poetry is delightful, the other that it is ethical. What William Wimsatt calls Horace's "hedonistic-pedagogic compromise"[19] remains just that, a compromise. For the Roman moralists pleasure and virtue are, very often, nearly opposites. Seneca writes, "Virtue is something high, lofty, and regal, unconquered, inexhaustible; pleasure base, slavish, weak, transitory."[20] Horace assumes that the ethical and the pleasurable have distinct kinds of appeal under even the best of circumstances:

Old men criticize anything lacking benefit,
Proud young men neglect serious poems;
He has obtained all the applause who has mixed the sweet
    with the useful.[21]

The artist's task, expressed in Horace's verb *miscere*, to mix, is one of juxtaposition—the combination of two unrelated terms. Thus Jonson represents their alliance, in *Pleasure Reconciled to Virtue*, as a political and aesthetic miracle. When he rehearses his apparently banal promise to "profit and delight," in other words, he commits himself to an extremely difficult enterprise; he needs to juggle and coax fundamentally refractory elements into some kind of working relationship.

IN his middle years, Jonson juggles and coaxes in a variety of interesting ways. His didactic aims in the comical satires had been very ambitious. He wanted not merely to present a various and interesting world for his audiences, but to make their experience of that comic world intense and persuasive enough actually to change their behavior, to "correct their

53

manners." The vividness and diversity of the humours characters, and the "energetic realism of detail"[22] in these plays,
contribute to the immediacy of their effect. Nonetheless, their
explicit didacticism creates major dramatic problems. The stark
moral choices Jonson presents seem simplistic, and his bul-
lying of the audience seems intolerable.

In the years after the comical satires, Jonson does not merely
develop new didactic strategies. He reassesses altogether
comedy's potential for "the correction of manners." Hortatory concerns gradually recede, as Jonson resigns himself to
the fact that his audience does not much want to be improved anyhow.

> Though this pen
> Did never aime to grieve, but better men;
> How e'er the age, he lives in, doth endure
> The vices that shee breeds, above their cure.[23]

The prologues, dedicatory epistles, and inductions to the
comedies written between 1605 and 1614 display a slow reo-
rientation away from an almost exclusive emphasis upon
"profit" toward a celebration of the pleasurable and the mimetic. It is no news that *Epicene*, *The Alchemist*, and *Bartholomew Fair* are more "relaxed" than his early plays,[24] but it
may come as a surprise how precisely Jonson's critical remarks, so often dismissed as insensitive to his own creative
evolution, register the dimensions and indicate the significance of the alteration.

In the dedicatory epistle to *Volpone*, Jonson firmly declares
"the principall end of *poesie*, to informe men, in the best
reason of living." He admits that his "*catastrophe* may, in the
strict rigour of *comick* law, meet with censure," but asks

> the learned, and charitable critick to have so much faith
> in me, to think it was done off industrie: For, with what
> ease I could have varied it . . . I could here insert. But
> my speciall ayme being to put the snaffle in their mouths,

that crie out, we never punish vice in our *enterludes*, etc.,
I tooke the more liberty. (115-117)

In *Volpone*, Jonson is willing to violate or at least strain
"comick lawe," disappointing the audience's expectation of
a joyful ending, in order to illustrate the triumph of virtue
and the punishment of vice. He wants his readers to know
how carefully the decision was made—a decision which suggests that when generic conventions conflict with didactic
requirements, the moral considerations are the ones to win
out.

The resolution of the issue is an uneasy one, however, and
Volpone himself reminds us, in his epilogue, of the disparity
between the sources of our profit and the sources of our enjoyment.

> Now, though the FOX be punish'd by the lawes,
> He, yet, doth hope there is no suffring due,
> For any fact, which he hath done 'gainst you;
> If there be, censure him: here he, doubtfull, stands.
> If not, fare jovially, and clap your hands.

Having thoroughly enjoyed Volpone's ingenious crimes, the
audience is hardly in a position to identify its interests with
Celia's or Bonario's.

Three years later, in *Epicene*, the balance seems to have
tipped decisively in the direction of comic pleasure:

> Truth sayes, of old, the art of making plaies
> Was to content the people . . .

Jonson begins his prologue with a clear emphasis upon enjoyment, and proceeds to develop a metaphor of good comedy as a public banquet, with courses to suit every taste.[25]
Jonson had used the metaphor of poetry as "cates" before,
in *Every Man Out of His Humour*, but there he stressed nour-
ishment, moral utility. Here he emphasizes pleasurable con-
sumption and, as Barish says, "for the first time . . . explicitly subordinates the 'utile' to the 'dulce' of the Horatian trio."[26]

55

Jonson has certainly not abandoned his original conception of the aims of art; in his second prologue he insists that the poet needs both to "profit" and to "delight," and to write "things (like truths) well fain'd" besides. It is not the formula, but the way Jonson uses the formula—the relative significance he accords to the different factors—that has changed between *Volpone* and *Epicene*.

The Alchemist makes even clearer the new order of Jonson's comic priorities. By now, the purely ethical attractions of comedy seem to be in eclipse. "This pen / Did never aime to grieve, but better men," asserts Jonson in his prologue, but how the moral lesson is to take effect is unclear.

> They are so naturall follies, but so showne,
> As even the doers may see, and yet not owne.
> (23-24)

If those guilty of the satirized "follies" merely laugh along with everyone else, failing to recognize their own culpability, how is the performance to reform them? Most telling is Lovewit's final speech to the audience:

> That master
> That had receiv'd such happinesse by a servant,
> In such a widdow, and with so much wealth,
> Were very ungratefull, if he would not be
> A little indulgent to that servants wit,
> And helpe his fortune, though with some small straine
> Of his owne candor. Therefore, gentlemen,
> And kind Spectators, if I have out-stript
> An old mans gravitie, or strict canon, thinke
> What a yong wife, and a good braine may doe:
> Stretch ages truth sometimes, and crack it too.
> (V.v.146-156)

Lovewit invokes his new "happinesse" to excuse himself from "candor" and "gravitie." The argument Jonson made in *Volpone* has by now been reversed; when "delight," or the comic expectation of a joyful finale, interferes with moral considerations, it is the morality that gives way. Rules are broken in the name of "a yong wife, and a good braine," not in the name of moral truth. *Bartholomew Fair*, a play "merry, as full of noise, as sport: made to delight all, and offend none," goes even further in its emphasis upon the enjoyable. In the induction and prologue, Jonson makes no mention of edification at all.

JONSON'S increasing concern for the pleasurable in his comedies is often taken as a sign that his youthful harshness has been tempered, and that he has achieved a more tolerant maturity. But it is dangerous to assume that Jonson's increasing concentration upon low-mimetic comedy, and his new emphasis upon comic pleasure, constitute firm evidence of a new geniality. It is just as likely to represent a way—not the only way, at that—of resolving Jonson's particular artistic dilemmas. Between the rib-splitting *Alchemist* and the uproarious *Bartholomew Fair*, Jonson writes *Catiline*, the Restoration revival of which Pepys calls "the worst upon the stage, I mean the least divertising, that ever I saw any."[27] Pepys evaluates the performance solely in terms of the pleasure it affords him, and entertainment is quite evidently not one of Jonson's primary goals in tragedy. Tragedy requires, he writes in the preface to *Sejanus*, "truth of Argument, dignity of Persons, gravity and height of Elocution, fulnesse and frequencie of Sentence" (19-20). "Truth of Argument," though conceived somewhat differently from comic mimesis, is important here, and so is moral seriousness—"fulnesse and frequencie of Sentence"—but "delight" goes unmentioned. In its stark presentation of ethical opposites and its straightforward portrayal of Roman moral paragons, *Catiline* (at least superficially) resembles the comical satires more than it does *The Alchemist* or *Bartholomew Fair*. Jonson's newfound geniality seems to be generically limited.

Perhaps Jonson's willingness to eschew straightforward "counsel" in the middle comedies is related to the increasing diversity of his artistic enterprises after around 1605. He be-

gins to write masques on a regular basis, and his new intimacy with members of the aristocracy creates both subject-
matter and audience for his verse epistles and epigrams. He
has other and perhaps more appropriate outlets than comedy
for the kind of artistic energies he had put into, say, Lorenzo
Junior's justification of poetry in *Every Man in His Humour*,
or the Lylyean opening scenes of *Cynthia's Revels*. It is only
natural that, at this stage in Jonson's career, his consciousness
of the particular context for which he creates a poem or play
should be heightened and refined. A comedy like *The Alchemist*, a tragedy like *Catiline*, a masque like *Oberon*, and a poem
like "To Penshurst" each serves a different purpose, has a
different aim, and therefore exploits different artistic resources.

It is not surprising, then, that after 1605 Jonson places increasing emphasis on the rules which govern different kinds
of artistic endeavor.[28] In *Every Man Out*, Cordatus had wel-
comed generic innovation; in the prologue to *Cynthia's Revels*, Jonson proudly advertises a Muse who "shunnes the print
of any beaten path." But in the prologue and preface to *Volpone* he emphasizes his regard for "needful rule," and in the
preface to *The Alchemist* inveighs against those "presumers
on their own Naturalls" who fail to "use election, and a
meane." Even as the moral fervor of Jonson's early years
fades from his comedy, in other words, his criticism seems
to become more rule-bound—not what one would expect
from someone who is supposed to be growing more tolerant
and genial.

The apparent contradiction results from the increasing significance, for Jonson, of generic boundaries and conventions.
His strict new attention to the requirements of genre provides a solution to the artistic dilemmas he confronts in comedies like *Volpone*, *Epicene*, and *The Alchemist*. It gives him
some way of assigning priorities to artistic means and ends
which would otherwise prove destructively competitive. He
need not fear that he is compromising moral and artistic
principles when he writes less-than-edifying comedy; he can

simply maintain that comedy is by nature less didactic than, say, tragedy or epigram.

Nonetheless, Jonson never allows his increasing emphasis upon delight to overwhelm entirely his other purposes. He conjures up perversely low-minded audiences—the "pretenders" in the dedicatory epistle to *The Alchemist*, the Stage-keeper in *Bartholomew Fair*—to make manifest the difference between his own artistic practices and those of playwrights who abandon moral concerns entirely. In the preface to the revised *Every Man in His Humour* he insists that he

> for want, hath not so lov'd the stage,
> As he dare serve th'ill customes of the age:
> Or purchase your delight at such a rate,
> As, for it, he himselfe must justly hate.
>
> (3-6)

"The Concupiscence of Daunces, and Antickes" lies beyond a boundary Jonson refuses to trespass.

THIS stubborn refusal to capitulate entirely to audience hedonism reflects the important fact that Jonson's appeal to generic conventions does not make troublesome questions about the morality of art disappear. It merely solves one set of problems by replacing it with another. For Jonson is no generic relativist; he conceives the artist's initial choice of artistic direction as itself a morally significant decision. In *Every Man Out* he condemns romantic comedy, for instance, because it is improbable, a false reflection of the real world. In the middle comedies and satiric epigrams, too, Jonson castigates the romantic imagination for its refusal to acknowledge the mimetic requirements of good art. Ignoring the facts, it supposes it can make virtue from vice, gold from lead, purses from sow's ears—running away from nature as if it were afraid of her. The writer of romantic comedy cannot plead that he is merely following the conventions of his genre, when that genre is itself corrupt.

At issue here is the complicated theory and practice of what

Jonson and his Roman moralist forebears call "decorum," propriety.[29] The Roman moralists place a high value on propriety in both its social and artistic manifestations. As orators, statesmen, and men of letters, they must be particularly sensitive to the way moral imperatives are modified and changed by circumstances, precedents, expectations, customs. But what precisely constitutes decorum, and what relationship holds between decorum and virtue, is controversial. On one hand, the decorous often overlaps with the morally good; it is decorous for a man to be temperate and pious, for example, or for a child to respect its parents. On the other hand, "decorous" behavior is often good not absolutely, but only under certain circumstances. In one country it might be decorous to run about naked or to grow one's hair long, even though it would be shocking elsewhere. Or it may be appropriate for an orator to use especially emotional rhetoric, or certain kinds of jokes, to some audiences but not to others. Or it may be proper to compromise some values because of a need to accommodate other values; thus in a work of art, which is supposed to "imitate life" as well as promulgate moral truths, some unedifying element may need to be introduced in the interests of plausible representation.

It is easy to see why the relationship between virtue and decorum should prove to be a difficult issue in classical times, and continue to stimulate endless debate during the Renaissance. On one hand, too wide a gap between the virtuous and the appropriate means that decorum degenerates into relativist expediency, a politic submission to immediate convenience. Such an admission would jeopardize one of the humanists' most treasured beliefs—that the philosophically educated, morally responsible individual is naturally the most effective in practical affairs. (We have already seen how potent a vision the union of virtue and rhetorical power had been for Jonson in his early years.) On the other hand, not to acknowledge any distance at all between absolutely and conditionally moral action seems to belie the ample experi-

ence both the Roman moralists and their Renaissance followers have adjusting their absolute values to the situation at
hand—popularizing, cajoling, exaggerating, temporizing.
Jonson's change of course after *Sejanus* reflects his willingness to undertake just such adjustments, to submit to the
requirements of propriety even when those requirements seem
to interfere with some of his most cherished artistic goals.

Jonson's admired Horace leaves the great question open;
the distinctive, eminently practical tone of the *Ars* is largely
due to his refusal to distinguish between the artist's responsibility to moral and philosophical truth in the abstract, and
the kind of prudential considerations which secure a large
public. One writes self-consistent poems, puts fitting speeches
into the mouths of one's characters, keeps the language life-
like not only in order to produce aesthetically satisfying results, but also in order to recommend oneself to a heteroge-
neous audience.

Jonson himself takes this optimistic view of the situation
in his prologue to *Epicene*:

But in this age, a sect of writers are,
   That, onely, for particular likings care,
   And will taste nothing that is populare.
With such we mingle neither braines, nor brests;
   Our wishes, like to those (make publique feasts)
   Are not to please the cookes taste, but the guests.
Yet, if those cunning palates hether come,
   They shall find guests entreaty, and good roome;
   And though all relish not, sure, there will be some
That, when they leave their seates, shall make 'hem say,
   Who wrote that piece, could so have wrote a play:
   But that, he knew, this was the better way.

                            (4-15)

In Book XI of the *Institutiones*, however, Quintilian makes a
kind of distinction that is often important for Jonson, between decorum and expedience.

It must be most strictly taught, that he only speaks suit-
ably, who has considered not only what is useful, but
also what is becoming. Nor do I forget, that these things
generally go together. . . . Sometimes, though, they are
at odds. Whenever they conflict, that which is becoming
prevails over that which is useful.[30]

Socrates' *Apology*, writes Quintilian, was manifestly inexpe-
dient; he easily could have obtained an acquittal from the
Athenian court if he had taken the character of his audience
into consideration, as orators are normally expected to do.
Socrates refused to do so because a conventional defense would
have violated a more fundamental kind of decorum, a propriety that transcends occasion. His speech, though inexpe-
dient, is therefore "becoming," *decens*.

It is this kind of appropriateness which Jonson invokes in
the passage already quoted from the revised *Every Man in
His Humour*, where he refuses to "purchase your delight at
such a rate, / As, for it, he himselfe must justly hate." Like
Quintilian, Jonson hopes that the "becoming" and the "ex-
pedient" will ordinarily coincide, but when they conflict he
tries to follow Quintilian's advice, and allows the "becoming" to prevail.

For the artist, the fact that works of art must satisfy a variety
of diverse criteria complicates the problem of appropriateness. We have already seen that the moral and the pleasurable
exist more or less in tension with one another, at least for a
Stoically inclined artist like Jonson. What is ethically appropriate might not be appropriate as entertainment, and vice
versa. Moreover, the Horatian-Ciceronian formula contains
not two prescriptions but three; the work must be moral, it
must be delightful, and it must imitate nature.[31] Where does
mimesis fit in?

Jonson's emphasis on verisimilitude as an aesthetic crite-
rion increases even as he becomes more solicitous for his
audiences' pleasure. The second prologue to *Epicene*, and the

preface and prologue to *The Alchemist*, both suggest that he is considering carefully the importance of mimesis in comedy. The fact that *Epicene* was suppressed for a time, because it supposedly slandered Lady Arabella Stuart, probably helped focus Jonson's attention upon the relationship between reality and artifice. But his sense of that relationship has changed since *Poetaster*, where he had considered the propensity of his audience to seek "applications" as a sign of their envy or perversity. Now that "Our *Scene* is *London*," rather than Venice or Gargaphie, Jonson can provide his audience with a precise and immediate depiction of the familiar, a depiction he assumes will delight them.

> For here, he doth not feare, who can apply.
> If there be any, that will sit so nigh
> Unto the streame, to looke what it doth run,
> They shall find things, they'ld thinke, or wish, were done.
> ("Prologue," *The Alchemist*, 19-22)

The audience, peering into the "streame" of the play, sees there its own unscrupulousness and gullibility, but like Narcissus it loves its reflected image.

The induction to *Bartholomew Fair*, the most frankly entertaining of Jonson's plays, likewise places a high value on mimesis. The author who, in the prefatory epistle to *Volpone*, had protested that he "trembled to thinke toward the least prophaneness," now scolds those who might "challenge the *Author* of scurrilitie, because the language some where savours of *Smithfield*, the Booth, and the Pig-broath." He jokes that

> though the *Fayre* be not kept in the same Region, that some here, perhaps, would have it, yet thinke, that therein the *Author* hath observ'd a speciall *Decorum*, the place being as durty as *Smithfield*, and as stinking every whit. (156-160)

"Decorum" here involves no special propriety of language or behavior; it is a synonym for naturalism.

Jonson's close association between the mimetic function of art and the pleasure of the beholders is a time-honored one that originates in Aristotle's *Poetics*:

> Imitation is natural to man from childhood . . . and it is also natural for all to delight in works of imitation. The truth of this second point is shown by experience: though the objects themselves be painful to see, we delight to view the most realistic representation of them in art, the form for example of the lowest animals and of dead bodies.[32]

In the *Ars poetica*, Horace observes that even poorly written poems will gratify the public when they provide an accurate representation of real life. Some Renaissance commentators go so far as to identify Horatian *delectio* with the pleasure Aristotle maintains is produced by imitations.[33]

At the same time, however, Jonson is aware that the pleasure of the audience is not *necessarily* dependent upon artistic verisimilitude. In the preface to *The Alchemist* he complains that "the Concupiscence of Daunces, and Antickes so raigneth, as to runne away from Nature, and be afraid of her, is the onely point of art that tickles the Spectators." Here the foolish public perversely prefers the antirealistic to the legitimate feigning of the responsible artist. But the difference between pleasing the audience and satisfying standards of verisimilitude is clearest in cases of outright flattery. The parasites in *Discoveries* 1587-1593, who "invent tales that shall please: make baites for his Lordships eares . . . fit their discourses to the persons, and occasions," possess irresponsibly narrow notions of appropriateness; they elevate the desire to please their audiences above other more legitimate priorities.

So the artist's mimetic responsibilities do not correlate in any simple way with his obligation either to instruct or to entertain his audience. Mimesis seems to be a third, distinct requirement. Yet Jonson seems unwilling to separate mimesis from his other *desiderata*, to make it an end in itself or even a privileged term in the Horatian formula. In the *Dis-*

coveries he writes that "the true Artificer will not . . . depart from life, and the likenesse of Truth, but speake to the capacity of his hearers" (772-774). The relationship of the crucial last clause—"but speake to the capacity of his hearers"—to the preceding part of the sentence is ambiguous. Is Jonson implying that the artist's faithfulness to "the likenesse of Truth" is a function of his sense of audience? Or are there rather two distinct constraints upon the responsible artist, who must *not only* convey the likeness of truth *but also* speak to the capacity of his hearers?

The ambiguity here reflects the uncertain role of mimesis in Jonson's theoretical framework—sometimes a good in its own right, sometimes a means to an end, sometimes a factor that gives way under the pressure of rival priorities. For mimetic accuracy is not, finally, the goal of certain kinds of poetry. In his *Epistle to Master John Selden* Jonson writes,

> I have too oft preferr'd
> Men past their termes, and prais'd some names too much,
> But 'twas with purpose to have made them such.
>
> (20-22)

The moral impulse, the desire to "correct manners" and to "better men," prevails in panegyric over values like representational precision or absolute sincerity. Jonson's attitude here is not idiosyncratic. The Roman moralists appreciate the educational value as well as the dangers of undeserved praise. In a passage preserved by Servius from Cicero's *De republica*, one of the interlocutors observes, "It is a difficult matter to praise boys, for not accomplishment, but expectation, deserves to be praised."[34] The best way to become good, the Roman moralists claim, is to keep a vision of an ideal always before one's eyes, even if that ideal is unattainable. Thus Seneca responds heatedly to the objection "Philosophers do not practice what they preach":

> Nevertheless they practice much of what they preach,
> which they conceive with a virtuous mind; for if their

actions matched their utterances, who would be more happy than they? At any rate there is no reason for you to belittle good words, and hearts full of good thoughts. . . . Why is it amazing, if they do not climb up to a height difficult to reach? But if you are a man, admire those who undertake great things, even if they fail. It is a noble trait to make one's efforts with a view not to one's own resources, but to those of nature herself, to attempt the heights and to conceive in the mind greater things than even those with mighty souls can accomplish . . . he who imagines, wills, attempts these things, makes a way toward the gods; and surely, even if he will not reach them, "Nevertheless he perished in a great enterprise."[35]

If satire is the Roman moralists' stick, panegyric is their carrot.

So while Jonson may call his comedies "speculum consuetudinis," and his masques "the mirrors of mans life,"[36] the reflected images serve different functions and are therefore drastically different. Jonson retains the image of the ideal in genres where compliment is taken for granted—masques and verse panegyric—and can portray virtuous characters straightforwardly in *Catiline* because tragedy traditionally calls for "dignity of Persons." Meanwhile, in the years between 1605, when he writes *Volpone*, and 1614, when *Bartholomew Fair* is performed, Jonson's comedy becomes more and more insistently low-mimetic. His art is increasingly specialized; its form increasingly depends upon the particular context for which it is intended, its purpose and its prospective audience.

Nonetheless, Jonson realizes that the line between the conventionally acceptable exaggeration he praises and the falsification he despises can become extremely thin. Since he commits in the name of decorum acts that would ordinarily incur his disapproval—shirking artistic pedagogy in the middle comedies, magnifying the virtues of his patrons in masques and poems—its morality remains troublesome for him. The

vividness of *Volpone*'s parasite-artist Mosca, and the harshness of his punishment at the end of the play, both perhaps
reflect Jonson's ambivalence about his authorial role in the
years when he is beginning to lighten his didactic emphasis
in order to cultivate the goodwill of his audiences. How much
should Jonson be willing to accommodate moral imperatives, such as his obligation to speak truth, with the requirements of different genres and the expectations of spectators,
readers, and patrons? Drummond's account of Jonson's conversation, though it does not pretend to be a verbatim tran-
script, contains a suggestive ambiguity: "And so he might
have favour to make one Sermon to the King, he careth not
what thereafter s[h]ould befall him, for he would not flatter
though he saw Death" (330-332). The last clause is sometimes quoted by itself, as evidence either of Jonson's sturdy
independence or of a masquewright's pathetic self-delusion.
But what is Jonson really saying here? Does he mean that he
would make a good preacher because he is not the sort of
man who flatters kings? Or is he maintaining that absolute
frankness is specially appropriate to sermons, though it might
be indecorous, say, in the masque? The passage supports either
reading. Jonson's artistic priorities—delightfulness, profita-
bility, truth to nature, appropriateness defined in a variety of
ways—exist in a state of unresolved mutual tension. Any one
term can, under certain circumstances, be subordinated to
another: profit cedes to delight, and delight to mimesis, in
the middle comedies; mimesis in turn cedes to profit in the
masques and panegyric poems.

So it is clear that Jonson's critical stance changes to reflect
changes in the direction of his creative energies. But the evolution of his critical position not only reflects but seems to
provide some of the impetus for his development as a playwright. In *Sejanus* and *Volpone*, as he begins to cope with the
collision between his original moral values and his theatrical
values, Jonson displays a characteristically Roman ambivalence toward the adaptable, inventive character; his most

memorable figures are time-servers, flatters, and parasites who, unhindered by any sense of personal integrity, exploit circumstances for all they are worth. They incarnate both the dangers and the attractions of the theater for Jonson at this point in his career. As Jonson gradually reconceives the function of comedy, however, minimizing both its didactic possibilities and its potential for corruption, his extravagant hypocrites begin to lose some of their moral menace. Face, Dol, and Subtle are opportunists and crooks, but they are not opportunists and crooks on the scale of Tiberius and Sejanus, or Volpone and Mosca. The action of *The Alchemist* is more limited and its consequences are far less grave. In *Epicene* and after, the really stubborn interpretive problems tend to center not on pure opportunists but on characters like Truewit in *Epicene*, Lovewit in *The Alchemist*, Cicero in *Catiline*, or Quarlous in *Bartholomew Fair*, for whom the articulation of moral truth is complicated by a highly developed sense of what is appropriate in particular circumstances. In other words, they are all characters in situations analogous to Jonson's own; the plays reflect the dilemmas of their author.

There is a striking lack of consensus among *Epicene*'s critics about the status of Truewit, Dauphine, and Clerimont. Some believe that Jonson presents the gentlemanly trio in a purely positive light, and that they embody the standards by which the other characters are to be judged.[37] Some think that Jonson's wholehearted approval for repulsive characters like these merely betrays his own psychological imbalance.[38] Others suggest that Jonson means the three friends to be perceived as seriously flawed,[39] others that Jonson himself could not make up his mind.[40] What criteria are we supposed to apply to these characters? As witty gentlemen, they are exemplary; as social beings they are more intelligent and successful than anyone else in the play. But their code itself sometimes seems inadequate; Dauphine's casual cruelty is disturbing, and so is Truewit's willingness to alter his conversational direction completely in the interests of maintaining a sprightly tone. Douglas Duncan observes perceptively: "To criticize Truewit's behavior is to swim against the tide of the play. But the more we capitulate to his brand of festivity the more we find ourselves cajoled into disregarding the serious ethical issues which the play persistently raises."[41] We have a sense, in *Epicene*, of being pulled two ways at once. Dauphine's delight in manipulating fools, Clerimont's preoccupation with pleasure, and Truewit's multifariousness and worldly sociability coordinate with the generic values of comedy—something "painless and ridiculous," as Jonson says, which mocks rigidity, affectation, and folly, and praises flexibility, wit, and unpretentious geniality. Dauphine, Clerimont, and Truewit are characters eminently suited to what Duncan calls "the tide of the play." But Jonson keeps his audience aware as well of the negative aspects of the comic spirit: its callousness, its triviality, its conformism.

The allusions to Latin literature in *Epicene* are crucial to this self-conscious examination of comic values. John Dryden complains that Truewit is too bookish to make a plausible London wit;[42] he differs from the Restoration comic hero, who is in many ways his descendant, in the unembarrassed way in which he calls upon his classical education. It is a freedom common among *Epicene*'s characters; the fatuous Jack Daw lays claim to extraordinary classical erudition, and even the barber and the bearbaiter sprinkle their speech with Latin tags. Morose, in perhaps his most sympathetic moment, admits:

> My father, in my education, was wont to advise mee, that I should alwayes collect, and contayne my mind, not suffring it to flow loosely; that I should looke to what things were necessary to the carriage of my life, and what not: embracing the one, and eschewing the other. (V.iii.48–52)

The ascetic preferences here, the imagery of collection and containment, suggest Seneca; and indeed Jonas Barish believes that "the victory of Truewit over Morose represents

Jonson's attempt to assert the values of the world and the flesh over the consolations of philosophy."[43] Nonetheless, Morose has misconstrued his sources badly. Seneca, like the rest of the Roman moralists, would be appalled by his anti-social egotism, his lack of urbanity, his ridiculously affected speech, his rejection of avuncular obligation.

Morose is not the only one to skew the Latin classics. If Truewit and his friends were to affiliate themselves with a Latin author, one might expect them to choose Horace—but it is not Horace whom Truewit quotes, but the mutually contradictory Ovid and Juvenal. Jonas Barish shows how Jonson systematically heightens the bizarre aspects of these texts, making them deliberately outrageous by quickening the pace of the Juvenalian satiric catalogue and transforming Ovid's gently practical advice on cosmetics into a fantasy of piecemeal feminine self-construction.[44] "Is it for us to see their perrukes put on, their false teeth, their complexions, their eye-browes, their nailes?" (I.i.117-119). The moderation of the Roman moralists disappears in a welter of extreme and incommensurable possibilities; Truewit is more mercurial than temperate, veering first one way, then the other. The classical synthesis of politeness and integrity has ruptured and its parts become estranged.

Ultimately our sympathies are with the three gentlemen—or at least our interests, as a comic audience, coincide with theirs. What Dauphine, Clerimont, and Truewit want out of life, we want out of the play. They embody the values that make *Epicene* work, and that make Jonson's middle plays so much more enjoyable than the early ones. Do we have any right to complain? Douglas Duncan claims that "the right way to respond to Truewit is not by denying our admiration for him but by recognizing the moral dilemma we are put in by accepting and enjoying him."[45] This formulation, though, is incomplete; part of our dilemma consists in our uncertainty as to whether we should find ourselves in a dilemma at all. Volpone obviously presents a threat to his society, and our enjoyment of him is patently amoral. We may feel uncomfortable about this, but at least the situation is clear-cut. Truewit and his friends, on the other hand, simply do not violate moral norms in the same blatant way. They are "decorous," and at the same time their conversation renders the concept of decorum problematic. Truewit quotes both Ovid and Juvenal on proper feminine behavior, but they provide no consensus at all. Decorum depends upon the existence of a stable set of assumptions, a framework of accepted values. This stable set of assumptions is precisely what Jonson denies his audience in *Epicene*.

Given his notion of comedy, Dryden is right to complain about *Epicene*'s classical freight. It disturbs comic decorum by calling that decorum into question. The allusions to Seneca, Juvenal, and Ovid bring to bear upon the action of the play a disconcerting range of alternative, irreconcilable proprieties, unsettling the confidence of the comic audience upon matters it might prefer to take for granted.

THE end of *The Alchemist* raises problems similar to those presented by *Epicene*. Once again, critics disagree on appropriate criteria for evaluating the final triumph of Lovewit and Face. A "moral" critic like Gabriele Jackson writes that "Lovewit, upon whose shoulders the responsibility would seem squarely to fall, shrugs it off by applying aesthetic, intellectual, and sensual, rather than moral criteria. He is a Falsewit rather than a Truewit."[46] Jackson's bleak reading of *The Alchemist* relies upon the assumption that moral issues ought to take precedence over "aesthetic, intellectual, and sensual ones"—the claims, that is, of pleasure. Richard Levin, on the other hand, who objects to what he calls "decomicalizing" readings of *The Alchemist*, polemicizes in the opposite direction. He refuses to "surrender the joyous pleasures that the immediate, felt experience of comedy can give us, in all of its rich and complex particularity, for a mess of platitudinous pieties."[47] To support his cheerful reading of *The Alchemist*, Levin represents moral issues as abstract and irrelevant—"platitudinous pieties"—while the aesthetic, intellec-

tual, and sensual considerations dismissed by Jackson become "joyous pleasures," "immediate, felt experience," and
"rich and complex particularity." As in *Epicene*, moral readings seem irreconcilable with comic ones. Critics disagree
upon the relative importance of moral absolutes versus generic expectations.

Levin is right that *The Alchemist* is a hilarious play and that
the last scene participates in its comic spirit. As Face himself
admits, "my part a little fell in this last *Scene*, / Yet 'twas
decorum." The question, then, is not whether the ending is
generically inappropriate but whether generic propriety is the
only relevant kind. Levin assumes that critics who introduce
moral criteria here are insensitive or perverse.[48] But surely
Lovewit's and Face's elaborate apologies for their action point
up the fact that comic decorum here necessitates a departure
from "candor" and "gravitie." Just as Jonson refuses to make
the clever, opportunistic characters of the middle comedies
agents of moral revelation, so he also refuses to fudge the
discrepancy between generic values and moral ones. Face says
in his epilogue:

> I put my selfe
> On you, that are my countrey; and this pelfe,
> Which I have got, if you do quit me, rests
> To feast you often, and invite new ghests.

Though the audience may be a bribed jury, willing to overlook "strict law" to further its own interests, it does not
necessarily follow that the law has been repealed.

Jonson does not deny pleasure its due; but even at his most
tolerant he remains aware (and keeps his audience aware) of
the context and limitations of that enjoyment. It is a complex
position. Critics like Richard Levin characteristically emphasize Jonson's willingness, in his most successful comedies, to
let his audience eat its cake, while critics like Gabriele Jackson stress his unwillingness to let them have it too. At one
end of Jonson's spectrum is *Bartholomew Fair*, characterized
by what Ian Donaldson calls "double-level appeal . . . ro-

bust, noisy farce, overlaid by cool, ironic reflections upon the implications of such entertainment."[49] At the other there is *Pleasure Reconciled to Virtue*, where—though the gross physical indulgence of Comus must be rejected—a more genteel Pleasure is made compatible with Virtue, "hir noted opposite." Even here, though, the alliance is temporary, a sort of vacation from ordinary life:

> Theis, theis are howres, by Vertue spar'd
> hirself, she being hir owne reward,
> > But she will have you know,
> > > that though
> > hir sports be soft, hir life is hard.
> You must returne unto the Hill,
> > And there advaunce
> > with labour, and inhabit still
> > > That height, and crowne,
> > From whence you ever may looke downe
> > > Upon triumphed Chaunce.
>
> > > (328-338)

The transience of the masque, often frustrating for Jonson, here becomes part of the moral lesson.

In *Catiline* Jonson considers from another angle the problem of reconciling moral absolutes with the limited possibilities for effective action. The special low-mimetic emphasis of Jonsonian comedy renders the contrast between the moral and the pleasurable particularly strongly marked; the high-mimetic focus of tragedy, on the other hand, can accommodate the straightforward presentations of virtuous protagonists. Jonson's heightened sense of the problematic relationship between absolutely moral and conditionally acceptable behavior, though, makes virtue in *Catiline* a more complicated phenomenon than it had been in the comical satires.

Catiline has two virtuous exempla, not one; Cato—the most outstanding classical example of unyielding integrity—and Cicero, noted rather for his eloquence and patriotic opportunism. They are friends and political allies, ranged against the forces of rebellion, but they represent different kinds of political virtue. Cato sees the right course and pursues it without regard to the consequences or to the likelihood of success. "What honest act is that, / The *Roman Senate* should not dare, and doe?" (IV.526-527). He wastes no words—his most common form of utterance in the play is a simple, heartfelt assent to something Cicero has already advocated in a long speech.[50] Cicero's heroism is far more flexible and politic. A self-made man (like Jonson), he is keenly aware of limitations upon his power, a power that (like the power of the playwright) ultimately rests upon the strength of his rhetoric. Though he is the moral and intellectual superior of his audience in the Senate, he derives his legitimacy and his purpose from that audience; thus his leadership must involve the persuasion, not the coercion, of the stupid, the lethargic, and even the perverse.

Thus Cicero must be willing to employ dubious expedients in a worthy cause. Though he despises the whore Fulvia, "a base / And common strumpet," he flatters her when he needs information.

> Here is a lady, that hath got the start,
> In pietie, of us all; and, for whose vertue,
> I could almost turne lover, againe: but that
> TERENTIA would be jealous. What an honor
> Hath shee atchieved to her selfe! What voices,
> Titles, and loud applauses will pursue her,
> Through every street! what windores will be fill'd,
> To shoot eyes at her! what envy, and griefe in
>   matrons,
> They are not shee!   (III.341-349)

Cicero the rhetorician gauges the level of his audience and pitches his appeals to that level; his calculated flirtatiousness here caters to the sexual competitiveness and love of public display which led Fulvia to abandon the Catilinarians in the first place, when she thought they considered her Sempro-

nia's inferior. Like Catiline, who hates "the dregs of mankind
. . . whores, and women" with whom he must collaborate,
Cicero exploits other people's vice for his own ends; but his
ends, unlike Catiline's, are morally impeccable.

Cicero's talent for capitalizing upon the opportunities provided him prove vital for the detection and defeat of the Catilinarian conspiracy. Jonson portrays Cicero much as Cicero
likes to portray himself, as the savior of the Roman state at
the apex of his political career. On the other hand, as Joseph
Bryant observes, our awareness of Roman history modifies
our sense of Cicero's victory.[51] In a major departure from
Sallust, Jonson makes Caesar an accessory to the Catilinarian
plot.[52] Both Cicero and Cato, in Jonson's *Catiline*, know that
Caesar is guilty; Cato presses for prosecution. Cicero, however, refuses—even to the point of throwing the charge out
of court when it is introduced. Cicero judges it impolitic to
alienate a powerful citizen when the state is weakened by
revolt; even Cato agrees he is right. On the other hand, we
know that Cato, who believes that all traitors should be punished regardless of circumstances, is in some ways the wiser
here. Cicero cannot perceive that his calculated disinclination
to confront serious dangers merely postpones them and
eventually contributes to the downfall of the system he now
triumphantly redeems.

Cato and Caesar, epic antagonists *in potentia*, lurk on the
edges of *Catiline*'s action, modifying our vision of the central
events. If, however, Roman history suggests that Cicero is
unwise to mimimize the Caesarian threat, it also suggests
that Cato's inflexibility presents a different kind of problem.
Ignoring Cato's advice may eventually lead to disaster for
the republic. But when Cicero accepts Cato's counsel, and
executes the Catilinarian conspirators, he gives his enemies a
pretext for exiling him the very next year, permanently crip-
pling his political power and ruining his effectiveness as a
virtuous public servant. The real threat to virtue in *Catiline*
is not Caesar but the social corruption of which the choruses

complain—the real-world messiness that makes Cicero's compromises necessary in the first place.

So although Cicero's purgation of Rome may be incomplete, at least he accomplishes something constructive. And he triumphs, moreover, without the sanction of the omnipotent authority Jonson had needed to guarantee the beneficence of fortune in the comical satires. Because it acknowledges a kind of virtue capable of adaptation and compromise, *Catiline* bridges, however unsteadily, the gap between integrity and efficacy which, in *Sejanus*, had seemed hopelessly absolute.

It is precisely the ability to bridge this gap which makes Jonson, in his middle plays, more successful than he was before or ever will be again. And yet the absolute morality of a Cato retains its own stern appeal; it furnishes an implicit criticism of Ciceronian flexibility. The Horatian artist seeks simultaneously to please and to instruct his audience, to gratify a sometimes undiscriminating public while maintaining his own artistic standards; he finds it virtually impossible to realize all his ambitions in any one poem or play. Compromise is inevitable. Yet in play after play Jonson, embodying in his protagonists his own artistic dilemmas, insists upon the provisional character of even his most brilliant compromises, and qualifies them with an awareness of impractical but attractive alternatives.

Roman Moral Psychology and Jonson's Dramatic Forms

THE COMEDIES

EARLY in his career as a dramatist, Ben Jonson informs his audience that his play will not make "a duke to bee in love with a countesse, and that countesse to be in love with the dukes sonne, and the sonne to love the ladies waiting maid: some such crosse wooing, with a clowne to their serving-man."[1] For much of his career, Jonson refuses to provide the kind of theater that the Elizabethan audience would have expected, and that Northrop Frye has taught modern readers to regard as quintessentially comic—plays in which young lovers overcome the arbitrary resistance of their parents and, aided by beneficent circumstances, unlikely conversions, and miraculous transformations, bring about the birth or regeneration of a happy community.[2] Jonson's protagonists rarely excel as lovers; courtship and marriage are not usually major issues in his plays. In fact, the fate of *Volpone*'s Celia and *Epicene*'s Morose is divorce. Jonson's characters are hardly given to sudden conversions or reversals—indeed, critics traditionally complain that Jonson's characters are incapable of development. Nor is generational conflict a major Jonsonian theme. Though in *Every Man in His Humour* a sympathetic son triumphs over an insensitive, repressive father, Jonson does not make father-son relationships primary again until he writes *The Staple of News* twenty-six years later—and this time the father is sympathetic and the son needs to be reformed.

WHY is Jonson's comedy so unusual? Many of its peculiar

aspects become comprehensible when some important psychological assumptions made by the Roman moralists are clarified. For the kind of comedy Northrop Frye describes is not ideologically neutral; it is based upon certain assumptions about human psychology and social organization. We do not recognize this fact only because various forms of these assumptions are so familiar to us. The Roman moralists' characteristic ways of thinking about psychological and political issues gives Jonson an alternative perspective, one that has a tremendous impact upon the kinds of artistic endeavor he finds congenial.

In the psychological systems to which we are most accustomed, the direction or orientation of an impulse determines its moral value. A Freudian might describe a child who graduates from playing with his feces to making mudpies; when he is older he collects stamps, and he grows up to be a banker. The energy involved in all these forms of behavior is, for the Freudian, derived from the same source. A single basic drive finds different outlets at various times in a person's life, and is disparately expressed by different people. The man who copes with his Oedipal complex by writing *The Way of All Flesh* is morally superior to the one who murders old men in subways, but the psychic origin of both actions is the same.

The most important classical proponent of a psychology like this one is Socrates in *The Symposium*.[3] Socrates describes *eros* as a general desire for the beautiful which may find any number of objects—from those promising immediate but transitory sensual pleasure, like a beautiful boy; to more intellectual and permanent pleasures, like the beautiful boy's soul; on up to the absolute gratification afforded by the idea of eternal beauty itself. Socrates' celebrated unseduceability is the consequence not of emotional sluggishness but of a keenly developed erotic impulse which has found its proper object in philosophy.

Augustine, whose own religious philosophy incorporates much of his earlier Platonism, Christianizes the same sort of psychological assumptions and uses them to distinguish himself from the Stoic ethical philosophers that Jonson's Latin writers find so attractive. In the *City of God* XIV, 7, he points out that in the Vulgate the words *amor* and *dilectio* are used indiscriminately for good and bad love. The most abandoned lust and the finest kind of sacred devotion proceed from the same source; it is their objects which differ. It is not surprising, therefore, that throughout the *Confessions* the verbs Augustine uses to describe his attainment of religious conviction imply a deflection of energy, not its suppression—*mutare* (to change), *convertere* (to change direction or to transform). In the *City of God*, he explicitly contrasts Stoic imperturbability with Christian sensitivity: "In our discipline it is not asked whether the pious spirit will be angry, but why it is angry; nor whether it is sad, but for what cause it is sad; nor whether it fears, but why it fears."[4] Desire is taken for granted by Plato and Augustine—the point is to find it an adequate outlet.

What constitutes that outlet? For many medieval and Renaissance writers the right management of libidinal energy becomes a primary religious concern. Insofar as the beloved is substituted for God, the lover is idolatrous, but insofar as the beloved is worshipped for her divine element, as a sort of symbol of God's love, she becomes not a hindrance but a help to religious enlightenment. The moral daring of Dante in the *Paradiso*, or Petrarch in his sonnets to Laura, is made possible by the Platonic-Augustinian assumption that sacred and profane love share a common impulsive base. "O glorious trial of exceeding love!" cries Eve in *Paradise Lost* as Adam reaches for the forbidden fruit, determined to join her in sin. What they both forget in the moment of the Fall is that strong emotion, considered in itself, has no moral value. Its rectitude or depravity depends upon the quality of the object.

A psychology something like this one is assumed by the kind of comedy Northrop Frye describes. Sexual desire is, in erotic comedy, the linchpin of the human psyche and the primary motive for community life. The forces of repression need to be overcome; the rule of the game is not to deny one's emotional nature but to employ it in some acceptable manner. To paraphrase Augustine, it is not whether one loves but what and how one loves that makes the difference. In Platonic and Augustinian philosophy, the beloved is finally supernatural, and thus *eros* is not really acceptable until its carnal nature has been transcended. Erotic comedy, which celebrates a secular, human love, is more liberal in this regard; but here, too, one proves one's moral status by one's attraction to something intrinsically good. The point is still to find some adequate outlet for libidinal energy. Although the psychological gymnastics performed by the comic hero and heroine are not as strenuous as those required of the Christian saint, the process of sublimation—the transference of sexual energy away from explicitly carnal aims—is nonetheless important in erotic comedy. After all, there are weddings in the fifth act, not orgies. In *As You Like It* the relationship between Rosalind and Orlando ranks higher than the relationship between Touchstone and Audrey; in all Shakespeare's comedies we think it is important that the unmarried heroines remain chaste through five acts. Premarital abstinence becomes symptomatic of true love.

Jonson rejects romantic comedy because the Roman moral philosophy he finds so attractive would lead him to regard as untenable the erotic dynamic it celebrates. Socrates' psychology in the *Symposium*, the Christian psychology of Augustine, Dante, or Petrarch, is a psychology of radical *dependence*. Both the Socratic philosopher and the Augustinian saint are motivated by a sense of incompleteness, and seek to find outside themselves a perfection they cannot supply from within. They share a sense of profound humility beside the ideal beloved; it is Satan in *Paradise Lost* who thinks that "the mind is its own place," forgetting that his moral nature is determined by the quality of his allegiances.

The Roman moralists utterly repudiate the Platonic-Augustinian strategy of abasement. The whole idea of sublimation is unintelligible to them because it makes moral status a consequence of what are, strictly speaking, external factors. They are hostile to desire in general, not merely the more sordid kinds of desire, because it undermines the self-sufficiency in which they believe true happiness and tranquillity reside. Seneca tells an anecdote about a youth who asks his philosophy teacher whether a man who was perfectly wise would fall in love. We need not concern ourselves with that question yet, the teacher replies. Certainly we, who are as yet imperfect, would be ill-advised to succumb to an impulse so "agitated, powerless, surrendered to another, vile in itself."[5] In the *Pharsalia,* Lucan introduces his ideal citizen, Cato, with a panegyric on his married life. After he has three children by his wife, Cato lends her to another man, that she might increase his family by her fertility. When this man dies the wife comes to Cato in her mourning garments and begs to be taken back into his household. Lucan writes admiringly:

These customs, these severe practices were characteristic of
  Cato's steadfast
Way of life; to keep well within limits and hold fast to his
  goals,
To follow nature, and to devote his life to his country;
He believed himself born not for himself, but for the whole
  world.

                              . . . His only use of sex
Was for progeny; he was a father for the sake of the city
  and a husband for the sake of the city;
He supported justice, preserved inflexible integrity,
And was good to everyone; in no act of Cato's
Did pleasure steal in and claim a part as its due.[6]

Far from deriving an ideal society from the comic triumph of eros, Lucan assumes that a commitment to personal integrity and the public good involves a sacrifice of sexual pleasure. Virgil's Aeneas, too, must renounce the erotic satisfactions of Carthage in order to realize his destiny as founder of Rome. This is the standard doctrine of the Roman moralists. In *De senectute* Cicero has Cato say that from lust is born "betrayals of the country, subversions of the commonwealth, hidden conversations with enemies."[7] "Really this whole thing ordinarily called love," Cicero writes in *Tusculan Disputations*, "—nor in truth can I devise another name by which it might be called—is of such triviality that I see nothing that I believe to be comparable." And then he adds signficantly, "There would be no comedy at all, if we did not approve of such disgrace."[8]

THIS is why, though Jonson is intensely interested in some traditional comic themes—community life, for instance—eros in almost all his comedies tends to be peripheral or non-existent. Wives are picked up casually, and women ordinarily exist only on the margins of the dramatic action. The exceptions—the women who play important or powerful roles in their comic societies—are, moreover, conceived differently from the women in other Jacobean comedies. Edmund Wilson chastises Jonson for the "remoteness" of his ideal women[9]—though one need not accept the pejorative thrust of Wilson's analysis, he is correct to say that Jonson ordinarily represents female virtue as a quality that would be violated, not completed, by sexual contact.

> Have you seene but a bright Lillie grow,
> Before rude hands have touch'd it?
> Have you mark'd but the fall o'the Snow
> Before the soile hath smutch'd it?[10]

In *Cynthia's Revels*, Cynthia is the virgin queen of a court devoted not to marriage but to chastity; the virtue of Celia, her later, less powerful incarnation, similarly involves a repudiation, not an acceptance, of her sensual nature. Her comic destiny is not happy marriage but perpetual celibacy—something Shakespeare will not even allow his militantly chaste Isabella.

The ideal plane disappears in the comedies after *Volpone*.

In *The Alchemist* and *Bartholomew Fair*, the centrally important women—Dol Common and Ursula Pig-Woman—are
whores who accept their sensual nature with a vengeance,
but for whom the conventional comic reward of respectable
sexual gratification is unavailable. There is a curious matter-
of-fact quality about Jonson's treatment of Dol and Ursula
which is very likely a product of Roman assumptions. Even
in the plays of Middleton, who treats his whores with a certain sympathy, there is ordinarily something particularly ob-
jectionable and unassimilable about these women. Even when
they sincerely repent they remain—unlike, say, prodigal
heirs—marginal or outcast in the comic society of the conclusion. The penitent Courtesan in *A Trick to Catch the Old
One* is coupled with an aged usurer; the reformed Bella-
fronte, in *The Honest Whore*, is wed to a spendthrift bully.
Jonson does not seem to feel the same compulsion to punish
his whores or to distinguish sexual vice from other sorts.
Dol's part of the "venter tripartite" does not differ in moral
kind from the coordinate activities of Subtle and Face; Ursula
exemplifies the values of her world rather than single-hand-
edly subverting them.

The squeamishness of most Jacobean dramatists surely derives from the assumption, in erotic comedy, that sexual desire rightly directed constitutes a primary social bond. Pros-
titutes, by perverting desire from its constructive potential,
are guilty of an extraordinary kind of social subversion. Since
Jonson does not recognize in sexual passion the positive value
attributed to it by other comic dramatists, he is not com-
pelled to protest so vigorously against its less attractive aspects. Prostitution for Jonson falls into a general class of vicious and incontinent behavior; he does not single it out as a
particularly gross scandal. In conventional Renaissance comedy the whore commonly has a polar opposite in the virtuous woman the hero eventually marries—Infaelice in *The
Honest Whore*, Beatrice in *The Dutch Courtesan*, the Niece in
A Trick to Catch the Old One. But the similarities between
Jonson's whores and his middle-class women are more strik-

ingly obvious than their differences. When Face and Subtle
need to show their eager "Spaniard" to a woman, and Dol
Common is otherwise engaged, they substitute in despera-
tion the young middle-class widow, Dame Pliant. And Dame
Pliant fits her role to perfection; Surly makes his fatal error
when he treats her like a romance heroine and fails to capi-
talize immediately upon his sexual opportunity:

> What an over-sight,
> And want of putting forward, sir, was this!
> (V.v.54-55)

Win Littlewit and Mistress Overdo are transformed into
whores by the end of *Bartholomew Fair*, and Dame Purecraft
reveals to Quarlous and the audience her own more discreet
form of prostitution. Indeed, Jonson's whores by their frank
self-knowledge achieve a kind of limited intelligence, and gain
our qualified sympathy when the hypocritical, self-deceptive
bourgeois women merely repel us.

It is not surprising that Jonson, who rejects in his drama
the firm distinction made by other playwrights between sub-
versive and socially constructive sex, likewise rejects the possibility of sublimation—the transference of erotic energy from
a base to a noble object. Donne's *Anniversaries*, he declares
to Drummond, are "profane and full of Blasphemies"[11]—
Donne's strategy, which is to refine the love felt for an earthly
woman until it is similar to the love of God, seems shocking
to Jonson, because he thinks the whole operation is an impossible one. In the comedies, dreams of grandeur inevitably
reduce to foolishness and greed. Volpone's and Mosca's fantasies, as well as those of the legacy-hunters they deceive, are
grounded in obsessive avarice; *The Alchemist*, with its false
transmutations, even more comprehensively savages the human yearning for positive metamorphosis. In Shakespearean
comedy disguise is creative; it makes possible a transformation of identity and is normally the prelude to marriage. But
in Jonson, disguise is hypocritical, and in *Epicene* it leads not
to marriage, but to divorce.

84

THE same Roman resistance to the psychology of sublimation is perhaps responsible for the oft-noted "corporeality" of Jonson's imagination. Jonson's debt to the materialist Roman humours psychology has already been mentioned, as well as the ambivalence toward the body that he inherits from writers like Seneca and Cicero. But the Roman moralists' general attitude toward the material world has additional important consequences for Jonson's art. Harry Levin remarks that in Jonsonian drama

> the imagery surprises us by being so tangible, by presenting its objects not as fanciful comparison, but as literal description. . . . The rich jewel in the Ethiop's ear belonged to Juliet only by metaphorical parallel; Jonson would have slashed off the ear, conveyed the jewel to Volpone's coffers, and dangled it before Celia as the price of her virtue.[12]

Crispinus is made to vomit his neologisms in *Poetaster*, Sir Pol's fantasies go up in real smoke, Epicure Mammon's voluptuous dream-world shatters in an actual explosion, Justice Overdo, the failed magistrate, sits in the stocks. And surely it is Jonson's close attention to the body, its cravings and its products, which leads William Hazlitt to complain, "In Ben Jonson, we find ourselves generally in low company, and we see no hope of getting out of it. He is like a person who fastens upon a disagreeable subject, and cannot be persuaded to leave it."[13]

Nineteenth-century critics have the same problem with many of Jonson's favorite Roman writers. In 1872 Edward Walford explains Juvenal's obscenity as a regrettable feature of Roman culture:

> The coarseness which does undoubtedly deface his pages in more than one instance . . . is the result of the times far more than of the individual temperament of the writer; and the same coarseness will be found not only in the pages of Horace and Persius, but also of philosophers

like Seneca and Pliny, to say nothing of such writers as Martial and Petronius.[14]

Juvenal writes about hemorrhoids, their causes and treatment; Horace imagines himself impotent with an ugly woman; Martial jokes about oral sex in terms so explicit that the Loeb editors print only Italian translations of many epigrams.

What is it about "the times" which is congenial to this kind of poetry? The Roman moralists' sense of propriety and its violation issues from their conception of desire and appetite. They can seem, in their Stoic phase, fiercely repressive, but they are not prudish—at least not in the Victorian sense—because they have nothing to gain from prudery. Appetite, the Roman moralists believe, cannot be legitimately channeled into "higher," more spiritual forms; they construe the objects of appetite in a narrowly carnal way. They stress the contrast between the insatiability of desire—its extraordinary ambitiousness—and what they believe to be its comparatively trivial or base forms of gratification. (This discrepancy can be exploited for purely comic effect, as it is in some of Horace's self-mocking odes, or for an ethical lesson, as in Seneca's *Moral Essays*, or it can be treated satirically, as it is in Juvenal and Persius.) When Volpone and Epicure Mammon employ hyperbole to convey what they believe to be the vastness of their acquisitive and voluptuous fantasies, they betray at the same time a truth they need to ignore: that any realization of these fantasies would inevitably prove disappointing.

> I will have all my beds, blowne up; not stuft:
> Downe is too hard. And then, mine oval roome,
> Fill'd with such pictures, as TIBERIUS tooke
> From ELEPHANTIS: and dull ARETINE
> But coldly imitated.
>
> (*The Alchemist*, II.ii.41–45)

But how pornographic can a picture be, how soft a bed? The satisfactions Sir Epicure and Volpone anticipate are limited by the necessarily physical form they take. After a certain point the organism surfeits, and a law of diminishing returns begins to apply. The voluptuous mind must devote itself to contemplating mere accretion—"I will make me, a back . . . to encounter fiftie a night"[15]—or to exquisite variations: Celia in a new dress every evening. The ultimately exhausting effect of Volpone's or Sir Epicure's rhetoric derives from the fact that their appetites offer them no escape. Even in their most extravagant flights of imagination they finally can only repeat themselves. When Volpone describes an exotic meal, he thinks of eating "the heads of parrats, tongues of nightingales, / The braines of peacoks, and of estriches"[16]—merely transferring into explicitly gastronomic terms his hunger for the substance of his stupid, prideful, and blind neighbors (as figured by the parrot, the peacock, and the ostrich) and his sexual appetite for Celia, who nearly suffers at his hands the fate of Philomel.

A resolute refusal to grant desire any but narrowly carnal aims keeps insatiability from becoming a romantic, tragic, or pathetic phenomenon for Jonson. Epicure Mammon, deliriously envisioning himself dining upon the udders of pregnant sows, betrays a closer kinship with Spenser's Grill than with Tamburlaine or Endymion. It is a conception of appetite which makes Jonson deceptively easy to psychoanalyze.[17] One would not dream of trying to classify Donne or Shakespeare or Spenser as "anal" or "oral," but that Jonson's imagery is "anal" in "The Famous Voyage," or that Penshurst, the edible estate, "satisfies oral cravings," is patently true. Instead of trying to classify Jonson's neuroses, though, it might be more interesting to ask why he makes things so obvious. By assuming that the body and its functions are the sole possible source and object of desire, Jonson has in a sense already performed the psychoanalyst's task for him, has already reduced appetite to its most energetically primitive, egoistic, inchoate forms. What to a Freudian seems to be a case of arrested or perverted development is for the Roman moralist a form of honesty.

This does not mean that the Roman moralists always, or even ordinarily, tolerate obscenity. They would have no sympathy, for example, with the modern liberal who claims that frankness about sex is a good, healthy thing because sex itself is a good, healthy thing. But the rationale they give for the suppression of sexually explicit language, or for the concealment of bodily functions, is different from that which Edward Walford, upset by Roman coarseness, takes for granted. If one believes that obscenity diverts impulses away from "high" spiritual aims, it is invariably a bad thing; it is vicious in and for itself. Furthermore, it is just as bad to choose an improper subject for one's art in the first place as it is to treat a noble one in a coarse way.

The Roman moralists, on the other hand, eschew obscenity because they believe that the shameful and degrading aspects of life should not be allowed to impinge upon more dignified occasions. It is a matter of uniformity of tone. Obscenity is not bad in itself, but bad in particular contexts. Of course, one can construe these contexts so broadly that "coarseness" is invariably improper (Cicero sometimes comes close to doing so).[18] But the Roman attitude is also consistent with a more permissive sense that content should dictate style. Jonson invokes this pretext when he addresses James in the prologue to *Bartholomew Fair*:

> Your *Majesty* is welcome to a *Fayre*;
> Such place, such men, such language, and such ware,
> You must expect.   (1-3)

Hazlitt would not be mollified by this explanation because he would maintain that Jonson should not have written about Bartholomew-birds in the first place. One imagines that Horace, or Juvenal, or Seneca, or Persius would have been more receptive.

JONSON'S use of traditionally polysignificant myths of metamorphosis, myths so important to Elizabethan and Jacobean comedy, reveals as surely as do his comic plots his general suspicion of the sublimatory process. One of the perennially intriguing features of the kind of psychology proposed by Plato, Augustine, or Freud is the way it allows noble and base possibilities to coincide simultaneously, paradoxically, in the same subject. Erotic desire, in particular, has an extraordinary range of potential; it seems obscene and grotesque on one hand, sacred and mysterious on the other. In the Middle Ages and the Renaissance the Ovidian mythological canon became particularly susceptible to a sort of bivalent allegorization. The story of Danae could suggest both prostitution and the descent of divine grace; the story of Ganymede both homosexual rape and the union of the good soul with God. Shakespeare habitually exploits both possibilities at once; Bottom in *A Midsummer Night's Dream* gets transformed into something that both exceeds and falls short of his ordinary identity.

Jonson, though, is usually more comfortable with the alternative Roman tradition of mythological exegesis. Although fully aware of the allegorical possibilities of the traditional stories, the Roman moralists insist that, nevertheless, there are myths and myths. The story of Pandora, for example, is admonitory no matter how it is understood; the moral valence of the symbolic and literal level is identical. The stories of Jove's metamorphoses, on the other hand, though they can be made edifying as allegories, still depict the gods in literally indecorous situations, and this makes the Roman moralists very uneasy. Seneca repeatedly deplores the ineptness of poets who excuse human vices by attributing them to the gods.[19] Cicero writes:

> I do not suppose the gods rejoice either in nectar or in Hebe who tends the cups, nor do I attend to Homer, who says that Ganymede was stolen by the gods on account of his beauty, in order to serve drinks to Jove; there was no just cause to do Laomedon such harm. Homer imagined these things and transferred human

qualities to the gods; I would prefer divine ones be given to us.[20]

Virgil departs from Homeric precedent by depicting the gods in generally dignified positions—unlike Ovid, who, Quintilian complains, is "lascivus . . . in herois," licentious in his treatment of heroic things.[21] Another way to deny the sanctity of the myth is to undermine the awe with which it is traditionally regarded. In *Satires* I, Juvenal ridicules the decadence and bombast of post-Augustan mythological epics. When Horace writes about Europa he writes not about mysterious metamorphosis and passionate consummation but about a girl left pregnant on an empty beach far from home, striken with panic and remorse after the fact.[22]

Jonson follows the Roman moralists' precedent by consistently associating metamorphic myths not with his virtuous, but with his vicious characters. In the *Epigrams* he warns Sir Voluptuous Beast, who trains his wife to take "varied shapes," that he is teaching her to be a whore. Volpone invokes the loves of Jupiter when he is trying to seduce Celia; she perceives the debased sensualism that motivates his beautiful language. In *The Alchemist* Epicure Mammon, mythographer *extraordinaire*, tries to win Dol Common's love by comparing her to Danae; the joke is on him, for while he thinks of himself as omnipotent Jove, pouring alchemical gold into the lap of his beloved, the audience knows that Dol is Danae the prostitute, extorting money from an enamored gull. In *Catiline* Fulvia invokes Danae once again as a whore's precedent:

> I'am not taken
> With a cob-swan, or a high-mounting bull,
> As foolish LEDA, and EUROPA were,
> But with the bright gold, with DANAE. For such price
> I would endure, a rough, harsh JUPITER,
> Or ten such thundring gamesters: and refraine
> To laugh at 'hem, till they are gone.
>
> (II.179-185)

And not only the myths of Jupiters' metamorphoses, in Jonson, are used to reveal the impossibility of sexual transcendence. Important to *Cynthia's Revels* is the story of Actaeon, whom Jonson portrays as a voyeur and potential rapist. The gates to divinity, Cynthia maintains, are not to be gained by erotic assault.

It is interesting in this regard to look at Jonson's portrayal of Ovid himself in *Poetaster*. A. C. Swinburne complains that Ovid's presence in the opening scenes lead the audience to assume that he is the bad poet after whom the play is named.[23] But the first scenes themselves set Ovid up as a New Comedy hero, complete with heavy father and ungratified love. Is Ovid a bad poet, or a comic hero—or a combination of both, like Orlando in *As You Like It* or Benedick in *Much Ado*? Ovid baffles the audience at the beginning of *Poetaster*, just as, later in life, he will baffle his readers with the ambivalent moral tone of the *Metamorphoses*. Eventually Jonson's Ovid holds a masquerade banquet of the gods, casting himself as Jupiter, the emperor's daughter as Juno, and his friends as various lesser deities. An outraged Augustus exiles Ovid in consequence.

What are we to think of this? On one hand Ovid—as Quintilian complains, and like the Homer whom Cicero and Seneca deplore—has degraded the gods to excuse human vices. Like Actaeon, he is punished for presumption; eros as a means of transcendence fails again. On the other hand, Ovid is certainly *not* guilty of treasonable designs on the imperial throne, as Augustus' informer has implied; the wise Horace thinks his sentence overharsh. The point is that Ovid is neither the exemplar of the good life nor a serious social threat, neither poetaster nor true poet. In the Augustan world of *Poetaster*, Ovid is socially marginal; Jonson's audience, conditioned by erotic comedy, has trouble with him because it fails to recognize a red herring when it sees one. In the War of the Theaters, *Poetaster*'s elaborately detailed Roman setting serves Jonson's polemical requirements; it constitutes a kind of reply to Thomas Dekker, who in *Satiro-Mastix* can make

"Horace" look ridiculous merely by dropping him into the middle of a flamboyantly romantic tragi-comedy. Jonson quite literally banishes Ovid from his play after a parodic balcony scene with Julia, and with him disappear all vestiges of romance. What supersedes it is the more typically Jonsonian process of exposure and purgation, a ritual overseen by the public poets Horace and Virgil, and sponsored by the authority of an emperor. This drama, and not the drama of frustrated love, produces the regenerate comic society of the conclusion.

If the Roman moralists reject sublimation as a means of transcendence, what do they put in its place? The benefits of their rationality—tranquillity, security, joyfulness, harmony with God—as well as certain side-effects, like the moderation of sensual desire, resemble those described by Augustine as the benefits of the Christian faith. And neither camp gives favorable publicity to vices like gluttony, lust, anger, envy, and avarice. But the Roman moralist and the Augustinian Christian employ radically different strategies both to obtain these spiritual benefits and to avoid these spiritual pitfalls.

The Roman moralists typically envisage the attainment of wisdom and virtue—two synonymous terms—not as a redirection of energy but as a replacement of one kind of thing by another. It is false to call their hostility to emotional indulgence merely repressive, because the whole concept of harmful repression involves the assumption, denied by Roman psychological theory, that an impulse unnaturally suppressed will pop out uncontrollably in some unexpected and usually grotesque fashion. Since they do not accept the Platonic-Augustinian-Freudian notion of an economy of drives, the Roman moralists see no reason for this to be true. "Is it possible for desire to be limited?" asks Cicero. "It is to be destroyed, and pulled out roots and all."[24] Seneca agrees that "it is easier to exclude vice than to rule it, and not to admit it at all than to restrain it after it is admitted."[25] Desire for things outside the self, the Romans believe, arises from the false conviction that such things will make one happy; thus it can be extinguished by virtuous intelligence, the wisdom that allows one to see one's moral actions as entirely free from external control. The Roman moralists, therefore, as the quotation from Seneca reveals, imagine desire as an alien intruder upon the tranquil, rational soul; Jonson expands upon this idea when he imagines a quasi-political conspiracy and betrayal in his *Epode*:

> For either our affections do rebell,
>   Or else the sentinell
> (That should ring larum to the heart) doth sleepe,
>   Or some great thought doth keepe
> Back the intelligence, and falsely sweares,
>   Th'are base, and idle fears
> Whereof the loyall conscience so complaines.
>   Thus, by these subtle traines,
> Doe several passions (still) invade the minde,
>   And strike our reason blinde.
>
>   (21-30)

Seneca and Cicero safeguard the ideal inviolability of the virtuous mind by adopting the Platonic distinction between the rational and irrational parts of the soul and assigning passion to the irrational part.

> I recall that the soul is composed of two parts; one is irrational, and this part suffers pain, annoyance, and sorrow; the other is rational, and this part has unshaken beliefs, is calm and unconquerable.[26]

Philosophy teaches one to maximize, so to speak, the rational part of the soul, which man shares with the gods, at the expense of the irrational part, which man shares with the lower animals. The wise man vanquishes his weakness to become a sort of god in little. The Roman moralists posit no continuity between reason and unreason; they reject, for example, the Platonic suggestion that love of knowledge has an erotic base. Augustine employs plainly sexual language to describe his intellectual life. He is *amator sapientiae*, a lover of wisdom, who wishes to embrace her "with no clothing between us, as if nude."[27] Cicero, by contrast, indignantly dismisses the possibility of an emotional affinity between metaphysical curiosity and sexual passion. "What! You call studiousness lust?"[28] Cicero praises Socrates for having overcome his innate tendency to sexual excess; Seneca admires the unchanged countenance with which he faces any and all eventualities.[29] The disciplined Socrates, indifferent to worldly fortune, captures their imagination. They ignore the ironic, erotic aspect of the Socratic personality, and the process by which, in the *Symposium*, he claims it is possible to achieve self-mastery.

Thus, though both Augustine and the Roman moralists illustrate their doctrine by exempla, there is a crucial difference in their techniques. Augustine conceives of bad and good moral states as episodes in the progress of the same soul. He writes autobiography, in which he can conveniently show himself first as a vicious heretic, then undergoing a conversion experience, then a regenerate Christian. Erotic comedy, too, is fond of miraculous conversions—energy suddenly deflected from a bad end to a good one. The Roman moralists, by contrast, though they certainly believe that a person can grow better or worse over time, tend to imagine either amelioration or decline as a slow process of education and habituation, a process difficult to portray convincingly and in its entirety within the narrow confines of an epistle, essay, satire, or play. Therefore they find it more convenient to use two different people or groups of people to depict moral opposites. Horace and Juvenal invoke the stern Romans of olden days with which to compare lax moderns; Cicero contrasts the temperate Laelius with the glutton Gallonius, and sensual Lucius Thorius with heroic Regulus.[30] Seneca is particularly fond of paired examples:

> I will set before your eyes two examples—the greatest of your sex and generation—one, a woman who per-

mitted herself to be carried away by grief, the other a woman who, struck with a similar misfortune and by a greater loss, did not however allow herself to be long overpowered by her hardships, but quickly restored her spirit to its usual state. . . . Choose, therefore, which example you suppose the more praiseworthy.[31]

The Roman moralists' sense that virtue and vice are of an entirely different psychological character is the intuition which lies behind Jonson's requirement that the poet have "the exact knowledge of all vertues, and their Contraries; with ability to render the one lov'd, the other hated, by his proper embattaling them."[32]

In the Jonsonian masque the antimasque grotesques are not ordinarily transformed into something nobler but are simply banished, and a new and higher order takes their place. Seneca, in order to stress the differences between virtue and vice, imagines them in different settings:

You will meet virtue in the temple, the forum, the senate building, or before the city walls . . . pleasure more often in hiding and in search of darkness, around the baths and sweatrooms and the places that fear the ediles.[33]

Likewise in the masques the lack of continuity between bad and good is emphasized by a change of scene and tone that accompany the shift from antimasque to masque proper. In the *Masque of Queenes* the witches' coven is unexpectedly interrupted:

In the heate of theyr *Daunce*, on the sodayne, was heard a sound of loud Musique, as if many Instruments had given one blast. With which, not only the *Hagges* themselves, but theyr *Hell*, into which they ranne, quite vanished; and the whole face of the *Scene* alterd; scarse suffring the memory of any such thing: But, in the place of it appear'd a glorious and magnificent Building, figuring the *House of Fame*. (354–360)

95

The masque as Jonson develops it is a Roman moralist equivalent of romantic comedy, demonstrating the triumph of the perfect society over the threats of its subversion.

The isolation of virtue from vice, of the high from the low, is not merely a matter of masque decorum; it occurs all through Jonson's art. Horace recommends to dramatists that their characters be self-consistent from one end of the play to the other,[34] and Jonson's idea of self-consistency involves a radical inability to be morally transformed. No one repents for ethical reasons in Jonsonian comedy until *The Devil Is an Ass*. Ordinarily exposure deflates the characters and forces the play to end. In *Every Man Out of His Humour* Cordatus revealingly compares the knocking of characters "out of their humours" to the felling of great trees; the perverse self is not to be changed but to be, at best, suddenly and violently demolished.

All this does not mean that Jonson's characters are necessarily "simple"; moral fixity does not preclude certain kinds of complexity. John Creasar has argued convincingly for the subtlety of Jonson's characterization of Corvino, Volpone, Mosca, and Celia.[35] A similar argument could be made for the main characters in all Jonson's middle comedies. They do not lack psychological complexity, but potential for change. The Roman moralists' sense of the substantial difference between virtue and vice makes conversion a difficult dramatic issue. They would not say that a personality had changed its orientation but that one personality had been substituted for another. Thus Jonson prefers to depict ethical alternatives not in terms of a choice offered one of the characters but as a stark juxtaposition of bad and good:

> The thing, they here call Love, is blinde Desire,
>   Arm'd with bow, shafts, and fire;
> Inconstant, like the sea, of whence 'tis borne,
>   Rough, swelling, like a storme:
> With whom who sailes, rides on the surge of feare,
>   And boyles, as if he were

In a continuall tempest. Now, true Love
  No such effects doth prove;
That is an essence, farre more gentle, fine,
  Pure, perfect, nay divine;
It is a golden chaine let downe from heaven,
  Whose linkes are bright, and even.

(Epode, 37–48)

Meagher rightly traces this sort of trope, used in masques like *Love Restored*, back to Pausanias' speech in the *Symposium* about the earthly and divine Aphrodite.[36] The myth is an appealing one for Jonson, because it conceives of the distinction as a difference in kind, not as a difference in orientation.

The Roman moralists' rejection of sublimation means that they conceive of no commerce between the sublime and the ridiculous; they harbor no paradoxical conviction that the bestial is identical with the divine. "Good is not born out of evil, any more than the fig from the olive tree," writes Seneca.[37] And Horace has in mind the irreconcilable opposition between virtue and vice when he maintains that "virtue is the avoidance of vice, and the first wisdom is to lack stupidity."[38] So does Quintilian, when he claims that "there is no association of the virtuous and the shameful within the same breast."[39] In Jonson's comic world "contraries are not mix'd";[40] fools are not unexpected vessels of wisdom, nor does the sexual ambivalence of characters like Androgyno in *Volpone*, or Mrs. Otter and Epicene in *The Silent Woman*, point the way to happy marriage as it does in *As You Like It* or *Twelfth Night*. Jonson's fools are stupid and often vicious, his sexual deviants are merely perverted, his deceivers are out to subvert and not to reconstruct their world.

In the induction to *Bartholomew Fair*, Jonson makes snide remarks about *The Tempest*, objecting particularly to Caliban.

> If there bee never a *Servant-monster* i' the *Fayre* who can helpe it? he sayes; nor a nest of *Antiques*? Hee is loth to

97

make Nature afraid in his *Playes*, like those that beget
Tales, *Tempests*, and such like *Drolleries*. (127-136)

Indeed, from Jonson's viewpoint Shakespeare's last play would
be morally and artistically incoherent. Caliban is distinctive
and sympathetic because, unlike the merely vicious Sebastian
and Antonio, he refuses to fit into ordinary moral categories.
Prospero, self-sufficient philosopher-king and masque author, has much in common with the Roman moralists' sage
which, by 1614, Jonson had long since despaired of making
dramatically viable. But Prospero ends the play by abandon-
ing his earlier authority, acknowledging his relationship to
Caliban, pleading infirmity and impotence, and throwing
himself upon the mercy of the audience. For the author of
romance, Prospero's final realization is the recognition of life's
realities. For Jonson, who construes these realities quite differently, *The Tempest* does indeed make nature afraid.

THE rigorous Roman separation of virtuous impulses from
vicious impulses does not abolish moral problems. It merely
conceives them differently. Someone like Augustine judges
the moral status of an emotion by the quality of its object.
Love of God is good because the object is a good one; lust
is bad because its object is base. Moral problems arise for the
Augustinian when the object of emotion is unclear; what exactly *is* the object of Donne's adoration in the *Anniversaries*?
The Roman moralists, on the other hand, characteristically
ignore the objects of emotional impulses. Cicero writes:

> There is only one method of cure: one must say nothing
> about what kind of thing disturbs the soul, but must
> address the disturbance itself. Thus first of all in dealing
> with an actual desire, since it matters only that it be
> eradicated, one must not inquire whether that which in-
> cites the desire is good or not, but one must eradicate
> the desire itself . . . even if it is an over-ardent desire
> for virtue itself.[41]

Cicero, and the other Roman moralists, locate the morally significant difference between good and bad behavior in the psychic source of that behavior. They tend to ask not "What is the aim of this impulse?" but "From what part of the soul does this impulse arise?"

This characteristic focus upon the origin, rather than upon the objects, of the passions leads the Roman moralists to consider as identical emotions that from other points of view seem to be opposites. "What appear to be different, are conjoined," writes Seneca; "These things, which are so unlike, go together."[42] Fear and hope, he maintains, both originate in the same irrational anxiety about the future. Cicero classes compassion and envy together as forms of an improper passionate reaction to the fortunes of one's neighbors.[43] E. Pearlman, in a psychoanalytic reading of Jonson, notes quite correctly that he ignores the usual demarcations between avarice and lust, lust and gluttony:

> Oral, anal, and genital references are confused, collapsed one into the other to produce a swill of indistinct bodily images . . . all the instinctive demands of the body, the appetites, whether oral, anal, or genital, are identical in that they conflict with order, superego, reason.[44]

Distinctions between forms of irrationality are not important to Jonson; what is important is the difference between irrational appetite and "order, superego, reason"—in Roman moral terms, the rational part of the soul. On the other hand, since the Roman moralists do not believe that virtuous and vicious behavior share a common emotional origin, they distinguish between phenomena which, to a Freudian, would look like manifestations of the same basic drive. Cicero, for example, distinguishes between rational wishes for the truly good, and irrational, immoderate desires for the merely pleasureable, and likewise between rational avoidance, or *cautio*, and *metus*, irrational fear.[45]

The problem for the Roman moralist is to make the proper distinctions between the virtues and the vices that imitate them. How is one to tell *cautio* from *metus*? Quintilian mourns "the proximity of vice to virtue: abusiveness is taken for freedom, rashness for strength, extravagance for fluency."[46] Seneca, in the *Epistulae morales*, describes the ease with which mistakes can be made:

> We embrace bad things in the place of good ones. . . . Vice cheats us under the name of virtue; rashness hides under the title of courage, laziness is called moderation, timidity is taken for caution; in these matters we stray with great danger.[47]

Catiline's chorus, lamenting the decadence of late republican Rome, likewise perceives wickedness as a failure to make accurate distinctions:

> What age is this, where honest men,
> Plac'd at the helme,
> A sea of some foule mouth, or pen,
> Shall over-whelme?
> And call their diligence, deceipt;
> Their vertue, vice;
> Their watchfulnesse, but lying in wait;
> And bloud, the price.
> O, let us plucke this evill seede
> Out of our spirits;
> And give, to every noble deede,
> The name it merits.   (IV.879-890)

Jonson habitually begins his poems of praise with a series of negative conditions; in typical Roman moral fashion he defines positive values in terms of their antitheses, carefully distinguishing the real from the specious.

> Not he that flies the court for want of clothes,
> At hunting railes, having no guift in othes,
> Cryes out 'gainst cocking, since he cannot bet,
> Shuns prease, for two maine reasons, poxe, and debt,
> With me can merit more, then that good man,

Whose dice not doing well, to'a pulpit ran.
No, SHELTON, give me thee, canst want all these,
But dost it out of judgement, not disease.

("To Sir Ralph Shelton," 1-8)

Thou art not, PENSHURST, built to envious show,
Of touch, or marble; nor canst boast a row
Of polish'd pillars, or a roofe of gold:
Thou hast no lantherne, whereof tales are told;
Or staire, or courts; but stands't an ancient pile,
And these grudg'd at, art reverenc'd the while.

("To Penshurst," 1-6)

Sonne, and my Friend, I had not call'd you so
To mee; or beene the same to you; if show,
Profit, or Chance had made us: But I know
What, by that name, wee to each other owe,
Freedome, and Truth, with love from those begot.

("Epigram. To a Friend, and Son," 1-5)

In early masques, Jonson depicts the imitation of virtue by vice in devices like the duel between Truth and Opinion in *Hymenaei*; Opinion steals Truth's clothing and has to be stripped. In later masques, antimasque characters are frequently impostors—bad artists or false courtiers attempting to usurp the power they are incapable of rightly handling. Eventually their fraud is exposed, and the genuine article replaces them. Throughout Jonson's career as a playwright, too, vice is parodic. In the drama, though, the parody becomes more and more thoroughgoing, and more and more threatening to the stability of the values it imitates.

Cynthia's Revels is Jonson's most explicit early treatment of this particular problem. Like *Poetaster*, *Cynthia's Revels* looks at first as if it is going to be an erotic comedy. Mercury and Cupid head for Cynthia's court disguised as pages; Cupid has designs on the courtiers, and something along the lines of Lyly's *Endymion* or Greene's *Arraignment of Paris* seems likely to follow. But as in *Poetaster*, romantic possibilities fizzle out. Cupid, like the naive morality-devil Pug years later in *The Devil Is an Ass*, finds himself ineffectual in the real world. Furious at his failure with the self-absorbed humours characters, Cupid decides to wreak his vengeance on Crites, the Stoic artist-hero. But he has no luck here, either, because Crites is friendly with Arete, or "Virtue," and as Mercury explains, her "favour makes any one shot-proofe against thee, CUPID."

Immunity to erotic temptation, in other words, can proceed either from extraordinary nobility or extraordinary baseness. However, though moral opposites have a similar (abortive) effect on a romantic comedy, it is still important that their differences be made apparent. At the end of the play, Crites presents Cynthia with a masque in which each vicious courtier is disguised as the virtue he or she pretends to possess—Moria, ignorance, as Aphelia, simplicity; Anaides, impudence, as Eutolmus, good audacity; Gelaia, frivolity, as Aglaia, pleasant conversation. Crites' masque makes visual the threat perceived by Seneca, Cicero, and Horace—the possibility that vice may parade as virtue. As in the later masques written for James, falsehood cannot long be sustained in the presence of genuine virtue. Cynthia, the ideal sovereign, detects the fraud and hands the delinquents over to Crites and Arete to be punished.

What is needed to make the necessary distinctions is a quality of judgment, the *iudicium* which the Roman moralists frequently use as an inclusive term for virtue in general. Jonson gives all his virtuous characters opportunities to display their abilities in this line; Crites' name, in fact, derives from the Greek *kritein*, to judge. However, since the importance of the Roman moralists' conception of judgment for Jonson needs to be understood in social as well as psychological terms, a full discussion will have to wait until the next chapter.

THE MASQUES

Though Jonson's masques and nondramatic verse show in many ways the impact of Roman moral assumptions, the fact remains that Jonson's treatment of eros is somewhat more lenient in the poems and masques than in the plays. In the *Haddington Masque* he writes:

> To night is VENUS *vigil* kept.
> To night no *Bride-grome* ever slept;
> And if the faire *Bride* doo,
> The married say, 'tis his fault, too.
> Wake then; and let your lights
> Wake too: for they'l tell nothing of your nights:
> But, that in HYMENS warre,
> You perfect are.   (426-433)

Like the poems to Celia in *The Forest*, this celebration of sexual love seems surprising, given the severely antiromantic attitude of Jonsonian comedy.

The few love poems in *The Forest* pose a far less serious challenge to the view of a characteristically unromantic Jonson than do the masques.[48] Since Jonson works in a variety of genres with a wide range of aims, it is not surprising that his accomplishment in different forms should vary somewhat. On the other hand, even when Jonson excels in forms apparently alien to the Roman sensibility, that sensibility nevertheless tends to make itself felt. For the greatest of Jonson's immediate predecessors and contemporaries—Sidney, Shakespeare, Spenser, Donne—a "lyric" is almost invariably a love poem, whether addressed to a man, a woman, or God. In this context, Jonson's tendency to "write not of love" is striking. The vast majority of the poems in *Epigrams* and *The Forest* are panegyric or satiric; poems of praise or blame which express judgmental affection or dislike, not uncritical desire or devotion.

The poems to Celia are inspired by or adapted from Catullus and the Greek Anthology, rather than from the authors upon which Jonson more usually relies. Jonson differs in his emphases, though, both from Catullus and from the great love-poets of the English Renaissance. Jonson writes not of a consuming passion, an extravagant attachment that gives the lover's life its primary meaning, but of a tender moment, complete but necessarily limited. For other Renaissance love poets, the experience of passion is a form of self-definition: " 'Fool,' said my Muse to me, 'look in thy heart, and write.' " The futile efforts to identify Shakespeare's fair young man or his dark lady may seem laughable, but they develop out of readers' understandable interest in the poet's elusive personality. Nor is it surprising that Donne's or Sidney's lyrics *seem* autobiographical, even if they are not. Against our "better critical judgment," our awareness of sonnet conventions and of the distance between fiction and real life, the lyrics tell us that we discover the nature of the lover when we comprehend the nature of the beloved. Jonson's lyrics imply nothing of the kind. No one inquires into the identity of Celia, because we sense that the information would not enhance our understanding of Jonson. The lyrics to Celia do not form a sequence because they neither relate nor require a history, biographical or otherwise. Their significance depends not upon relationship but upon the context in which they are articulated and the occasion they commemorate. Thus they acquire a radically different import when that context is altered. "Come, my Celia," which seems well-meaning enough in *The Forest*, becomes sinister on Volpone's lips.

Jonson's attitude toward eros in the masques is much more complex. His outlook changes considerably, moreover, between 1605 and 1615, the period during which he is writing his greatest plays. In the 1606 *Hymenaei* Reason, not Eros, is the master of ceremonies, and has to banish the unruly Humours and Affections before the marriage can proceed. The Roman moralist psychodrama, not the psychological assumptions of erotic comedy, gives this masque its shape. Likewise, in the 1608 *Masque of Beauty*, Jonson is careful to distinguish between the kind of Cupids that accompany the noble participants, and the blind gods of wanton love. The Cupid who helps Hymen officiate at the *Haddington Masque*, however, is a more obstreperous youngster, ordinarily the enemy of Minerva and the Muses. By 1611 and 1612, Love of a plainly erotic nature is a main character in such produc-

tions as *Love Freed from Ignorance and Folly* and *Love Restored*.
Given the peripheral place of eros in the nondramatic poetry
Jonson writes during the same years, and the resolute anti-
romanticism of the plays, why does love play a comparatively extensive and honorable role in the masque?

During the early years of his preferment at court, Jonson's
increasingly acute sense of audience, genre, and context
doubtless contribute to his flexibility of outlook. In his prefaces and interlinear commentary, the issue of decorum looms
even larger for the masques than it does for the plays in these
years; Jonson sees it as "my first, and speciall reguard, to see
that the Nobility of the Invention should be answerable to
the dignity of [the] persons." He remarks upon the wedding
song at the end of *Hymenaei*:

> Because I made it both in *forme*, and *matter* to emulate
> that kind of *poeme*, which was call'd *Epithalamium*, and
> (by the ancients) us'd to be sung, when the *Bride* was
> led into her chamber, I have here set it downe whole:
> and doe heartily forgive their ignorance whom it chan-
> ceth not to please. Hoping, that *nemo doctus me jubeat*
> *Thalassionem verbis dicere non Thalassionis*. (436-443)

Obviously if Jonson is commissioned to write a wedding
masque for an aristocratic young couple, or a production in
which the queen and her ladies appears, he will not take the
occasion to point out the similarities between loose women
and apparently respectable ones. But there is more than com-
monsensical tact behind Jonson's comparatively favorable
treatment of eros in the masques. The issue is worth exploring in some detail, because it can help illuminate both the
relation between Jonson's work in different genres, and the
complexity of his use of the Roman moral tradition.

THE activity of masque-writing has great appeal for Jonson;
like a number of his Roman moralist predecessors, he finds

laureateship a deeply satisfying condition. He adopts whole-sale the Roman moralists' emphasis on the artist's civic responsibility, and their tendency to regard certain kinds of poetry as forms of statecraft.[49] The wise Augustus, in *Poetaster*, proclaims that "CAESAR, and VIRGIL / Shall differ but in sound"; a character like Crites, in *Cynthia's Revels*, can reform his society by presenting a masque.

The threat to this exalted conception of masque-writing is the triviality and ephemerality of the genre, both of which Jonson makes strenuous efforts to overcome. Even as he deemphasizes the element of edification in his comedies, he stresses the seriousness of his masques, insisting upon "profit" where mere delight might have been deemed sufficient.[50] And Jonson strengthens his claim for the significance of the masque as literature when he introduces the antimasque; it gives his productions at court more emotional range, and allows the virtuous element to appear both as a remarkable surprise and a miraculous solution. But the antimasque has to be carefully handled, since the requirements posed by a celebration of absolute virtue tend to conflict with artistic *desiderata*. Aesthetically, a certain unity of conception is desirable; on the other hand, the contrast between the vicious or foolish antimasque world and the world of the masque proper must be very strongly marked. It would not do, in the *Masque of Queens*, to suggest that the ladies who populate the House of Fame participate in the grotesqueness of the witches that precede them.

One way to provide more cohesiveness without endangering the exalted tone of the later part of the production is to provide a witness for the antimasque, a character who actually belongs to the high world of the masque proper but who is forced to look on in amusement or disgust while the low characters disport themselves. At the beginning of *The Golden Age Restored*, Pallas descends in her chariot, promising the return of Saturn, Astraea, and the golden age in the reign of James I. She is interrupted, however, by Iron-Age and the Evils; the antimasque then proceeds until it is banished as usual, the scene changes, and the masque proper takes its place. The point of the antimasque is made clear from the beginning, because the positive values against which it reacts have already been firmly stated. Virtue and vice remain, in orthodox Roman moral fashion, polarized and segregated. Pallas in *The Golden Age Restored* is no more implicated in the rebellious ambitions of Iron-Age than Seneca, viewing the promiscuity of Baiae, is tainted by the lewdness there.[51]

Sometimes, however, Jonson relates antimasque to masque in ways that depart from the Roman moralist sense of the relation between virtue and vice. When he writes *Oberon* in 1609, Jonson creates for the first time an ambiguous character who can participate both in the antimasque and in the masque proper. Silenus is a "lover of wine," friend and mentor of the mocking, sensual, unsophisticated satyrs—"but in the *Silenes*," Jonson assures us in note "c," "was nothing of this petulance, and lightnesse; but on the contrarie, all gravitie, and profound knowledge, of most secret mysteries." The antimasque is eventually superseded by "the nation of fays"; a sylvan orders the satyrs to

> Give place, and silence; you were rude too late:
> This is a night of greatnesse, and of state;
> Not to be mixt with light, and skipping sport.
>
> (319-321)

But of course the night *is* mixed with light and skipping sport; it is pleasurable as well as profitable. Silenus comprehends within himself both the festive and morally serious aspects of court entertainment; formally a part of the antimasque, he can nevertheless appreciate the virtue of the monarch. How he can possess both a grotesque and refined aspect is left unclear; Jonson takes refuge in citation of the impeccable Virgil to defend himself against charges of incoherence or indecorum.[52]

In fact, however, the doubleness of Silenus is only one symptom of a new way of relating the two parts of the masque. Even as the sylvan comes forward to tell the satyrs to "give place and silence," the song of the fays suggests an entirely different logic of transition:

> Melt earth to sea, sea flow to aire,
>   And aire flie into fire,
> Whilst we, in tunes, to ARTHURS chaire
> Bear OBERONS desire.
>
> (300-304)

The emphasis here is not simply upon supersession and triumph but upon a kind of chemical evolution upward. For Jonson, this constitutes an unprecedentedly favorable view of metamorphosis. The satyrs are limited by nature, as they freely admit: "Every one / Cannot be ENDYMION." On the other hand, as Jonson points out in a marginal note, the Greeks call satyrs *pheras* or *phereas*, "from whence, it were no unlikely conjecture, to thinke our word *Faeries* to come." The antimasque satyrs and the fays of the masque proper may, in other words, represent "low" and "high" manifestations of the same phenomenon.

Jonson can hardly be said to embrace with enthusiasm the form of transition with which he experiments in *Oberon*—at least until late in life, when his long-held antipathy to romance begins to dwindle on all fronts. Even some of the more endearing and harmless antimasque characters are often quite harshly dismissed.[53] In the second decade of the seventeenth century Jonson does, however, experiment a number of times with a masque unified by a central, morally ambiguous character. In *Love Freed from Ignorance and Folly*, Cupid enters in the clutches of the sphinx, fails to solve her riddle, and is condemned to death. He is saved at the last minute by the Muses' Priests, who give him the clue that liberates him from his captor. Love in this masque is a morally neutral agent, endangered by ignorance but rescued and ennobled when he cooperates with the forces of wisdom. The conception owes more to Plato than to Cicero or Seneca. Jonson exploits the same organizational principle in *Lov-*

ers Made Men, and in the remarkable *Vision of Delight* stresses the polymorphic quality of the poetic imagination: Phant'sy bodies forth the shapes first of ridiculous things, then of sublime ones.

IN many ways, as we have already noted, the appeal of the masque for Jonson is a conservative one; the genre allows him to preserve intact features of the Roman moral vision which he finds difficult to represent on the comic stage. The Roman moralists' sense of the arbitrary relationship between virtue and fortune had required, in the comical satires, an alliance between Jonson's virtuous protagonist and a sovereign power—Queen Elizabeth, Cynthia, or Augustus. In the masques, however, where the king is supposed to possess both virtue and power at the same time, the very conjunction that seems fortuitous in the comedies becomes a fundamental premise, both cause and subject of the celebration.

So it may seem strange that the masque is susceptible to such innovation, that Jonson should even tentatively accept a sublimatory psychology in a masque like *Love Freed from Ignorance and Folly*. Like comedy, however, the masque requires a certain adjustment of Roman attitudes, albeit in a different direction. The Roman moral outlook, particularly in its Stoic phase, is a profoundly defensive one, designed to cope with an indifferent or even hostile world. "To live, Lucilius, is to serve as a soldier," writes Seneca to his friend. And in another letter: "One must cast off the desire for life, and learn that it does not matter at what time you suffer, since at some time one is bound to suffer."[54] It is better to face the inevitable bravely than to succumb under it. In fact, ill fortune becomes an opportunity for the virtuous man:

> Virtue withers without an adversary; it is clear how great and powerful it may be, when it has displayed by endurance what it can do. . . . [Fortune] searches out the strongest, those equal to her; she passes by others with disdain. She attacks the most stubborn and the most up-

right, and asserts her power against them; she tests Mucius with fire, Fabricius with poverty, Rutilius with exile, Regulus with torture, Socrates with poison, Cato with death. One does not discover a great example without bad fortune.[55]

Seneca's conception of life as a test and fortune as the crucible is fundamentally alien to the masque. In the masque, fortune is not virtue's adversary but her cooperative partner, an alliance that renders Seneca's spiritual combat-readiness beside the point. The myth of the monarch's omnipotent goodness, the very feature which makes the masque so conducive to the straightforward dramatic portrayal of virtue, also inevitably alters the essential character of that virtue.

This does not mean that Jonson doubts the validity of Roman moral principles. Indeed, their validity must be taken for granted if the compliments of the masques are to seem sufficiently extravagant. Jonson makes Prince Henry "Oberon the Fair" in 1610, the same year he makes Dapper, in *The Alchemist*, nephew of the Fairy Queen. Unless one knows that fame and virtue are often at odds, that alchemy is generally fraudulent, that pleasure and virtue are ordinarily opposites, that the golden age is gone forever, the masque is pointless. Jonson shows James enforcing harmony among intransigent materials, purging them of their dross, surmounting the insurmountable.

When fortune is rendered utterly reliable, desire becomes unproblematic. The Roman suspicion of desire is founded upon the intuition that everything outside the self is untrustworthy, and that any sort of dependency is therefore perilous. Love is safe in the masque because a virtuous authority guarantees the beneficence of the external world. "How neere to good is what is faire!" exclaim the Muses' Priests in *Love Freed from Ignorance and Folly*. In most of Jonson's comedies, however, no such guarantee pertains. Dependency is still dangerous, and the capacity of desire to transform either lover or beloved remains a mere illusion.

Jonson and the Roman Social Ethos

BEN JONSON conceives of the poet's role as one of public service. In *Discoveries* he repeats Aristotle's claim that poetry "dispose[s] us to all Civill Offices of Society" (2388), and in the prefatory epistle to *Volpone* he calls the poet "a master in manners" who "can alone (or with a few) effect the businesse of man-kind" (29-30). As many critics have noted, Jonson prefers to work in genres that deal explicitly with social issues or social relations: the epigram, epistle, comedy, and masque.[1] Tragedy, in his hands, dramatizes the possibility of certain kinds of political action in a corrupt or morally enervated society.

Jonson's form of social commitment, however, has its bizarre aspects. What Geoffrey Walton calls Jonson's characteristically "dignified and courteous tone"[2] sometimes gives way to invective that seems anything but dignified and courteous. In *Poetaster*'s "apologetical dialogue" Jonson's aggression against his literary rivals takes weirdly extravagant forms:

> They know, I dare
> To spurne, or baffull 'hem; or squirt their eyes
> With inke, or urine . . .
> . . . .
> I could stampe
> Their foreheads with those deepe, and publike brands,
> That the whole company of *Barber-Surgeons*
> Should not take off, with all their art, and playsters.
>   (158-167)

Jonson is more the public executioner here than the "master in manners." In *Volpone*'s preface, the same fantasies of revenge on detractors recur in the midst of his declaration of true poetry's exalted aims. Occasionally, too, Jonson seems curiously prone to the misanthropic hypersensitivity he attributes to some of his comic butts; other people's talk, for instance, can grate upon his senses intolerably:

> they fly buzzing, mad, about my nostrills:
> And like so many screaming grasse-hoppers,
> Held by the wings, fill every eare with noise.[3]

These outbursts of loathing, while elicited in their most violent form by the War of the Theaters, are hardly phenomena confined to Jonson's youth. Near the end of his life he causes a stir with his notorious "Ode to Himself." His social impulse seems to coexist somehow with a sense of exclusivity, a desire to "sing high and aloofe."

Something more complicated than an amiably extrovert personality, therefore, seems to underlie Jonson's commitment to social art. Several critics have remarked upon the Roman roots of his social consciousness,[4] and there are clues to suggest that Roman moral writing affects the misanthropic side of Jonson as well. In *The Staple of News*, Jonson adapts from Seneca a speech for the antisocial Penyboy Senior; the passage reappears nearly verbatim in *Discoveries* as a comment of Jonson's own.[5] Properly understood, Roman social assumptions and categories can illuminate not only Jonson's distinctive ambivalence about his social role, but also a whole range of apparently unrelated critical problems: his sense of what constitutes an appropriate poetic subject, his characteristic construction of a comic plot, his unusual relations with his audience.

It is difficult to imagine a group of writers more impressed than the Roman moralists with their public responsibilities. Senators, consuls, administrators, advisors—they provide models for Renaissance men of letters like Jonson, who envy their ability to find socially beneficial employment for their artistic and philosophical expertise. Rome as a military power, as a civilized ideal, as a cultural and political entity, engages both their practical and their intellectual energies to the fullest.

Like other people who think about social organization in theoretical terms, the Roman moralists are curious about the motives that draw human beings into communities. Political philosophers have suggested a whole range of such motives, each of which tends to privilege a certain kind of human relationship. If, for instance, one considers the basis of society to be economic, the relation between the producer and consumer of goods becomes primary, and other relationships—family bonds, class and religious loyalties—tend to get explained in terms of economic factors. If social organizations arise from one party's need for reliable protection and another's need for dependable service, then the interdependence between king and subject, lord and servant is crucial. If the need to produce offspring is a fundamental motive, then the relation between the sexes is of paramount importance, and the creation of families a primary social goal.[6] The Roman moralists, too, tend to perceive certain relationships as exemplary or fundamental, and their perceptions here are consistent with their general understanding of human nature. While Plato in the *Symposium*, and Augustine in the *Confessions*, make desire ethically and psychologically crucial, the Roman moralists tend to belittle the importance of desire and recommend its suppression. It is not surprising that they refuse to acknowledge eros, sublimated or otherwise, as a primary socializing force.

To the question "What makes human beings form communities?" the Roman moralists answer "reason" or "human nature" or "the social instinct." People form associations with one another not because they are passionately attracted to one another but because individuals naturally seek out other individuals like themselves. Birds of a feather flock together, Seneca informs Lucilius: "By nature everything good is dear to good men, so that every good man is friendly with other good men as with himself."[7] The virtuous man relieves a neighbor in distress, Cicero maintains in *Tusculan Disputations*, not because he participates emotionally in that distress—which would be a weakness—but because he generalizes certain truths about himself and must logically assume that they apply to similar entities.[8]

The Roman moralists' identification of "reason" with "instinct" may seem peculiar to modern readers. Many post-classical thinkers tend to put "instinct" in the same psychological category with "passion" and "emotion," and consider reason to be a separate faculty.[9] But for the Roman moralists or their predecessors, the Greek Stoics, instinct has nothing to do with passion; it is rather a kind of proto-reason, the inborn equipment that allows animals and men to cope effectively, if unthinkingly, with their environment. When songbirds build beautifully designed nests, or newborn chickens flee from the hawk they have never seen, their instinct is leading them to behave in apparently intelligent ways even though they do not possess the ability to reason. Since both instinct and reason are "according to nature," they are in no essential conflict.

Passion, however, is not according to nature and has nothing to do with instinct; it is the result of false beliefs about the world. Cowardice, for example, which some would describe as an intensification of the instinct for self-preservation, the Roman moralists consider to arise from a wrong opinion about the sources of happiness. Selfishness, too, represents a kind of error—either one misapprehends the true state of affairs and fails to notice the similarities between oneself and other people, or else one notices the similarities but irrationally prefers oneself.[10] Thus Jonson depicts egoism as a kind of perceptual handicap; as Mosca says of his gulls in *Volpone*:

> Too much light blinds 'hem, I thinke. Each of 'hem
> Is so possest, and stuft with his owne hopes,
> That any thing, unto the contrary,

114

Never so true, or never so apparent,
Never so palpable, they will resist it.

(V.ii.23-27)

The plays make comic capital out of this kind of self-aggran-
dizing impercipience—Corbaccio's intimations of immortality, Dapper's serene acceptance of fairy ancestry, Overdo's
faith in his superlative cunning.

Human fellowship, then, is founded upon an accurate assessment of similarity—a much more dependable basis, the
Roman moralists believe, than passionate whim. In *De amicitia*, Cicero makes Gaius Laelius maintain that friendships
are closest and most permanent among those who are completely self-sufficient: "For he who trusts greatly in himself,
and is fortified by such great wisdom and virtue that he lacks
for nothing and believes that everything he owns lies within
himself, to that degree does he excel in seeking out and cultivating friendships."[11] For the Roman moralists, perfect love
cannot require dependency. An association based upon un-
fulfilled needs and desires, they maintain, will cease as soon
as those needs and desires are fulfilled. "A sense of community with the human race, affection, friendship, justice, and
the rest of the virtues," writes Cicero, "cannot exist at all
unless they are free."[12] A Platonist or an Augustinian would
distinguish here between kinds of need, kinds of dependency. An association to promote only the material advantage
of both parties would not constitute friendship for them any
more than it would for the Roman moralists. But the Platonist or the Augustinian Christian would recognize a kind
of good dependency, based upon mutual affection and esteem, and ultimately upon a recognition of the incompleteness of the self. For the Stoically inclined Roman moralists,
on the other hand, all dependency and incompleteness implies moral weakness. Sociability, being in itself a good, must
arise out of a virtuous disposition; it cannot be the consequence of what the Roman moralists perceive as a defect.

Thus, like Cicero's Laelius, Seneca attributes the special talents of the wise man—that "master of the art of making friends"—to his complete self-sufficiency.[13] The best social relations exist among people who could live happily without them.

JUST as Marx privileges economic relationships and Hobbes the relations between the powerful and the weak, because they believe that those associations are socially fundamental, the Roman moralists give a certain priority to the social relations that seem most obviously to exemplify their theory of community. The affection among blood relatives, for instance, is easy to explain in terms of a familial intuition of similarity. So it is not surprising that filial bonds loom large for the Roman moralists—much larger than they do for such contemporaries as Ovid or Propertius.[14] When Quintilian describes his suffering upon losing a cherished wife, he subsumes the marital to the paternal relationship· "[She was] so young, especially compared to me, that it was like losing a daughter."[15] Similarly, though he is writing to a bereaved husband, Jonson imagines heaven as a place where not marital but filial bonds are reestablished:

> And each shall know, there, one anothers face,
>   By the beatifick vertue of the Place.
> There shall the Brother, with the Sister walke,
>   And Sons, and Daughters, with their Parents talke.[16]

Parental love especially appeals to the Roman moralists because it seems so obviously the consequence not of need but of disinterested generosity issuing from a perception of likeness.[17]

But even filial relationship, based as it is upon mere physical resemblance, pales before the association of good men, the alliance founded upon spiritual similarity. "He who looks upon a true friend, contemplates as it were a likeness of himself."[18] The Roman moralists ridicule the Platonic description of friendship as merely a hypocritical form of homosex-

116

uality.[19] They glorify instead friendship among virtuous men drawn together not by desire but by a general compatibility of moral taste:

> Nothing is more attractive or joins two people together more effectively than similarity of character in good men; for among those who share inclinations and attitudes, each comes to value the other as himself; and as Pythagoras maintains regarding friendship, one is made out of many.[20]

This is the kind of relationship Jonson celebrates in his ode "To the immortall memorie, and friendship of that noble paire, Sir LUCIUS CAREY and Sir H. MORISON," when he emphasizes that

> No pleasures vaine did chime,
> Of rimes, or riots, at your feasts,
> Orgies of drinke, or faign'd protests;
> But simple love of greatnesse, and of good;
> That knits brave minds and manners, more than blood.
>
> (102-106)

The records the Roman moralists leave behind them reveal the energy they devote to this sort of friendship. Ovid and Propertius may versify their erotic escapades, Catullus his passion for Lesbia—but Cicero's writings testify to his friendship with Atticus, Cato, Calpurnius Piso, and Brutus; Seneca's to his affection for Lucilius and Serenus. Horace's cheerfully promiscuous bisexual affairs seem emotionally undemanding compared with his friendship with Maecenas. Jonson follows their example, writing epigrams and epistles to Donne, Beaumont, the Roe brothers, Carey, Squib, Camden, and numerous other associates, bestowing upon his friendships an attention unprecedented in English poetry.

THE Roman moralists are not alone, of course, in their appreciation of filial intimacy and close nonerotic friendship. But their distinctive understanding of the way these relationships work leaves its mark on Jonson's life and art. Certain apparent paradoxes and contradictions in Jonson's social attitudes vanish, and others appear in a different light, when the terms in which he understands personal relations are clarified.

Fundamental to the Roman moralists' rational altruism is a process of assessment; the sociable man gauges the degree of similarity between himself and others. In *De amicitia*, Laelius stresses the temporal and logical priority of the judgmental moment: "You should love after you have judged, not judge after you have begun to love."[21] We habitually consider "judgment" the coldblooded opposite of "sympathy," "inspiration," or some such unpredictable but superior attribute. Likewise "justice" often seems a (usually unsatisfactory) alternative to "mercy." This is not how the Roman moralists, or Jonson after them, ordinarily delimit the concept. Cicero's Piso articulates a Roman commonplace when he claims that "it is called justice, to which are connected dutiful loyalty, benevolence, generosity, friendliness, kindness, and every trait of the same kind."[22] Judgment *is* true sympathy, true fellow-feeling, not the withdrawal or rejection of fellow-feeling. In his preface to *Volpone*, Jonson defines "the office of a *comick-Poet*, to imitate justice, and instruct to life, as well as puritie of language, or stirre up gentle affections" (119-121). The syntax here is strange. Is the imitation of justice an alternative to the stirring up of gentle affections, or is it a corollary? Jonson's grammar makes it impossible to decide. The ambiguity, however, is significant—the simple opposition between "sympathy" and "judgment," invoked at least implicitly by many critics who find Jonson too "cold" and "intellectual," is not an intelligible one to the Roman moralists.[23]

Sometimes, too, Jonson's critics assume that his attraction to Stoicism must be at odds with his social commitment, even when they recognize the same combination of traits in his Latin predecessors.[24] But for the Greek Stoics, and for the more eclectic Roman moralists after them, self-sufficiency does not involve a withdrawal from society; indeed, it is a prerequisite for the best kind of social intercourse. Jonson praises his truest friendships by calling them "free"; like Laelius in *De amicitia*, he deplores flattery as a corruption of the independence upon which real friendship is based.

The proper relation between independence and friendly generosity can, of course, be difficult to ascertain. Cicero devotes a large part of *De amicitia* to establishing boundaries beyond which self-respecting people may not go in their loyalty to their acquaintance.[25] Geoffrey Walton remarks upon the way Jonson's fine sense of balance in this regard informs poems like *The Underwood* 26, in which he rebukes a friend for duelling.[26] Occasionally, though—as in the beautiful "On My First Son"—the very difficulty of achieving the ideal equilibrium becomes Jonson's subject.

Filial affection, one of the exemplary relations for the Roman moralists, poses particularly grave challenges for a parent. He must think of the child simultaneously as a likeness of himself and as a separate, independent consciousness—even though the child's physical and emotional development is not yet complete and though the filial relationship, unlike friendship, cannot be fully reciprocal. The Roman moralists, therefore, regard with awe those who can accept the death of children with relative equanimity—those like Seneca's Telamon or Cicero's Anaxagoras, who say at their sons' funerals, "When I begat him, then I knew he was to die."[27] Even Tacitus, who disapproves of the more severe Stoic prescriptions of absolute emotional calm, cites Agricola's restraint upon the death of his son as a proof of his sound character.[28]

So when Jonson writes "On My First Son," he portrays himself in a situation the Roman moralists consider particularly difficult and revealing. And the special significance of parenthood in the Roman scheme of things affects the way he experiences his bereavement.

> Farewell, thou child of my right hand, and joy;
> My sinne was too much hope of thee, lov'd boy,

> Seven yeeres tho'wert lent to me, and I thee pay
>   Exacted by thy fate, on the just day.
> O, could I loose all father, now. For why
>   Will man lament the state he should envie?
> To have so soone scap'd worlds, and fleshes rage,
>   And, if no other miserie, yet age?
> Rest in soft peace, and, ask'd, say here doth lye
>   BEN. JONSON his best piece of *poetrie*.
> For whose sake, hence-forth, all his vowes be such,
>   As what he loves may never like too much.

He regards the child as his own production: "child of my right hand," "Ben Jonson his best piece of poetrie." In the less intensely felt "On My First Daughter," both mother and father mourn the loss of their infant. Here, though, there is no hint of maternal bereavement, of collaborative authorship. Since Jonson thinks of the child as so completely his own, his moral situation is somewhat ambiguous.

> My sinne was too much hope of thee, lov'd boy.

Does this mean only that Jonson realizes, in retrospect, that he was unwise to stake so much on a mortal object? In this case there is no causal relation between the father's excessive ambition and the son's decease. But the line might also mean that Jonson perceives young Benjamin's death as a kind of punishment visited upon a doting father. In this case, he is directly responsible for the boy's death.

A suggestion of paternal guilt persists, although Jonson is quick to supply an alternative description.

> Seven yeeres tho'wert lent to me, and I thee pay,
>   Exacted by thy fate, on the just day.

The father seems absolved; not his excessive hopes but an impersonal fate, an unnamed creditor, demands the child's life.[29] Even as he insists that his ownership of the boy is incomplete and conditional, however, Jonson interprets the death in terms of his own action: "I thee pay." "I," not the boy, his fate, or the just day, is the grammatical subject.

> O, could I loose all father, now. For why
>> Will man lament the state he should envie?
> To have so soone scap'd worlds, and fleshes rage,
>> And, if no other miserie, yet age?

Jonson realizes that the boy is not unfortunate, and acknowledges that the consolations appropriate for all deaths should apply to young Benjamin's as well. "When I begat him, then I knew he was to die."

Nonetheless, the universal forms by which grief is alleviated seem beside the point, and the logic of Jonson's argument breaks down in a cry of pain. "O, could I loose all father, now." The Roman moralists characteristically encourage the mourner to forget his own sense of deprivation by assessing the consequences of death from the point of view of the person who experiences it. In *De amicitia* Laelius describes the way he comforts himself upon the death of his closest friend:

> I suppose nothing bad to have happened to Scipio—it has happened to me, if it has happened to anyone—but someone deeply distressed for his own inconveniences loves not his friend, but himself.[30]

Jonson fails to find such a technique effective because it depends upon separating the mourner's experience from the experience of the person whom he mourns. And Jonson has trouble imagining the boy except as an extension of himself. The Roman moralists praise parental love for its pure generosity, and it is precisely this generosity which presents a stumbling block for the bereaved father. Simply because he takes all affectionate initiative—authoring, joying in, hoping for, borrowing, paying back his child—it is difficult to think of the boy as a thing apart, a human being with his own destiny and point of view. Thus in line 5 Jonson believes that only by renouncing completely his paternal feelings can he temper his grief.

Jonson struggles closer to the Roman ideal of the heroically bereaved parent when he begins to grant his son some separate identity.

> Rest in soft peace, and, ask'd, say here doth lye
> BEN. JONSON his best piece of *poetrie*.
> For whose sake, hence-forth, all his vowes be such,
> As what he loves may never like too much.

He no longer considers repudiating his sense of responsibility for his child, his masterpiece. On the other hand, he manages to moderate his fierce sense of exclusive ownership. He imagines the dead boy answering the questions of some curious third party; for the first time the son is allowed dealings with someone other than the father, dealings that take place in the public, impersonal rhetoric of gravestone verse. Perhaps young Benjamin merely speaks words designed for him by his father, but at least he now becomes some sort of agent in his own right, rather than simply a passive recipient of fatherly affection. Once Jonson can conceive of his son as another human being with a distinct point of view, the way is cleared for effective consolation.

The final vow, distinguishing as it does between paternal love and dangerous self-involvement—a distinction Jonson found impossible earlier in the poem—strives toward the Roman ideal of disinterested affection. The poem he writes is restrained, understated; it implies rather than exhibits his grief. On the other hand, Jonson has by no means gained a passionless equilibrium. "As what he loves may never like too much." It is clear both what the last line has to mean— that Jonson's emotional recovery will require a separation of real "love" and selfish "liking"—and also that this separation is unstable and difficult to maintain. Jonson is translating here from Martial: "quidquid ames, cupias non placuisse nimis" (Whatever you might love, wish that you may not be overly pleased with it).[31] *Amare* and *placere*, two very different words in Latin, make the difference between love and gratification seem quite clear-cut. "Like" and "love" in English, though, overlap a great deal—so much so that Jonson's formulation reads like a paradox. The language of the last line implies the difficulty of acting upon his resolution, without suggesting that there is any alternative.

THE importance of parenthood for the Roman moralists makes them characteristically eager to distinguish true sources of filial pride and affection from false sources. Scorning mere fortune, they are unwilling to concede moral advantages to an exalted family background. "A hall full of sooty images does not make a nobleman," Seneca counsels Lucilius.[32] Juvenal writes:

> One can adorn one's entrance-hall on all sides with wax
> busts
> Of ancestors, but virtue is the one and only nobility.
> . . . .
> Are you pure,
> Someone who holds fast to justice, meritorious in word
> and deed?
> I acknowledge you a lord.[33]

Jonson, as much a "new man" himself as Cicero, Horace, or Tacitus, is forever echoing these sentiments. He tells Drummond that he "never esteemed of a man for the name of a Lord," and informs Sir William Jephson that merit is "not entail'd on title": "To live great, was better, then great borne."[34]

Actually, though, the Romans redefine rather than diminish the importance of inheritance. Jonson's advice to the Digby children is translated from Juvenal:

> Hang all your roomes, with one large Pedigree:
> 'Tis Vertue alone, is true Nobilitie.

But he does not conclude that the paternal example should be ignored—quite the opposite, in fact.

Which Vertue from your Father, ripe, will fall;
Study illustrious Him, and you have all.[35]

Even as Cicero boasts to his son, in *De officiis*, of an ascent
to power unaided by family connections, he assumes the boy
will strive to perpetuate the paternal glory.[36] Jonson uses the
same logic, invoking the family laurels in order to encourage
the young William Sidney *not* to rest upon them:

Your blood
So good
And great, must seeke for new,
And studie more:
Not weary, rest
On what's deceast.
For they, that swell
With dust of ancestors, in graves but dwell.

'T will be exacted of your name, whose sonne,
Whose nephew, whose grand-child you are.[37]

Inheritance, far from being denied, is in fact crucially important, but it is the spiritual and not the physical bequest which
really matters. Horace informs Maecenas that he would not
trade his freedman father for a wealthier or more distinguished one, since he has received from him a morally sound
upbringing, the only thing a son should rightly ask.[38]

But if this is so—if the true bond between relatives is spiritual, not physical—why draw any distinction at all between
filial ties and ties of friendship? Indeed, the Roman moralists
often conflate them. Unlike modern meritocrats, they never
want to render ancestry irrelevant, but rather at most to make
filial bonds elective. Adoption was a fact of Roman life, and
Roman moral writers quite naturally extend the concept of
adoptive affiliation to intellectual and moral spheres. Seneca
suggests to Paulinus that he consider Socrates or Zeno his
spiritual father:

We generally say that it was not in our power, which
parents fell to our lot; that they are given to mankind
by chance; but actually, it is permitted us to be born
according to our choice. There are families of the most
excellent characters; choose the one into which you would
like to be adopted.[39]

The adoptive relationship combines the purely spiritual emphasis of Roman friendship with the intimacy and emulative
ambition of the filial bond. Juvenal encourages effete modern
Romans to take Paulus, Drusus, or Cossus as their models:
"Put them before the images of your ancestors."[40] Quintilian
wants pupils to love not only the subjects they study but also
their teachers, the "parents of their minds."[41] Early in life
Jonson, reputed to have argued with his bricklaying step-
father, follows Quintilian's advice and attaches himself to his
teacher, William Camden, "best parent of his muse."
"Alumnus olim, aeternum amicus," he calls himself in the
dedication to *Cynthia's Revels*: "a student once, a friend forever." In this case, filial piety and friendship have become
identical. And even at the age of nearly fifty Jonson finds it
quite natural to think of Vincent Corbett as "both . . . a
friend and Father."[42] Increasingly in later years he assumes
the parental role himself, extending to the "sons of Ben" a
distinctively Roman, adoptive friendship between self-sufficient but compatible individuals.

> Sonne, and my Friend, I had not call'd you so
>   To mee; or beene the same to you; if show,
> Profit, or Chance had made us: But I know
>   What, by that name, wee to each other owe,
> Freedome, and Truth; with love from those begot.
>   ("Epigram to a Friend, and Son," 1-5)

Though the uses Jonson makes of the Roman moralists change
in many ways over the course of his career, the kinds of

relationships they endorse remain unvaryingly important to him from one end of his life to the other.

THE BASIS OF COMMUNITY

THE Roman moralists have considerable philosophical prec-edent for the emphasis they place on filial relationships and disinterested friendship as the basis of community life. In *De finibus* the Stoic Cato and the Academician Piso both insist that civic responsibility arises from the natural love of par-ents for children; Cicero points out to them that the doctrine ultimately derives from Aristotle.[43] Friendship, too, is so-cially basic. *De amicitia*, written from Cicero to Atticus— bosom friends and pillars of the Roman republic—presents doctrines that are supposed to come from the great jurist Quintus Mucius Scaevola, who in turn gets them from his renowned friend Laelius, who claims to be repeating what his even more renowned companion Scipio believed. "By making his participants in the dialogue famous men," Earl Miner observes, "Cicero makes without stating it the Aris-totelian point that friendship is the basis of the concord of the state."[44] Hugh Maclean notes the same phenomenon in Jonson's poems, which "lay stress on the virtues of friend-ship between good men, and in the strong resources such friendships constitute for the ordered society and the secure state."[45]

The community, in other words, is the single social rela-tionship writ large. Private virtues and public virtues are identical. Qualities of disinterestedness, generosity, and fair-ness, which characterize the relations between friends, sim-ply find a more general and diffuse expression in the good society as a whole. "Judgment" and "justice" are as funda-mental to the entire community as they are to the relation-ship between two compatible people; in Jonson's drama, the moment of public judgment becomes climactic.[46]

Jonson is not, of course, the only playwright to recognize the dramatic potential of the trial scene, or its plausibility as

a way of collecting all characters onstage for a satisfying finale. What is unusual about Jonson is his insistence upon the
device in play after play after play. The role of judge is oc-
cupied by such varied characters as Justice Clement, Crites,
Horace, the Roman senate, the Venetian avocatori, Lovewit,
Cicero and Cato, Justice Either-Side, Penyboy Senior, Pru-
dence. Even when there is no real trial there is often some
vestige of one. Cordatus, the ideal member of the audience
in *Every Man Out*, takes over some of the functions of the
judge. Tom Otter and Cutberd conduct a mock judicial investigation at the end of *Epicene*. In *Bartholomew Fair* Justice
Overdo, Rabbi Busy, and Humphrey Wasp dream of dis-
pensing perfect justice, although each must eventually relin-
quish his claims to authority.

The significance of Jonson's comic trials becomes clear when
one grasps the importance of justice in Roman social thinking. In erotic comedy the love of the young couple generally
confers benefits beyond the personal gratification of hero and
heroine; the progress of their relationship is both cause and
symbol of a more general change in the nature of their society.[47] The attempts to interrupt their courtship, and its
eventual success, attest to the threatened subversion and subsequent renewal of social and familial bonds. The wedding,
at which the lovers' alliance is made permanent and potentially fertile, is an appropriate ritual for a comic conclusion—
once this primary relationship is assured by marriage, social
regeneration seems to follow as a matter of course. The society founded at the end of the comedy will presumably succeed because it acknowledges and celebrates libidinal energy,
instead of suppressing or perverting it. But for the Roman
moralists, who believe society to be founded upon reason,
not upon desire, the trial rather than the wedding is the fundamental social ritual. As Cicero writes, "We are inclined by
a natural impulse to esteem other people, and this is the
foundation of the law."[48] In Jonsonian drama, the trial at its
most effective becomes the recognition scene that makes the
truth manifest and civilized community possible. Jonson's best

men—Crites, Horace, Cicero—are those who can take command of the legal process and use it to implement the best social order.

The revelations that occur in Jonson's trials, however, are not always those intended by characters in positions of judicial power. As Jonson's career progresses, his comic trials become more and more ironic; instead of displaying the authority of his judges, they show up their weaknesses. Just as in erotic comedy our attitude toward the newly wedded couple in the fifth act governs our assessment of the world they inhabit, so the quality of Jonson's judicial authorities, and the circumstances of his fifth-act trials, control our sense of his endings. In *De legibus*, Cicero argues that because justice is so fundamental to any society, its legal machinery provides an index of its moral rectitude.[49] The legal impotence of good characters in *Sejanus* or *Volpone* constitutes an indictment of the social order in these plays, just as the legal power of Horace in *Poetaster* or Cicero in *Catiline* suggests the ultimate triumph of healthy elements in republican and Augustan Rome. In plays where the ideal element disappears altogether, as it does in *Epicene*, *The Alchemist*, or *Bartholomew Fair*, the fifth-act trial becomes a parody. At the same time, Jonson's characters become more and more resolutely solipsistic, so that the humor of their situation arises largely from their inability to make connections with one another.[50] Volpone and Face can count upon their gulls' failure to cooperate and expose their hoaxes; Truewit can exploit the mutual impercipience of Daw and La-Foole for the amusement of the Collegiate Ladies and the audience. Where acute judgment is impossible, so is genuine sympathy.

WHAT are the consequences of analyzing a comic society in terms of its justice rather than in terms of the opportunities it gives couples in love? To some extent the Roman moralists' "justice" serves exactly the same social purposes for Jonson as sublimated eros does for romantic comedy. When the Roman moralists are in an expansive mood, they make the wise man's sense of community obligation, his idea of justice, into a doctrine of the brotherhood of all men. "Men are born for the sake of mankind."[51] The virtue that the Roman moralists most admire is always public both in its motivation and in its consequences.

> We know that the duties prescribed by justice are to be preferred to the zeal for knowledge and the duties prescribed by it; for the duties of justice relate to the welfare of mankind, and nothing should be more fundamental to men than that.[52]

It is not merely contempt for death which makes heroes like Regulus and Cato noteworthy; their true claim to fame is the patriotic single-mindedness with which they identify the public good with their own.[53] When they write philosophy, history, or poetry, Cicero, Seneca, Tacitus, Sallust, and even Horace feel obliged to mention the social benefits that accrue from their apparent retirement, and to point out that for one reason or another they are effectively disqualified from more obviously political pursuits.

Conceived in this way, as rational unselfishness, justice is perhaps the most important aspect of virtue for the Roman moralists: "In which virtue there is the greatest splendor, because of which men are called good."[54] On the other hand, just as charitable Christians quail at the sight of the unregenerate, and just as the most indulgent of comic communities find themselves unable to assimilate their Shylocks and Malvolios, the Roman moralists' sense of universal brotherhood begins to falter when they consider the vicious, the stupid, and the perverse.

Opinion can vary as to how irredeemably vicious the great mass of mankind really are; Quintilian and Horace are more optimistic than Seneca and Juvenal. In fact, though, Roman social theory inevitably presents more difficulties in the way of indiscriminate human bonding than does *eros* or *caritas*. Good judgment—the art of making valid distinctions—has

129

not only a positive aspect, the acknowledgment of the similar, but also an inevitable negative corollary.

Once a man perceives that another man shares his nature, the Roman moralists claim, he is rationally obliged to treat that man as he would treat himself. But if there is no shared nature, there is no motive for community. Only vicious men want to keep vicious men company; the virtuous, having nothing in common with thieves and murderers, see no reason to cultivate their acquaintance. In fact, as Seneca maintains, "association with unlike people disturbs what is quite tranquil and renews passion and irritates whatever in the mind is weak or not yet healed up."[55] The Romans stress in this connection their identification of vice and disease:

> Just as during a plague we are careful not to associate with infected bodies and with those burning with the sickness, because we would put ourselves in danger and suffer from their very breath, so, when we choose friends, we will pay attention to their character, so that we might accept the least contaminated; the beginning of disease is to mix healthy people with sick ones.[56]

Jonson echoes both the sentiment and the metaphor in his "Epistle to Lady Aubigny," when he writes of the superior virtues of solitary life:

> In single paths, dangers with ease are watch'd:
> Contagion in the prease is soonest catched.
>   (57-58)

In Luke 18, Jesus deplores a Pharisee who, when he prays at the temple, thanks God for his superiority to other men. The parable represents the Pharisee's attempt to set himself apart as complacent and self-deceptive. For the Roman moralists, however, a sense of exclusivity is the foundation of the moral sense. Horace takes it for granted that moral education develops the youth's faculty for disgust:

> The best of fathers pointed out to me
> Examples of the vices that I might avoid them.
> When he would urge me to live thriftily,
> Content with what he had provided, he would say,
> "Don't you see how miserably Albius' son lives, and
> How destitute is Baius? A good lesson, not to squander
> One's patrimony." When he wished to deter me from the
>   shameful
> Love of a whore: "Don't be like Scetanus."
> . . . .
> Just as a neighbor's funeral makes sick gluttons
> Spare themselves out of the fear of death,
> So the shame of others often deters young minds
> From vice.[57]

The sociability of the Roman moralists, in other words, is a highly discriminatory phenomenon. The virtuous wish to distinguish themselves from the vicious as heartily as they wish to affiliate themselves with the like-minded.

> I doe but name thee PEMBROKE, and I find
> It is an *Epigramme*, on all man-kind;
> Against the bad, but of, and to the good.[58]

Jonson's own *Epigrams* separate his acquaintances into the virtuous, whose real names and titles attest to their full humanity, and the vicious who are merely parts of people—Groyne, Cod, Lippe—or poor imitations—Ideot, Mime, Shift, Motion, Poet-Ape, Courtling.

Again and again the Roman moralists divide humanity into two groups: the depraved majority against an elite class of wise and virtuous men. "I hate the common rabble and keep it at a distance," writes Horace.[59] Fame, honor, power, and all the other rewards of public life are worth obtaining only from the latter group, the natural ally. The public-spiritedness of the Roman moralists almost always implies a positive contempt for most people. "We are destroyed by the examples of others," Seneca claims. "We will become healthy, simply by separating ourselves from the crowd."[60] Jonson's apparent misanthropy in the plays and satiric poems is not a violation of his social commitment, but one way in which that social commitment is realized.

> For it is Vertue that gives glory: That will endenizon a man every where. It is onely that can naturalize him. A native, if hee be vitious, deserves to bee a stranger, and cast out of the Common-wealth, as an Alien.[61]

In the comical satires, Jonson's trials punish or expel not merely a single recalcitrant scapegoat, but most of the characters in the play. The final, healthy community in the early plays is a tiny one—Crites, Arete, and Cynthia in *Cynthia's Revels*, Horace, Virgil, and Augustus in *Poetaster*. The true courtiers close ranks against the false ones, the true poets against the poetasters. The Roman moralist need to distinguish between genuine and imitation never seems so pressing as in the social realm. In the same way, Juvenal distinguishes himself from the absurd imitators of Virgil, Quintilian separates true orators from specious ranters, and Seneca sets people like himself and Lucilius apart from the degraded logic-choppers and etymologists in the philosophical world.[62]

After *Sejanus* Jonson is less rigorous about separating the sheep and the goats, and *Bartholomew Fair* ends with an admission that the project is impossible. This increasing lack of rigor goes hand in hand with Jonson's growing perception, during the same part of his career, of a fundamental discrepancy between moral and theatrical, especially comic, values. Increasingly he tends to stress the pleasurable element in his comedy, allowing the decorum of the theatrical situation to prevail over the more austere and insistent pedagogical aims of the earlier plays. At the same time, even as Jonson celebrates flexibility and adaptability, he retains—like his Roman moralist forebears—a certain nostalgia for the uncompromising Stoic alternative. Nowhere is this simultaneous concession-and-reservation clearer than in the trials with which the plays conclude, precisely where one would expect an affirmation of community values.

The point of strict judgment is to safeguard the virtuous few. If even that remnant has entirely disappeared, and everyone is a fool or a rogue, there is no particular necessity for discrimination or moral care. In Jonson, the unjudgmental endings of plays like *The Alchemist* and *Bartholomew Fair* are always bought at a price, and that price is human dignity. When characters are present to incarnate the finer moral possibilities, Jonson's comic denouements are—and by Roman moralist logic must be—severe. The most ferocious scenes of purgation occur in the comical satires, where the ideal is still firmly delineated. In *Volpone*, where the forces of virtue are less prepossessing, we are uneasy about the severity of the punishments meted out at the end, and we feel some pity for the convicts. Still, the relationship between the presence of virtue and the punishment of vice is made clear both by the mechanics of the plot and by the nature of the audience's half-reluctant sympathies. If Celia's virtue had not been outraged, or Bonario's patrimony threatened, Volpone would have gotten away scot-free—and we would have been content to see him do so. We do not mind much if he commits crimes against the likes of Corbaccio, Corvino, or Voltore. As it is, however, his compulsive destructiveness not only leads him into more and more perilous straits, but has more and more dangerous consequences for the innocent. We regret his punishment, but would also feel uncomfortable with acquittal or pardon.

The plays after *Volpone*, by excluding characters like Celia and Bonario, make ruthless precision of judgment less necessary and less pressing. Dame Pliant's virtue, or Surly's motives, are simply not worth elaborate vindication. Nonetheless, the mood at the end of *Epicene*, *The Alchemist*, and *Bartholomew Fair* is not really celebratory; there is precious little to celebrate. Jonson's newfound tolerance here is intimately bound up with his increasingly uncompromising low-mimetic emphasis. The inclusiveness of the denouement becomes possible only when all grounds for moral optimism have been firmly dashed. Thus, even after Jonson abandons the harsh punishments of the comical satires and *Volpone*, his comedy lacks what C. H. Herford calls "pure humour . . . innocent laughter . . . sheer fun."[63]

Bartholomew Fair, the most extreme case, shows this development most clearly. Justice fails here because all "warrants," all claims to moral authority, prove invalid or arbitrary—not because society has become regenerate but because no such regeneration is possible.[64] Overdo's blanket dinner invitation issues not from his vision of an ideal community, but from his recognition of the universality and inescapability of human imperfection. Quarlous, advising Overdo to "drowne the memory of all enormity in your bigg'st bowle at home," looks forward to no redemption, but rather suggests Lethe, or a Flood—a reduced version of liquid annihilation, appropriately stripped of the dignity of epic punishment. At the Fair, the subhumanity of the puppets had enabled them to escape Puritan censure; the human characters' limitations allow them a similar sort of freedom. Meaningful judgment becomes pointless or impossible in a morally diminished world. Thus bleakness of moral prospect in Jonson does not interfere with comic values like laughter and forgiveness; indeed, it is their corollary and prerequisite.

The Artist and His Audience

For the Roman moralists, as for Jonson, moral, social, and aesthetic values are ordinarily indistinguishable. Since "judgment" is practically synonymous with virtue in both its personal and social aspects, it is not surprising that Jonson considers it fundamental to aesthetic experience as well. In prologues, prefaces, and epigrams, legal metaphors dominate his discussion of the reader's or spectator's response.

> May others feare, flie, and traduce thy name,
>   As guiltie men doe magistrates: glad I,
> That wish my poemes a legitimate fame,
>   Charge them, for crowne, to thy sole censure hye.
>   ("To the Learned Critick," 1–4)

Judgment is indispensable to the artist too. In *Cynthia's Revels* the name of the artist-protagonist comes from the Greek *kritein*, "to judge." Drummond reports that Jonson resurrected the name in his lost commentary on the *Ars poetica*, where he made Donne appear under the name "Criticus."[65]

Thus it is not surprising that throughout his career Jonson describes criticism and creation as aspects of the same poetic gift.

> To judge of Poets is only the facultie of Poets; and not of all Poets, but the best. . . . Such was *Horace*, an Author of much Civilitie; and (if any one among the heathen can be) the best master, both of vertue, and wisdome; an excellent, and true judge upon cause, and reason.[66]

Good poets and their audiences—if indeed they are not the same people—can at least be described in the same terms: wise, judicious, good, pure, learned. Jonson conceives of his relationship with his audience in terms of the Roman moralists' theory of judgmental altruism, as a kind of fellowship ideally based upon similar talents and interests. Cordatus, the perfect spectator in *Every Man Out*, is "the Authors friend; A man inly acquainted with the scope and drift of his Plot: Of a discreet, and understanding judgement."[67] For Jonson, all three clauses are synonymous. Cordatus' critical infallibility derives from his moral affinity with Asper, the virtuous playwright. The approval of the audience is socially basic in the same way that friendship between good men is; it exemplifies the kind of bond that holds good communities together.

THE significance of the relation between author and audience makes Jonson understandably eager to make himself available to a public. Unlike many of his contemporaries, he is not content with the circulation of his manuscripts among a small group of sympathetic acquaintances, or with the ephemeral glory of a theatrical performance. Just as Cicero publishes his speeches (somewhat amended and improved) for the benefit of those not present at their original delivery, Jonson conceives of the written word as a way to extend and enhance, and eventually even to supersede, the oral version. His literary forebears—Cicero, Seneca, Horace, and Pliny— had given to the public even their supposedly private letters to friends, and Jonson follows their example. The simultaneity of private and public virtue for the Roman moralists makes the personal relations between good men socially significant; thus the expanded audience does not violate, but actually enhances, the fundamental character of the original relationship.

In fact, publication becomes a literary equivalent of heroic action for the Roman moralists—a socially significant achievement that creates an audience unlimited by the usual accidental constraints of time and place. Thus Cicero praises literary men for keeping the memory of the past alive and for gaining themselves immortality in the process.

> For virtue desires no reward for its trouble and perils except that of praise and glory; indeed, when this is withdrawn . . . what is there in the course of life, so short and brief, to encourage us in such efforts? . . . Now a kind of virtue is fixed within every excellent person, which . . . suggests that our name's memory should not be measured out by the duration of a lifetime, but should be made equal to all the future ages.[68]

Jonson, too, admires and sympathizes with those who desire a glorious reputation with posterity. "They that seeke *Immortality*, are not onely worthy of leave, but of praise," he writes in the *Discoveries* (176-178). When the London theatergoing public disappoints him, he makes his readers his jury, telling himself that "An other Age, or juster men, will acknowledge the vertues of his studies."[69]

Jonson's special social orientation makes rhetorical conceptions of art even more attractive to him than they are to other English Renaissance artists and critics. One of the most distinctive features of Jonson's published work is the overwhelming assertiveness of his authorial presence. He surrounds his plays, masques, and poems with an unprecedented weight of prefaces, prologues, dedications, inductions, footnotes, epilogues, and afterwords; he shatters any theatrical convention which demands that playwrights retire behind their fictions. At the same time, he is acutely aware that he designs his art to produce an effect upon an audience; he wants to excel at "moving the minds of men, and stirring of affections."[70]

Nonetheless, since the relation between artist and audience is governed by the same laws that determine other forms of social interaction, it suffers from the same uncertainties. Jonson may glorify the bond between the ideal spectator and the ideal artist, and may be willing to go to extraordinary lengths to make his work available to connoisseurs wherever they may be, but he knows very well that not all spectators are ideal. The Roman moralists would claim, in fact, that the percentage of good auditors in any group is probably extremely small. Their characteristic elitism prevents them, and Jonson, from relying too wholeheartedly upon the taste of any public. "Who can please the people, if virtue pleases him?" asks Seneca.[71] Though decorum is a major moral and aesthetic concern for all the Roman moralists, they realize that their idea of virtuous propriety often entails a rejection of majority preferences.[72] Horace thinks of the poet as a priest, addressing himself only to a small initiate group; Juvenal insists that his moral ideals are drawn not from the present but from Rome's virtuous past.[73] Cicero reveals why an artist like Jonson might be willing to court audiences far removed

137

in time or place, while nonetheless disdaining spectators closer to home:

> When the virtuous mind conceives that it is not confined by city walls to some particular place, but is a citizen of the entire world, as if it were one city . . . how it will correctly discern and despise, how it will suppose worthless, that which the crowd calls excellent![74]

For the Roman moralists cosmopolitanism and selectivity are closely allied. If one can conceive of "all the world as if it were one city," one may find oneself at a disadvantage with the less enlightened locals.

Jonson shares the Roman concern with decorum. When he calls the good poet "the interpreter, and arbiter of nature, a teacher of things divine, no less than humane, a master in manners,"[75] he does not mean the last phrase to sound anti-climactic. Yet he often insists, with a fastidiousness that annoys some modern critics, upon separating himself from popular taste, upon declaring that he works, and must be judged, according to different standards. He is almost always careful to qualify the terms upon which he will find the sympathy of his audience acceptable. In *Every Man Out* he presents "Cates . . . not season'd / For every vulgar Pallat, but prepar'd / To banket pure and apprehensive eares."[76] In *The Magnetic Lady*, thirty-three years later, he still claims to be "carelesse of all vulgar censure, as not depending on common approbation . . . confident [his play] shall super-please judicious Spectators."[77] The Roman moralists' altruism, as we have already seen, tends to separate the human race into sheep and goats; Jonson, extending Roman social assumptions to his relationship with his audience, distinguishes everywhere between "free souls" and "illiterate apes," "understanders" and "mere pretenders," "Schollers" and "the vulgar sort of Nutcrackers," "the learned critick" and the "meere English censurer." He no more wishes to attract a large and indiscriminate following than Horace, or Cicero's

Laelius, or Seneca wish to befriend the whole world without distinction.

THE audience for Jonson, then, is simultaneously, paradoxically, crucial and dispensable.[78] The traditional nature of his ambivalence should not obscure the fact that both he and his literary forebears are in a serious bind. Roman moralists, following the Stoics, describe virtue as a radically private phenomenon, unaffected by accidental external circumstances. But their sense that virtue entails social involvement leads them into extrovert expressions of that virtue. This causes them a number of problems. The most obvious social use for verbal talents is oratorical: the persuasion of other citizens to virtuous action. The Roman moralists thus tend to see their work—poems, histories, and philosophical essays as well as speeches and guides for public speaking—as forms of a general suasory enterprise. Horace stresses, in the *Ars poetica*, the inseparability of philosophic virtue, poetic talent, and social responsibility.

The origin and source of correct writing is wisdom.
The Socratic writings can reveal subject-matter to you;
And words come forth, not reluctantly, when the subject is
   already provided.
He who has learned what is due to the fatherland, and what
   to friends;
How he should love a parent, a brother, and a guest;
What should be the duties of senators, what of judges, what
Of generals sent to war; having learned this,
He knows how to render appropriate characters.[79]

Thus the Roman moralists resist any imputation that persuasive efficacy somehow involves a compromise with or disregard of truth; Cicero and Quintilian prescribe philosophical training for their ideal orator and, like Horace and Seneca, maintain that strength and beauty of expression can only enhance the true and the good.[80] Jonson follows this distinguished lead. On one hand he insists upon the philosophical respectability of poetry:

> Wheras they entitle *Philosophy* to bee a rigid, and austere *Poesie*: they have (on the contrary) stiled *Poesy*, a dulcet, and gentle *Philosophy*, which leades on, and guides us by the hand to Action, with a ravishing delight, and incredible Sweetnes.[81]

On the other hand he calls the poet, in *Discoveries*, "the neerest Borderer upon the Orator" (2528), and translates Quintilian's instructions to the rhetorician as guidelines for the artist.

Rhetoric, though, is finally judged by its effects. It requires attentive hearers as well as a talented speaker—or more precisely, the talent of the speaker is judged by the attentiveness of the hearers.[82] How can the virtuous man reconcile the need for an audience with his ideal self-sufficiency?

Jonson has no illusions about the dispensability of fortune for artistic success. "Never," he writes in the preface to *Volpone*, "had any man a wit so presently excellent, as that it could raise it selfe; but there must come both matter, occasion, commenders, and favourers to it." On the other hand, he is committed to a philosophical stance which denies the necessity of matter, occasion, commenders, and favourers. In *Pro Archia* Cicero perceptively diagnoses what will become his own philosophical dilemma in later years:

> In the very books which they write to belittle fame, those philosophers inscribe their names; in that very place where they condemn advertisement and renown, they wish to advertise themselves and be called by name.[83]

The difficulty of the position is well captured in Drummond's snide comment that Jonson "of all stiles . . . loved most to be named honest, and hath of that ane hundred letters so naming him."[84] John Creasar remarks that despite Jonson's Stoic pretensions he "seems to have had a quite unstoical need for other's esteem and admiration."[85] But this paradoxical combination of self-sufficiency and interest in the responses of others, both in public and private relationships, itself constitutes part of Jonson's classical inheritance.

IT is unfair to see the conflict between private virtue and public effectiveness as an inevitable one for the Roman moralist sensibility. In the ideal masque world Jonson brings pleasure and virtue, traditionally irreconcilable, into harmonious relations; fame, too, can coincide unproblematically with virtue in *The Masque of Queens*. Even under less than perfect conditions, the responsible artist or virtuous orator can find himself an audience of good men, people who accurately judge his merit because they share it. Unless society is hopelessly corrupt, in fact, there should be enough virtuous individuals to constitute an appreciative public. Cicero loves to recall his consulship, even though he is exiled afterward on charges of malfeasance; all right-minded men, as he says, approved of his conduct in the Catilinarian crisis. Seneca, out of favor with the increasingly depraved Nero, falls back upon a restricted but loyal circle of acquaintances. Horace's gratitude to Maecenas and Augustus, Jonson's to Aubigny, Pembroke, or James I, is the gratitude of men who find they do not have to compromise their principles to obtain patrons.

What happens, though, when the small-but-appreciative audience fails to materialize? The good man, Seneca writes to Lucilius, must bear in mind the words of Democritus: "A few are enough for me, one is enough for me, none is enough for me."[86] The Roman moralists believe that virtue is prior to all social convention—in *De legibus*, for instance, Cicero posits an anterior natural law, an absolute justice which particular sets of statutes may approximate, and by which they may be compared and evaluated.[87] Certain kinds of behavior are good, noble, and according to nature, even if a depraved individual or an entire decadent society chooses to ignore them. Most men are invariably deluded; in the worst conceivable case, all of them may be so.

The nightmarish possibility of absolute isolation thus haunts the Roman moralists. Some Christian groups, like the Romans, see themselves as a tiny elect group set apart from, and often unrecognized by, an immoral majority (the Puritan rhetoric Jonson despises often resembles his own to a startling degree). These groups, however, cultivate a reassuring faith in an omniscient divine spectator, whom they expect—at life's end, on the Last Day—permanently and dramatically to set right the defects of earthly judgment. Christians need only bide their time. But as a rule the Roman moralists lack any keen imaginative sense of a powerful proprietary deity. If they wish to have some practical effect, therefore, they must rely upon the consent of their hearers—a consent they know in advance is unreliable and defective.

So even when he conceives of his poems as the products of solitude—"Things, that were borne, when none but the still night, / And his dumbe candle saw his pinching throes"[88]—Jonson yearns for some absolutely convincing public demonstration of his superiority. In the apology after *Poetaster*, he swears that his experiments with tragedy will "give cause to some of wonder, some despight, / And unto more, despaire, to imitate their sound" (231-232). Almost thirty years later, in "An Ode to Himself," he departs from the stage still resolving upon new, literally astounding public displays of poetic virtuosity:

> They may, blood-shaken, then,
> Feel such a flesh-quake to possesse their powers:
> As they shall cry, like ours
> In sound of peace, or warres,
> No Harpe ere hit the starres.
>
> (54-58)

To the Roman moral writers, so attracted by the virtues of absolute self-reliance, the very importance of the audience makes its intransigence profoundly disturbing. In "An Ode to Himself," a poem that seems to declare the poet's self-sufficiency in its title, the poet's ambivalent need for and hatred of his recalcitrant audience crystallizes into a fantasy of literary rape in which his enemies are no longer seduced, but coerced, by his poetry's "ravishing delights."

If Jonson believes in the merit of his own art, he must also believe that the spectators' dislike of it reveals their moral and artistic depravity.

> Say, that thou pour'st them wheat,
>   And they will acornes eat:
> 'Twere simple fury, still, thy selfe to waste
>   On such as have no taste!
> . . . .
> If they love lees, and leave the lusty wine,
> Envy them not, their palate's with the swine.
>
> ("Ode to Himself," 11-20)

When the Roman plebs exile Shakespeare's Coriolanus, he exclaims, "I banish you!" In precisely the same way, and for the same reasons, Jonson denies the apes, spawn, swine, and parrots who disapprove of his work even the consolation of a human identity. The bad audience, however numerous, "deserves to bee a stranger, and cast out of the Commonwealth, as an Alien." Where he is, the virtuous and talented artist, there must the good community be. Thus even the isolated Jonson, in "Ode to Himself," rededicates himself to his social role, renouncing the theater in order to sing the glories of Charles I—a stingy patron and an indifferent poetic subject. The Roman moral tradition provides no more comforting alternative.

JONSON, then, conceives his relationship to his audience in terms of Roman moralist social assumptions, as a relationship between more-or-less like-minded people:

> . . . if I prove the pleasure but of one,
> So he judicious be; He shall b'alone
> A Theatre unto me.[89]

The "theater" here is not a place, but a transaction in which the playwright and the audience are principals, and the play is a sort of test by which they recognize their compatibility.

143

Nonetheless, the theater audience responds not to the author *in propria persona* but to the play; despite the manifold ways in which Jonson manages to suggest an unmediated relationship, the public inevitably perceives the author in and through his art. When discussing the relationship between author and audience, one has to take into account as well the relationship between the audience and the author's poetic or dramatic fictions.

In Jonson's work this relationship between audience and artwork is particularly close; indeed, he often identifies the two. The Roman invocatory habit—Horace's "Ne perconteris, fundus meus, optime Quincti"; Martial's "Cotille, bellus homo es"; Catullus' "Quaenam te mala mens, miselle Ravide"—becomes in Jonson's hands "How like a columne, RADCLIFFE, left alone" or "UV'DALE, thou piece of the first times" or "ROE (and my joy to name)." Even the non-living are accosted in the second person: "It will be look'd for, booke, when some but see / Thy title"; "Thou art not, PENSHURST, built to envious show." The subject of the poem is the person to whom it is addressed. This procedure has its parallel in the masque, where members of the audience become performers, and in the drama, the locally colorful *speculum consuetudinis* in which the spectators may see themselves and their community reflected. The poetic imagination bodies forth the shapes of its audiences.

In the panegyric poetry, the poem creates and celebrates the familiar sympathy between virtuous individuals so valued by the Roman moralists. Of course the actual readers of *Epigrams* or *The Forest* are not themselves addressed in the poems to Roe or Uvedale or Pembroke. But if they can share an appreciation for the qualities that evoke those poems, they become by virtue of such appreciation worthy of inclusion in the best sort of society.

When the image reflected in the *speculum consuetudinis* is less than ideal, though, the situation becomes more complicated. The relationship between virtuous people and imperfect people is, in the broad Roman sense of the word, a social one, based on an intuition of a common humanity. But in the stricter sense, since the virtuous and the vicious have so little in common, their sense of fellowship is tenuous and their association can be morally dangerous for the good. When a virtuous artist creates morally suspect characters, he thus makes two mutually exclusive responses available to the audience. It may, on one hand, affiliate itself with the author, joining him in satiric mockery of folly and vice. Alternatively, it may identify its interests with the created world, sympathizing not with the author against the characters, but with the characters themselves.

The first solution is, broadly speaking, that of the masques, satiric poetry, and comical satires; the second, increasingly, that of the middle and late comedies. In the masques the identification of the audience with the created world is only partial. The aristocrats confine their appearances to the masque proper, after the antimasque—the province of the professional actor—has been noisily banished. The satiric epigrams similarly loosen the close bond between audience and subject which is characteristic of the panegyric poetry. In some of the satiric epigrams Jonson addresses his subject directly, scolding undesirables like Brayne-Hardie, Doctor Empirick, Court-ling, and Proule the Plagiary. But while in the poetry of praise Jonson invariably invokes his subject in the second person, in the satiric epigrams he often deliberately implies a gap between the subject of the poem and its proper audience:

> See you yond' Motion? Not the old *Fa-ding,*
> Nor Captayne POD, nor yet the *Eltham*-thing. . . .
> ("On the New Motion," 1-2)

> You wonder, who this is! and, why I name
> Him not, aloud, that boasts so good a fame:
> Naming so many, too!
> ("On the Town's Honest Man," 1-3)

> Would you beleeve, when you this MOUNSIEUR see,
> That his whole body should speak *french,* not he?
> ("On English Monsieur," 1-2)

The "you" in these lines is not the satirized individual, but an imagined bystander, really or potentially sympathetic to Jonson. It is a strategy Jonson tends to prefer in his most scathing invective—in *Poetaster*'s "To the Reader," in "An Epistle to Sir Edward Sackville," in "An Epistle to a Friend, to Persuade Him to the Wars." The effect is to segregate the object of satire from even the minimal social relationship implied by a direct rebuke. The virtuous close ranks against the vicious—defining themselves, in typical Roman fashion, by a rigorous exclusion of the unfit.

Jonson can therefore follow Horace and Juvenal in claiming that the virtuous have no reason to take offense at satiric portraiture. Since they recognize no similarity between themselves and the satiric exempla, they should feel no reason to protest:

> And, the wise, and vertuous, will never thinke any thing belongs to themselves that is written, but rejoice that the good are warn'd not to bee such; and the ill to leave to bee such. The Person offended hath no reason to bee offended with the writer, but with himselfe; and so to declare that properly to belong to him, which was spoken of all men, as it could bee no mans severall, but his that would willfully and desperately claime it. It sufficeth I know, what kinde of persons I displease, men bred in the declining, and decay of vertue, betroth'd to their vices.[90]

The Roman moralists see no conceivable reason for the virtuous to champion the cause of the vicious. For Jonson it is necessarily a proof of the spectators' moral and aesthetic incompetence if, instead of affiliating themselves with the censorious artist, they make the mistake of identifying with the characters onstage.

Nonetheless, in Jonsonian drama, the relationships between author and audience, audience and artwork change in very significant ways over the course of Jonson's career. Traditionally, comedy is an inclusive genre, which often makes gestures to admit the audience into its final convivial rites. "Give us your hands, if we be friends"[91]—the applause of the onlookers makes them a part of the fifth-act festivity. Jonson, though, by importing satire into comedy, renders problematic this identification of stage world and audience; for satire, as Horace maintains, makes its moral point by cultivating an audience's capacity for disgust, and teaching it what best to avoid.

In Jonson's early plays the relationship between the audience and the dramatic fiction hinges upon the satiric artist-spokesman, who establishes a bond with the audience based on a shared contempt for vice and folly.[92] Jonson uses the relationship between Asper and Cordatus, Crites and Cynthia, Virgil and Augustus to refocus the traditional gregariousness of comedy away from the sympathy between spectator and character, to concentrate on the bond between the dedicated artist and the discerning audience. As his comedy becomes more and more insistently low-mimetic, however, both more pessimistic about human potential and at the same time less rigorously censorious, Jonson begins to close the moral gap between the spectators and the action they witness. *Epicene*, *The Alchemist*, and *Bartholomew Fair*, set in contemporary London and crammed with local reference, stress the continuity of the world onstage with the world in which the author and his audience really live. A sense of distance from the characters becomes more difficult to sustain.

In Jonson's hands, this more traditionally "comic" identification of onstage and offstage worlds shocks rather than reassures. Do we really want to embrace the society of these characters? We are uneasy, for example, when we discover, along with Morose, Truewit, and the Collegiate Ladies, that Epicene's true identity has been hidden from us for five acts. C. H. Herford writes:

> The sudden and simple solution of an apparently impossible problem produces a pleasant kind of surprise;

but if we have reason to think that the problem was not fairly proposed, the pleasure is crossed with a certain mortification like that of the victims of Columbus' well-known feat with the egg. A shade of such mortification has probably always qualified the pleasure produced by Jonson's denouement. Very possibly it is reflected in the bad temper ascribed to the audience who experienced this rebuff for the first time.[93]

The denouement, in other words, seems like a violation of an implicit contract, a breach of the hospitality with which Jonson, in his prelude, invites his audience to share in his comic feast. He has encouraged us to consider ourselves a privileged group, secure in our superiority to the characters, and now we turn out to be just on their level.

Jeremy makes the same unwelcome suggestion of collusion at the end of *The Alchemist*, where he seems to issue a perfectly ordinary "invitational" epilogue:

> I put my selfe
> On you, that are my countrey, and this pelfe,
> Which I have got, if you do quit me, rests
> To feast you often, and invite new ghests.

In context this invitation seems an insult to the audience; their applause, Jeremy tells them, constitutes acceptance of his bribe. The fundamental condition for social intercourse, in the imperfect London of the play, is a willingness to tolerate and even encourage vice, provided such tolerance accrues to one's benefit. Jeremy assumes that his audience is at best on a moral plane with his master Lovewit.

Jeremy's epilogue is not disturbing merely because it seems amoral. Plenty of Restoration comedies depict an amoral world, but the audience views its own inclusion there as a sign of cheerful hedonism or urban sophistication—qualities the plays encourage their spectators to admire from the beginning. If an audience is outraged by *The Country Wife*, say, or *Marriage-à-La-Mode*, it will be outraged from Act I, scene i, at the whole scheme of values the comedy celebrates. *The Alchemist* does not work this way. Jeremy seems presumptuous because we have been thinking of ourselves as part of another moral universe, as the "judging Spectators" addressed by the playwright in the prologue. We therefore experience Jeremy's apparently hospitable invitation as a demotion, a subtle betrayal, an assault on our complacent assumption of moral inviolability.

In the later plays, little indeed remains of the audience's formerly privileged status. If the withholding of crucial information in *Epicene* really did offend its original audience, as Herford suggests, Jonson seems to have ignored its ruffled feelings. In all his late plays—*The Staple of News, The New Inn,* and *The Magnetic Lady*—the audience remains unaware of at least one individual's true identity until it is revealed to the other characters onstage. In *The New Inn* the deception is massive: almost every character, unbeknownst to the audience, is in disguise until the fifth act.

Jonson's increased willingness to identify his audience with his limited, low-mimetic characters does not, however, mean that he abandons his older conception of an ideal association between poet and public. He continues throughout his career to insist upon the primacy of the relationship between author and spectator or reader, a relationship which in the low-mimetic comedies necessarily competes with the relationship between the audience and the characters onstage. This is perhaps why Jonson is so frequently seen as fundamentally hostile to his own characters—from the viewpoint of someone accustomed to ordinary comedy, he seems to be trying to upstage his own creation.

What changes in Jonson's sense of his dramatic audience is not his ideal, but his conception of the likelihood of achieving that ideal in the theater. As his career proceeds, he portrays his audience in less and less flattering ways. In *Every Man Out* one member of the audience-chorus is critically penetrating, and the other, though a little dim, is easily led. After *Sejanus,* Jonson begins to conceive of his spectators as moral equals of Truewit and Face—and in *The Staple of News* introduces a chorus that is evidently no guide to the moral or aesthetic significance of the action.

His disillusion with the theater audience goes hand in hand, as might be expected, with his increasing awareness that the Roman moralists' conception of virtue resists dramatization. The delusive possibilities of rhetoric interest him in *Volpone*, *Epicene*, *The Alchemist*, and *Bartholomew Fair*, because the popular theater as he understands it renders particularly acute the problem of relating truth and efficacy in a defective society. Like Cicero and Seneca, Jonson perceives the difficulty sharply but is ambivalent about its solution, since he is unwilling to abandon either his moral ideals or the possibility of effective social action. So he compromises and wavers. He praises Greek comedy repeatedly, but defends Horace's low opinion of Plautus by attacking the irreverence of Aristophanes or, more precisely, of Aristophanes' audience:

> What could have made them laugh, like to see *Socrates* presented, that Example of all good life, honesty, and vertue, to have him hoisted up with a Pullie, and there play the Philosopher, in a basquet? . . . This was *Theatricall* wit, right Stage-jesting, and relishing a Play-house.[94]

He creates theatrically compelling immoralists like Volpone and Mosca, but assumes a vigorously antitheatrical stance in his preface to their play. And even as late as *The New Inn* and *The Magnetic Lady*, he searches his unprepossessing audience for "judicious Spectators" to constitute his elect.

The Late Jonson

WHEN in 1629, a few years before his death, Jonson writes his first romantic comedy, *The New Inn*, he departs from the characteristic modes both of the comical satires, and of the great plays of midcareer. Courtship and marriage, conceived primarily in erotic and not financial terms, provide the focus of the main plot. The miraculous rediscovery of misplaced family members plays a similarly prominent role. And as Anne Barton observes: "In *The New Inn*, Jonson jettisoned another long-standing artistic habit. He replaced the old . . . essential names associated with his earlier comedies . . . by a nomenclature more mixed, flexible, and ambiguous."[1] Names like "Frampul" (which can mean both perverse and high-spirited) and "Sylly" (which implies perhaps blessed inno-cence and perhaps stupidity) refer not to fixed traits but to potentials, aspects of personality subject to mutiple, morally distinct realizations. *The New Inn*, in other words, endorses precisely those psychological possibilities that Jonson in his earlier plays had rejected as implausible or hypocritical.

Several critics, aware of Jonson's earlier hostility to ro-mantic comedy, have supposed that this unusual play is an incompetent parody—but this conclusion is unwarranted.[2] Though his best plays, all written before 1615, reflect the Roman moral sense that sexual passion is at best trivial and at worst immoral, Jonson's attitude begins to change in the second decade of the seventeenth century. He has already used something like a principle of sublimation to unify masques like *Love Freed from Ignorance and Folly*. Later in his career a more positive attitude toward eros begins to affect his nondramatic verse as well. Many of the lyrics in *The*

Underwood, almost all written after the publication of the folio *Works,* concern themselves with love in both its sexual
and religious manifestations. Jonson writes verses like "Oh
doe not wanton with those eyes" and "A Nymphs Passion";
elegies like "Though Beautie be the Marke of praise" and
"By those bright Eyes, at whose immortall fires"; religious
meditations; long poems so "metaphysical" in tone that they
are sometimes ascribed to Donne. The short poems to Celia
in *The Forest* describe limited erotic occasions rather than the
history of an extended involvement; "A Celebration of Charis
in Ten Lyric Pieces," however, approaches more closely the
Renaissance norm—an Aristotelian passion with a beginning,
middle, and end.

Likewise, the plays written after 1615—*The Devil Is an
Ass, The Staple of News,* and *The New Inn*—display a growing interest in courtship as a primary feature of comic plot.
Jonson had virtually ignored domestic comedy until *Bartholomew Fair*—and even here, as in *Volpone, Epicene,* and *The
Alchemist,* rituals of courtship are still closely tied to the strategies of intrigue. Quarlous wins himself a fortune by imper-
sonating Trouble-All and securing the wealthy but otherwise
undesirable Dame Purecraft for his own. His triumph is economic, not sexual. In Jonson's next play, *The Devil Is an Ass,*
courtship and intrigue are separated for the first time; the
lover Wittipol's connection with the "Projector" Meercraft
is slight and accidental. For the first time, too, the lovers
seem genuinely romantic. Wittipol's passion for Mrs. Fitzdottrel is not "chaste and fair" in its origins and essence; his
motives at first are emphatically carnal, and his goal is simple
seduction. Eventually, though, he rejects a course that would
purchase his enjoyment at the price of his mistress' ruin. His
passion is deflected toward an admiration of her virtue: "Lady,
I can love *goodnes* in you, more / Then I did *Beauty*" (IV.vi.37-
38).

The similarities between *The Devil Is an Ass* and *Volpone*
make their differences especially striking, and suggest important changes in Jonson's comic objectives. Lady Taile-

bush, a well-connected woman of dubious virtue who parades her indiscriminate cultural attainments, reminds one of Lady Would-be. Fitzdottrel is a version of Corvino; an obsessively jealous husband who keeps his wife under lock and key, he is nonetheless easily led to exploit her attractions for material gain. The seducer Wittipol, in disguise, captivates an audience (which includes his beloved) by reciting complicated recipes for miraculous rejuvenating cosmetics. The foolish and mercenary husband loses financial control over his wife—although he claims she is guilty of adultery, feigns madness in court, and nearly convinces a corrupt judge of his case against her. Here, though, the parallels end. In *The Devil Is an Ass*, the lover Wittipol—who plays the role of the seducer until the middle of act four—eventually renounces his original plans, rescues his beloved from the clutches of her husband, and stands falsely accused with her in court. Volpone transforms himself into Bonario. As in *Volpone*, Jonson denies his virtuous characters any promise of sexual union at the comedy's end. But clearly, the psychology of erotic sublimation required by a comedy like *The New Inn* has begun to seem a more attractive dramatic possibility to Jonson as early as 1616.

In the drama he writes in his prime, Jonson subscribes heartily to the orthodox Roman-moralist position on erotic love. Why does he depart from it in his old age? The question is perhaps best approached in what might seem an oblique way, to illuminate the general alteration of attitude of which it is symptomatic. A climactic moment in *Bartholomew Fair* provides a clue to Jonson's changing sensibility. In act five, scene five, Dionysius the puppet refutes the antitheatrical arguments of Zeal-of-the-Land Busy with what Edgeworth calls "plaine demonstration": "*The Puppet takes up his garment.*" Busy has objected to the transvestitism of the Elizabethan theater, in which "the male among you putteth on the apparel of the female." The puppet silences his Puritan antagonist by revealing that he has, of course, no sex at all. Jonas

Barish contends that "Jonson is hereby intimating the essential innocence of the theater,"[3] a reading that seems excessively wishful. Even if the disturbing implications of Dionysius' revelation remain merely latent here, the gesture is ambivalent in ways that will become extremely important for Jonson's later work.

Busy charges onstage at the beginning of the scene intending to "remove *Dagon* there . . . that *Idoll*, that heathenish *Idoll*." As the audience knows by this point in the play, Busy uses "idol" not in its restricted (Anglican or Catholic) sense to mean an image made specifically to be worshipped, but in the more general Puritan sense, referring to any overestimation of objects in the carnal world. Busy is defeated because he uses arguments against the puppet which apply only to human agents; the very terms upon which he takes up Leatherhead's challenge necessitate his acceptance of the puppet as a real person. Even as he rails against the confusion of male and female on the stage, he himself falls into far more profound error, treating the nonhuman as human, the inorganic as organic. This provides an opening for Dionysius, whose final gesture convicts Busy of the very idolatry for which the Puritans castigate the theater. "I know no fitter match," as Grace says, "than a *Puppet* to commit with an Hypocrite!"

So Busy loses not because his denunciation of the theater is groundless but because his criticism is not radical and comprehensive enough. Dionysius does not refute him; he merely turns his arguments back against him—if actors are "Pages of *Pride*, and waiters upon *vanity*," as Busy claims, then what about "feather-makers i' the *Fryers*, that are o' your faction o' faith?" Like Wasp and Overdo, the other pretenders to authority in *Bartholomew Fair*, Busy is not so much incorrect as outrageously unjust, singling out particular "enormities" and "profanations" for denunciation while ignoring others just as flagrant. *Bartholomew Fair* absolves its fools and rogues not by proving their intelligence or innocence but by tarring everyone with the same brush. Dionysius does not argue for

the innocence of the theater; he argues rather that since the-
atricality is everywhere it is pointless to object to the stage
as if it presented a unique moral threat.

DIONYSIUS' self-vindication therefore leaves the theatrical enterprise profoundly problematic. Jonson's reservations not only
about the theater but about all spectacular appearance in the
latter part of his life differ somewhat from the standard ones
rehearsed *ad infinitum* in contemporary antitheatrical tracts.
Jonson is made anxious not so much by the deceptive quality
of spectacle, its concealment of a true essence, as by its capacity to exist without any essence at all. There is nothing
under the puppet's garment, nothing behind "the mere perspective" of Inigo Jones's inch-board, nothing inside the
splendid clothing a servant fondles in *The Underwood* 42:

> An Officer there, did make most solemne love,
> To ev'ry Petticote he brush'd, and Glove
> He did lay up, and would adore the shooe,
> Or slipper was left off, and kisse it too,
> Court every hanging Gowne, and after that
> Lift up some one, and doe I tell not what.
> Thou didst tell me; and wert orejoy'd to peepe
> In at a hole, and see these Actions creepe
> From the poor wretch.
>
> (53-61)

The voyeurist and the fetishist—men who mistake symp-
toms for causes and who prefer false or partial gratifications
to real or complete ones—figure again and again in the later
poetry, plays, and masques. Busy, ambiguously "commit-
ting" with his "fit match" Dionysius, is a forerunner of the
tailor in *The Underwood* 42, whose "Letcherie / [Is], the best
clothes still to praeoccupie"; and the tailor turns up once more
as Nick Stuffe in *The New Inn*.

Jonson was never the clothier's friend, and he has always
been explicit, too, about the way magnificent or varied attire
titillates the beholder. In the epigram to Sir Voluptuous Beast,

155

or in Volpone's address to Celia, the attraction of women in splendid disguise figures as a subspecies of metamorphic indulgence. Excessive concern with clothing in the earlier Jonson is, however, merely one form of more general vices—affectation, effeminacy, or sensuality—and as such remains a secondary satiric target. Nor does it present extraordinary moral dangers. In the preface to *Cynthia's Revels* Jonson announces that "it is not pould'ring, perfuming, and every day smelling of the tailor, that converteth to a beautiful object: but a mind, shining through any sute, which needes no false light either of riches, or honors to helpe it" (13-15). On one hand, an undue concern with appearance is indecorous; on the other, Jonson is perfectly confident in the mind's capacity to render its beauty visible. Jonson's emphases change in later years, so that rich clothing and lavish spectacle become much more highly charged topics.[4] "False light" seems far more likely to blind the spectator.

What has happened to Jonson's view of the world? Jonson has always shared the Roman moralists' anxiety about the body and its relation to the virtuous soul; like his Latin predecessors, he is unsure whether the body should be classed as a part of the "real self," or rather as a part of the external world, excluded from selfhood. In Jonson's later years the Roman moral sense of the body as fortuitous and accidental, a mere excrescence, increasingly takes precedence over the alternative Roman materialism.

It is not surprising that a sickly, paralyzed, grossly obese old man should feel himself alienated from his own body; a celestial soul, in Cicero's phrase, "shut up inside a fleshly frame."[5] But the change in Jonson's attitude begins to be evident years before his own physical degeneration. John Lemly, writing on *The Underwood*, remarks that "Jonson's personality increasingly intrudes upon his art" in the poetry written after 1615.[6] This may seem a peculiar statement; Jonson's adaptation of Roman social ideas to his own situation has always led him to strive for a special quasi-personal relationship with the good audience. Jonson the classical scholar,

Jonson the responsible artist, Jonson the friend of virtuous men and women invariably manages to convey a sense of distinctive personality in his art. But something *is* new in the way Jonson presents himself in the late poetry. We get descriptions of the authorial persona as an object as well as a subject—the poet not only as he conceives himself, but also as he imagines others see him. In *The Forest* the reader gets a momentary glimpse of Jonson objectified, so to speak, as the glutton at table in "To Penshurst." This kind of self-portrayal becomes the rule rather than the exception in *The Underwood*. Even when the sight of Charis takes "my sight, / And my motion from me quite," the most significant aspect of the experience for the suffering lover seems to stem from the presence of observers:

> So that, there, I stood a stone,
> Mock'd of all: and call'd of one
> (Which with griefe and wrath I heard)
> *Cupids* Statue with a Beard,
> Or else one that plaid his Ape,
> In a *Hercules*-his shape.
>   ("How He Saw Her," 27-32)

The people nearby see only Jonson the unwieldy physical object, not Jonson the inspired lover. This discrepancy between the physical, observable self and the subjective, inward self is crucial to Jonson's self-portrayal in the second half of his career. In "An Elegy" he admits that he may be "as *Virgil* cold; / As *Horace* fat; or as *Anacreon* old," but he insists upon his prerogative "in Rithme to bee / As light, and active as the youngest hee." The wit in "My Answer: The Poet to the Painter" depends upon a similar contrast between "My Superficies . . . one great blot" and the gifted mind within. He sends Lady Covell his muse, "nimble, chast, and fair," in place of himself, "a tardie, cold, / Unprofitable Chattell, fat and old." Paralyzed and bedridden, he insists indignantly in the "Ode to Himself" that no palsy's in his brain.

THE contrast between body and soul, as these passages reveal, locates poetic talent firmly on the soul's side. Jonson's
physical self-irony invariably accompanies artistic self-exal-
tation; he is cold, fat, and old in the select company of Virgil,
Horace, and Anacreon. In "My Answer: The Poet to the
Painter" his apparent self-denigration fails to conceal his pride
in the superior authenticity of the poetic medium:

> But, you are he can paint; I can but write:
> A Poet hath no more but black and white,
> Ne knows he flatt'ring Colours, or false light.
> (19-21)

Language becomes the medium by which Jonson can communicate the invisible inward self and, when he is lucky,
effectively counteract the disabilities of his appearance. The
encounter between painter and poet is a fairly frequent one
in *The Underwood*, and the painter, limited to the representation of the material world, always comes out second best.[7]
Poetry's lack of sensual appeal seems a positive advantage to
the late Jonson.

The dramatic artist, though, unlike the lyric poet, must
use more—or less—than black and white. In earlier years,
Jonson had conceived the visible and audible aspects of the
drama as interdependent. In the induction to *Every Man Out
of His Humour* Asper promises to "hang my richest words /
 As polisht jewels" in the audience's ears, and also to show
them "objects / Worthy their serious, and intentive eyes."
The heroes of the comical satires, and the rogues of the middle comedies, exploit both language and spectacle for their
purposes. The "Image of the times" Jonson provides his audience is visually as well as verbally compelling. But in the
late plays Jonson prefers to dissociate himself from the visual
aspects of the drama. The messenger-prologue in *The Staple
of News* relays an authorial admonition:

> For your owne sakes, not his, he bad me say,
>   Would you were come to heare, not see a Play.

Though we his *Actors* must provide for those,
   Who are our guests, here, in the way of showes,
The maker hath not so; he'ld have you wise,
   Much rather by your eares, then by your eyes.

(1-6)

The seen and the heard no longer supplement one another in the later plays; physical reality has little to do with spiritual truth. Jonson is increasingly inclined to think of the theater as combining two unlike or even mutually destructive elements: poetry and spectacle.

For the younger Jonson the complex relationship between author and audience, and between moral and hedonistic imperatives, had determined the way he thought about his work in various dramatic genres. Masque subjects differ from comic subjects, and masque audiences differ from comic audiences. As a result the themes shared by Jonson's masques and comedies tend to get treated in different, often virtually complementary, ways. *The Alchemist* repudiates sublimation both as a chemical and a psychological process, but *Mercury Vindicated* makes successful alchemy a royal prerogative. In Jonson's late work the relationship between masque and comedy alters. The antagonism he now perceives between language and spectacle affects masques as much as plays—perhaps affects masques even more, given their traditionally more lavish visual appeal.

Showes! Showes! Mighty Showes!
  The Eloquence of Masques! What need of prose
Or Verse, or Sense t'express Immortal you?[8]

It is not surprising that in the 1620s Jonson's comedies and masques occupy a much larger common ground than they had previously. The comedies become less resolutely "low," the masques less inevitably "high." In some cases, as in the highly successful *Gypsies Metamorphosed*, the line between antimasque and masque is exceedingly fine, and the less-than-flattering implications of the antimasque insinuate themselves

in an unprecedented way into the final assertion of aristocratic ideals. Subjects common to the masques and plays Jonson writes in the 1620s are no longer treated in complementary ways; they simply duplicate one another. The
information-mongers from *News from the New World*, and
the pretentious cook from *Neptune's Triumph*, appear once
more in *The Staple of News*. The disguised gypsies from *The
Gypsies Metamorphosed* show up as Penyboy Canter in *The
Staple of News* and the Host in *The New Inn*. And Jonson's
old disillusion with his theater public begins to extend to the
masque audience as well. In the 1623 "Epistle Answering to
One That Asked to Be Sealed of the Tribe of Ben," Jonson
displays an uncustomary contempt for the aristocratic masqu-
ers, the "Christmas Clay, / And animated *Porc'lane* of the
Court." He is declaring the same independence from their
judgment that he had been asserting all along on the public
stage.

JONSON'S conviction that no physical contingency can possibly give access to the inner, "real" self, the privileged locus
of moral value, has profound effects upon the kind of drama
he writes. Meaningful theater ordinarily presumes some correlation between motive and deed, intention and action, but
it is just this correlation which Jonson now finds extremely
problematic. There are two courses open: either to cease
writing plays altogether, or to find some way of accommodating this unpromising metaphysic to dramatic expression.
In 1616 Jonson, who has been bringing out a play every year
or two for almost twenty years, unexpectedly abandons the
theater for what will become nearly a decade, although he
continues to be active as a poet and writer of masques. In
the latter half of the 1620s, when he finally returns to comedy with *The Staple of News* and *The New Inn*, he must forge
some link, discover some relationship, between the physical
world and the spiritual realities from which it is alienated.

Jonson's late plays each attempt to find and exploit some tenuous possibility of an alliance.

The Staple of News is as carefully naturalistic in its details— as saturated with local color—as *The Alchemist* or *Bartholomew Fair*. But the naturalism extends neither to characterization nor to plot. Jonson's antijournalistic satire emphasizes the meaninglessness of mere occurrences, events like those the News Staple files into its patently specious categories: "*Tailors Newes, Porters,* and *Watermens newes . . . vacation newes, / Terme-newes,* and *Christmas-newes . . . Reformed newes, Protestant newes, /* and *Pontificiall newes.*" The physical world in *The Staple of News* has meaning only insofar as it is made to stand for something else. Metaphor and allegory provide the link Jonson needs between the spiritual and the bodily, the unseen and the seen. As the gossips observe between the acts, the play resurrects the methods of the morality play, with lively but abstractly typical "*Vices,* male and female"— Prodigality, Miserliness, Idolatry.[9] These characters, like Jonson's earlier humours characters, are single-minded and predictable; but whereas the humours characters had been bizarrely individual, these derive their entire identity from the concept they incarnate.

The early and middle Jonson insists upon the physical—a chemical explosion coincides with dashed hopes in *The Alchemist*; sweat, grease, vomit, and urine spill from the morally incontinent in *Bartholomew Fair.* In *The Staple of News*, Jonson renders spiritual reality physical in a very different way. Instead of focusing upon instances where the soul and the body concur or overlap—upon the "humours," for example—Jonson emphasizes real or potential discrepancies between tenor and vehicle, allegorical sense and visible dramatic fact. He treats his characters "realistically" for part of a scene, then abruptly shatters the naturalistic illusion and reduces them to symbols. When the princess Pecunia and her train, tippling at Jonson's favorite Apollo, refuse to depart with Penyboy Senior, the servants enumerate their complaints:

> Statute. . . . he cramb'd us up in a close boxe,
>   All three together, where we saw no *Sunne*
> In one *sixe moneths*.
> Wax. A cruell man he is!
> Band. H'has left my fellow *Waxe* out, i' the cold,
> Sta. Till she was stiffe, as any froste, and crumbl'd
>   Away to dust, and almost lost her forme.
> Wax. Much adoe to recover me.
>   (IV.iii.44-50)

Jonson here deliberately confuses allegorical and literal sense—the normal fate of wax when it is the seal on a business document becomes comically incongruous when applied to "Wax" the simple-minded chambermaid. It is the kind of incongruity most allegorists would prefer to play down, but Jonson is eager to demonstrate the limitations of his symbolism.

The failure of the News Staple similarly disrupts the realistic tone established in previous scenes. Tom the barber comes bustling up to inform Penyboy Junior of the recent turn of events:

>   Heard you not
>   The cracke and ruines? we are all blowne up!
> . . . .—
> Our *Emissaries, Register, Examiner,*
> Flew into vapor: our grave *Governour*
> Into a subt'ler ayre; and is return'd
> (As we doe heare) grand-*Captaine* of the *Jeerers.*
> I, and my fellow melted into butter,
> And spoil'd our Inke, and so the Office vanish'd.
>   (V.i.39-50)

The "explosion" and "dissolution" of the Staple are rendered literal, but at the same time blatantly nonnaturalistic. Even (or especially) at what might have been a climactic moment, a deliberate lack of realism drives home the insignificance of the physical world.

The characters in *The Staple of News*, unaware that their world makes sense only in allegorical terms, suffer like the journalists that exploit them from a materialist obtuseness: a naive faith in the truth of the visible. The only character who possesses any real moral sense is Penyboy Canter—the father in gypsy disguise who eventually reforms both prodigal son and miserly brother, and who exposes the imposters with which the play is rife. He alone understands the difference between truth and appearance; denying both explicitly (in his homiletic speeches) and implicitly (in his role as tattered beggar) his son's equation of wit with clothes, his brother's equation of virtue with wealth. Near the end of the play he becomes quite patently a mouthpiece for the author, defending the appropriateness of the satiric targets in *The Staple of News* in familiar Jonsonian fashion:

> For these shall never have that plea 'gainst me,
> Or colour of advantage, that I hate
> Their callings, but their manners, and their vices.
> A worthy *Courtier*, is the ornament
> Of a *Kings Palace*, his great *Masters* honour.
> This is a moth, a rascall, a Court-rat,
> That gnawes the common-wealth with broking suits,
> And eating grievances!
>
> (IV.iv.137-144)

He rehearses the same defense Jonson used twenty-five years before, when soldiers and actors objected to the way members of their professions were portrayed in *Poetaster*.

The gypsy in disguise becomes an extremely attractive figure for Jonson in his last years. In *The Staple of News* and *The New Inn* he becomes the kind of authorial spokesman that has been absent from Jonson's comedy since the comical satires. The poet-scholar of the comical satires had been a gypsy of sorts—an insightful, somewhat shabby, superficially eccentric outsider. But while the comical satires chart the hero's acceptance into powerful circles, the gypsies of Jonson's old age—Buckingham, Penyboy Canter, Lord Frampul—are already secretly, independently, powerful. They are only apparent outsiders, free to resume the comforts of affluent respectability whenever they please. For an author who, by the time he writes his last plays, finds himself isolated from most of his former sources of social and financial support, the myth of the quasi-gypsy who chooses rather than suffers independence must provide a special kind of consolation.

The New Inn, with which this chapter began, attempts as does *The Staple of News* to find a way of mediating between body and spirit, visible and actual. Like *The Staple of News*, it takes unrelieved materialism as its primary satiric target. Nick Stuff, idolator of spectacle, receives extremely harsh treatment; appearance turns out to be an invariably untrustworthy guide to reality; play-acting is mistaken for sincerity, and sincerity for play-acting. Action is minimal, but speech is crucial to the play's resolution; Lovell's long and formal addresses, not any turn of the plot, convert Lady Frampul from flirt to faithful wife.

Yet the claims of the physical are not quite so firmly dismissed here as they were in *The Staple of News*. As C. G. Thayer observes, "In the illusory world of *The New Inn* nothing, in fact, is what it appears to be, and yet the appearance has considerable relevance to the reality."[10] Disguise can be constructive as well as obfuscatory. Frank, dressed as Laetitia, turns out to be Laetitia indeed. Pru, in the gorgeous clothes of a noblewoman, eventually marries a lord. Lovell's first speech in court makes a harsh distinction, in standard late-Jonsonian fashion, between body and soul.

> But put the case, in travaile I may meet
> Some gorgeous Structure, a brave Frontispice,
> Shall I stay captive i' the outer court,

Surpris'd with that, and not advance to know
Who dwels there, and inhabiteth the house?
. . . .
The bodyes love is fraile, subject to change,
• And alters still, with it; The mindes is firme.

(III.ii.140-160)

Nonetheless, the Court of Love makes its own claims for the body—swearing in the plaintiffs on the *Ars Amoris*, and permitting them to "beare about you, thing, or things, pointed, or blunt," provided only they are "naturall." Lovell's address, adapted from Pausanias' speech in *The Symposium* on the sacred and profane Aphrodite, is qualified—as it is in the original—by Aristophanes' bawdier story, retold by the sensual Beaufort.

Erotic love in *The New Inn*, just as for Socrates in *The Symposium*, constitutes a potential. Lovell's description of lust as "degenerous," "oblique," and "deprav'd" etymologically implies the possibility of a rightly directed sexual passion. The newly enamored Lady Frampul exclaims:

> By what alchimy
> Of love, or language, am I thus translated!
> His tongue is tip'd with the *Philosophers stone*,
> And that hath touch'd me thorough every vaine!
> I feele that transmutation o' my blood,
> As I were quite become another creature,
> And all he speakes, it is projection!

(III.ii.171-177)

This is the rhetoric of sublimation, which in Jonson's earlier drama had invariably proved chimerical. The imagery, which recalls Epicure Mammon's or Mosca's, and the pun on "projection" makes plain the physical element in the Lady's attraction. "Beware," warns Pru, "you do not conjure up a spirit / You cannot lay." But passion here, unlike desire in Jonson's earlier plays, is not necessarily limited to or by the body. Lady Frampul responds, after all, to what she per-

165

ceives as the eloquence and wisdom of a man "somewhat strooke in yeares, and old / Enough to be my father." She is a Charis with possibilities. Purely carnal affection in *The New Inn* leads to moral dead ends—the fetishism of Stuff or the crassness of Beaufort, who tries to disown his new wife when he comes to believe she is poor. But sexual love in its higher manifestations has a constructive aspect unprecedented in Jonsonian drama. It provides some hope of harmony between the body and the soul. The hope may be very faint—*The New Inn* is improbable even as romantic comedies go—but it is there nonetheless.

THE romanticism of *The New Inn*, which is shared by other works of Jonson's last years—*Love's Triumph Through Callipolis*, *The Sad Shepherd*—is not a mode congenial to the Roman moralist sensibility. Jonson, though, does not seem to believe that his newly appreciative view of romance constitutes an abandonment of Roman moral principles. He writes not only erotic comedy during the 1620s, but also his *Discoveries*—translations from Seneca, Quintilian, and other old favorites. His sensibility in these years, even more than in the past, is synthetic rather than exclusive; Lovell's first speech draws on Plato and Ficino, but the second, on valor, is almost entirely translated from Seneca's *De constantia*. The valiant man, Lovell declares,

> . . . can assure himselfe against all rumour!
> Despaires of nothing! laughs at contumelies!
> As knowing himselfe advanced in a height
> Where injury cannot reach him, nor aspersion
> Touch him with soyle!
>
> (IV.iv.134-138)

Jonson has found "valor" in this special sense—not knightly bravado, but Stoic fortitude—inspiring since the days of the comical satires, when Crites in *Cynthia's Revels* and the Author in the apology for *Poetaster* quoted the same passages.

In fact, Jonson's last work is continuous with, though not

similar to, what has gone before. Some critics believe that Jonson's new outlook on sexual love in his last years reflects the neo-Platonism of the Caroline court.[11] But Jonson's interest in eros predates the ascendancy of Henrietta Maria; it goes back to the years of *The Devil Is an Ass* and the poems to Charis. It constitutes an attempt to reintegrate a universe in which the soul is radically estranged from its surroundings and even from its own body.

The problem, though not the solution, is characteristically Roman. Jonson's later views ultimately derive from Stoic notions promulgated by the Roman moralists; the lack of meaningful relation between virtue and fortune, desert and destiny, has presented difficulties for Jonson from the beginning of his career as a dramatist. But though they may originate in Stoic convictions, Jonson's late experiments take him further and further away from the complex network of psychological and social assumptions in which the art of his earlier years had been rooted. In Jonson's prime, too, tense compromise had characterized his art—a typically Roman awareness of the often-incommensurable demands of virtue and efficacy. His late art, by contrast, develops not out of principled compromise but from an insurmountable sense of alienation which tends to subvert the fundamental character of theatrical production. The fixity of this conviction makes the brilliant truces of Jonson's earlier career impossible to negotiate in his last plays.

NOTES

Chapter I. Introduction: Jonson's Classics

1. John Dryden, *Of Dramatick Poesie, An Essay*, in *The Works of John Dryden*, ed. Samuel Holt Monk et al. (Berkeley: University of California Press, 1971), XVII, 21. Contemporary discussions of classical influence upon Jonson's poetry include Wesley Trimpi, *Ben Jonson's Poems: A Study in the Plain Style* (Stanford: Stanford University Press, 1962); Earl Miner, *The Cavalier Mode from Jonson to Cotton* (Princeton: Princeton University Press, 1971), 84-95, 256-275; Richard Peterson, *Imitation and Praise in the Poems of Ben Jonson* (New Haven: Yale University Press, 1981). Trimpi discusses the Latin precedents for Jonson's poetic style; Peterson focuses upon Jonson's use of traditional tropes in his poems of praise; Miner describes the adaptation of Jonsonian classicism by the "Sons of Ben." For classical influences on the masque, see D. J. Gordon, "*Hymenaei*: Ben Jonson's Masque of Union," in *The Renaissance Imagination*, ed. Stephen Orgel (Berkeley: University of California Press, 1975), 157-184; John C. Meagher, *Method and Meaning in Jonson's Masques* (London: University of Notre Dame Press, 1966). For Jonson's use of the Greek author Lucian in the middle comedies, see Douglas Duncan, *Ben Jonson and the Lucianic Tradition* (Cambridge: Cambridge University Press, 1979).

2. By the time he was fourteen the Elizabethan schoolchild would have had seven or eight years of training in the Latin language. He would be familiar with Horace, Virgil, Martial, Quintilian, Juvenal, and Pliny the Younger; he would have read some of Cicero's epistles and orations, and most of the extant Ciceronian philosophical treatises (*De re publica*, with the exception of the *Somnium Scipionis*, was unavailable in the Renaissance). Persius, Lucan, and Seneca were sometimes taught in the grammar schools; Seneca became progressively more important in the late sixteenth and early seventeenth centuries, and he eventually replaced Cicero as the major ethical philosopher read on the grammar school level. For information on the Elizabethan grammar school curriculum, see T. W. Baldwin, *William Shakespere's Small Latine and Lesse Greeke* (Urbana: University of Illinois Press, 1944).

169

3. For the humanist sense of historical distance from ancient culture, see Thomas Greene, *The Light in Troy* (New Haven: Yale University Press, 1982), esp. 264-293, which deal primarily with Jonson. For the contemporary political resonance of Jonson's Roman tragedies, see B. N. de Luna, *Jonson's Romish Plot: A Study of Catiline and Its Historical Context* (Oxford: Oxford University Press, 1967); and Annabel Patterson, "Roman-cast Similitude: Ben Jonson and the English Use of Roman History," in *Rome in the Renaissance: The City and the Myth*, ed. P. A. Ramsey (Binghamton: Medieval and Renaissance Texts, 1982), 381-394.

4. For the dispute between the "Ciceronians" and the "Senecans" see Morris Croll, "Attic Prose: Lipsius, Montaigne, Bacon" and "The Baroque Style in Prose," *Style, Rhetoric, and Rhythm* (Princeton: Princeton University Press, 1966), 167-202, 207-233. Croll, who posits a close relationship between prose style and philosophical preference, tends to overstate the ideological difference between Cicero and Seneca, and also to enroll in the "Senecan" school the many Renaissance writers who disapprove of the slavish imitation of Cicero. Wesley Trimpi adopts Croll's distinctions when he discusses Jonson's Latinity in his *Ben Jonson's Poems*.

5. Vives, *De tradendis disciplinis* IV, iv; Erasmus, *Ciceronianus*, p. 625 in *Opera Omnia* I, 2 (Amsterdam: North Holland Publishing, 1971). Vives classes Cicero and Seneca together as moral philosophers in IV, iv, and V, iii. Lipsius uses both philosophers together in *De constantia*, *Politicorum*, and *Manductionis ad Stoicam*. Even while defending his stylistic imitation of Seneca he insists that "Ciceronem amo" (*Epistularum selectarum centuria II miscellanea*, 10). For an English example of the same emphasis upon Cicero's philosophical doctrine, see Gabriel Harvey's *Ciceronianus* (1577), ed. Harold Wilson (Lincoln: University of Nebraska Press, 1945). Richard Peterson discusses Jonsonian eclecticism and its intellectual sources in his *Imitation and Praise*, 4-20.

6. Compare, e.g., Seneca's belief in the soul's immortality, as expressed in *Epistulae morales* CII, with the agnosticism of *Ad Polybium de consolatione* and *De brevitate vitae*. Cicero likewise wavers between belief (*De senectute*, *Somnium Scipionis*) and uncertainty (*De finibus*, *Tusculan Disputations*). Seneca's position on material wealth in *Epistulae morales* XVII differs from his opinion in *De vita beata*. In the *Ars poetica*, Horace is more willing to subject the artist to the

demands of a large audience than he is in the *Odes* or in *Epistles* I, xix, where he stresses his indifference to mere popularity. And so on.

7. Helpful discussions of the general characteristics of the humanist movement, and of its debt to Latin texts, include William Harrison Woodward, *Studies in Education During the Age of the Renaissance: 1400-1600* (Cambridge: Cambridge University Press, 1906); Paul Oskar Kristeller, *Renaissance Thought: The Classic, Scholastic, and Humanist Strains* (New York: Harper, 1961); Hanna Gray, "The Pursuit of Eloquence," *Renaissance Essays*, ed. P. O. Kristeller and P. P. Weiner (New York: Harper, 1968), 199-216; Jerrold Seigel, *Rhetoric and Philosophy in Renaissance Humanism: The Union of Eloquence and Wisdom, Petrarch to Valla* (Princeton: Princeton University Press, 1968).

8. Compare the experience of sixteenth-century English writers—More, Spenser, Marlowe, Shakespeare—of whom Stephen Greenblatt remarks: "All of these talented middle-class men moved out of a narrowly circumscribed social sphere and into a realm that brought them in close contact with the powerful and the great. All were in a position as well . . . to know with some intimacy those with no power, status, or education at all." *Renaissance Self-Fashioning* (Chicago: University of Chicago Press, 1980), 7.

9. *Discoveries*, 622-633. All quotations from Ben Jonson's works are taken from C. H. Herford, Percy and Evelyn Simpson, *Ben Jonson*, 11 vols. (Oxford: Clarendon, 1925-1952), hereinafter referred to as "Herford and Simpson." *I, j, u, v,* and *y* have been regularized.

10.   "Me libertino natum patre et in tenui re
           maiores pinnas nido extendisse loqueris

           . . . .

           me primis urbis belli placuisse domique."
           (Horace, *Epistles* I, xx, 20-23)

All quotations from classical texts are from the Loeb editions. The translations are my own; in passages of poetry I have tried to preserve line endings where grammar permits.

11. "Ego vero, quoniam forensibus operis, laboribus, periculis non deseruisse mihi videor praesidium in quo a populo Romano locatus sum, debeo profecto, quantumcumque possum, in eo quo-

que elaborare ut sint opera, studio, labore meo doctiores cives mei."
Cicero, *De finibus* I, iv, 10.

12. Henry Peacham, *The Complete Gentleman* (London, 1622), ed.
Virgil Heltzel (Ithaca: Cornell University Press, 1962), 14, 16.

13. For an analysis, in Freudian terms, of these "myths of the
artist," see Ernst Kris and Otto Kurz, *Legend, Myth, and Magic in
the Image of the Artist* (New Haven: Yale University Press, 1979),
esp. 1-60. It is important to note that the availability of an archetype
does not mean that the autobiographical accounts Horace and Cicero provide are *untrue*; in classical Rome, and in Renaissance Italy
and England, ambitious youths needed to work within established
systems of patronage. The availability of a "standard story," however, undoubtedly qualifies the way Horace, Cicero, or Jonson conceive of their own lives.

14. Justus Lipsius, "De vita et scriptis L. Annaei Senecae," *L.
Annaei Senecae philosophi opera, quae exstant omnia* (Antwerp, 1605),
xiii; and "C. Cornelii Taciti vita, honores, et scripta," *Cornelii Taciti opera quae exstant* (1600). In a Restoration English translation the
editor complains about Lipsius' refusal to acknowledge the promi-
nence of Tacitus' family (*The Annals and History of Cornelius Tacitus
. . . Made English by Several Hands* [London, 1698], 2).

15. "Virtus, etiamsi quosdam impetus ex natura sumit, tamen
perficienda doctrina est." Quintilian, *Institutiones* XII, ii, 1.

16.   "Ego nec studium sine divite vena,
      nec rude quid prosit video ingenium: alterius sic
      altera poscit opem res et coniurat amice.
      Qui studet optatam cursu contingere metam,
      multa tulit fecitque puer, sudavit et alsit,
      abstinuit Venere et vino; qui Pythia cantat
      tibicen, didicit prius extimuitque magistrum."
                        (Horace, *Ars poetica*, 409-415)

17. The analogy between blacksmith and artist is a favorite one
with Jonson. See, e.g., *Discoveries*, 2442-2443.

18. For the far-reaching social consequences of humanist attitudes
toward education and statecraft, see Mark H. Curtis, *Oxford and
Cambridge in Transition 1558-1642* (Oxford: Clarendon, 1959); "The
Alienated Intellectuals of Early Stuart England," *Past and Present* 23

(1962), 25-43; and Lawrence Stone, "The Educational Revolution in England 1560-1640," *Past and Present* 28 (1964), 41-80.

19. "Nihil enim interarescere, nihil exstingui, nihil cadere debet eorum, in quibus vita beata consistit. Nam qui timebit ne quid ex his deperdat beatus esse non poterit." Cicero, *Tusculan Disputations* V, xiv, 40-41.

20. "To the World: A Farewell for a Gentlewoman, Virtuous and Noble," 65-68. Cf. Seneca, *Epistulae morales* XXVIII, and Horace, *Epistles* I, xi, 25-30.

21. Cicero, for example, who claims to be an "Academic," has strong Stoic leanings. Though he sometimes takes issue with the Greek Stoics' claims to originality, and he does wish they wrote more attractive prose, he never attacks them as unethical. Both he and Quintilian after him represent Stoic faults as relatively minor beside fundamental Epicurean or Cyrenian misconceptions. While Horace makes fun of the humorless Stoic, Damasippus, in *Satires* II, iii, no Stoic would object to the moral sentiments he voices in the majority of the satires and epistles. Tacitus, though wary of everything doctrinaire, regards the Stoic position as basically sound. Like Juvenal, he attacks philosophical hypocrisy not because he objects to Stoic doctrine but because he resents the perversion of a noble teaching by unworthy practitioners. Relevant texts are: for Cicero, *De finibus* IV and V, *Academica* II, xliii-xlvi, and *Tusculan Disputations* IV, all of which discuss Stoicism and its relation to other major philosophical systems (Cicero comes to different conclusions in different treatises); for Quintilian, *Institutiones* XII; for Horace, *Satires* I, i; II, ii, iii, vi; and *Epistles* I, i, ii, vi, xvi; for Tacitus, the treatment of the "Stoic opposition" to imperial excess in the *Annals* and *Histories*, and the presentation of Seneca's suicide in *Annals* XV; for Juvenal, *Satires* II (on hypocritical Stoicism), VIII, X, XIII, and XIV.

22. "Nullum numen habes . . . nos te / nos facimus, Fortuna, deam caeloque locamus." Juvenal, *Satires* X, 365-366.

23.   "Nil admirari prope res est una, Numici,
        solaque quae possit facere et servare beatum."
                        (Horace, *Epistles* I, vi, 1-2)

24. "Vir igitur temperatus, constans, sine metu, sine aegritudine,

sine alacritate ulla, sine libidine, nonne beatus?" Cicero, *Tusculan Disputations* V, xvi, 48.

25. "Nullo modo magis potest deus concupita traducere, quam si illa ad turpissimos defert, ab optimis abigit." Seneca, *De providentia* v, 2-3.

26. Jonson, introduction to the *Epigrams*, 40-42.

27. Thomas Greene dicusses this aspect of Jonson's work in "Ben Jonson and the Centered Self," *Studies in English Literature* 10 (1970), 325-348.

28. "Quae enim tanta gravitas, quae tanta constantia, magnitudo animi, probitas, fides, quae tam excellens in omni genere virtus in ullis fuit, ut sit cum maioribus nostris comparanda?" Cicero, *Tusculan Disputations* I, i, 2. For the relation between the Roman sense of national identity and the widespread respect for Stoicism in late republican and imperial Rome, see Donald Earl, *The Moral and Political Tradition of Rome* (Ithaca: Cornell University Press, 1967).

29. Vives, *In libros disciplinis praefatio*, uses passages from Seneca, *Epistulae morales* XXXIII, 10-11, and from Quintilian, *Institutiones* III, i, and X, ii, 3-13. Cf. Cicero, *De oratore* II, xxii-xxiii; *De natura deorum* I, v, 10; *Tusculan Disputations* IV, vii. For Cicero's defense of the vernacular, see the introductory section of almost any of his philosophical works, e.g., *De finibus* I, ii-iii; *Academica* I, ii-iii; *De natura deorum* I, iv, 8; *Tusculan Disputations* I, i-ii.

30. See, e.g., Robert Knoll, *Ben Jonson's Plays: An Introduction* (Lincoln: University of Nebraska Press, 1964), or Freda Townsend, *An Apologie for Bartholomew Fayre: The Art of Jonson's Comedies* (London: Oxford University Press, 1947).

31. *Controversiae* I, praefatio 6.

32. Peterson, *Imitation and Praise*, xiii.

Chapter II. Virtue and Vice

1. Remarks by Jonson's contemporaries, and by selected critics from the Restoration to the nineteenth century as well, are collected in C. H. Herford, Percy and Evelyn Simpson, *Ben Jonson* (Oxford: Clarendon, 1952), XI, 307-569. The comments from Shadwell and Oldham are reproduced in this section.

2. Oldham, "Upon the Works of Ben. Johnson" (1678). Shadwell, Preface to *The Sullen Lovers* (1668).

3. Harry Levin, "An Introduction to Ben Jonson," *Ben Jonson: A*

Collection of Critical Essays, ed. Jonas Barish (Englewood Cliffs: Prentice-Hall, 1963), 56.

4. The only recent exception to this rule is, I believe, John Creasar, who discusses Jonson's methods of characterization in *Volpone* at considerable length in his introduction to the play (New York: New York University Press, 1978). He is particularly interesting on Celia and Corvino.

5. See, e.g., Henry L. Snuggs, "The Comic Humours: A New Interpretation," *PMLA* 62 (1947), 114-122. See also Herford and Simpson, I, 340-345; John Enck, *Ben Jonson and the Comic Truth* (Madison: University of Wisconsin Press, 1957), 44-49.

6. Seneca, *De ira* II, xix.

7. Induction to *Every Man Out of His Humour*, 102-104. For Cicero's protest against a too-literal humours psychology, see *Tusculan Disputations* IV, x, 23.

8. Cicero, *Tusculan Disputations* III, iii, 6.

9. *Cynthia's Revels* III.iii.32-36. Cf. Seneca, *De constantia* xiii, 2: "Hunc affectum adversus omnis habet sapiens, quem adversus aegros suos medicus." Seneca repeats this in *De ira* II, x, 7-8: "Omnia ista tam propitius aspiciet quam aegros suos medicus."

10. "Quid ergo est bonum? Rerum scientia. Quid malum est? Rerum imperitia." Seneca, *Epistulae morales* XXXI, 6.

11. *Every Man in His Humour*, prologue, line 24.

12. Seneca, *De providentia* iv, 9.

13. "Fluminibus innatant, non eunt, sed feruntur." Seneca, *Epistulae morales* XXIII, 8.

14. *Catiline* III.247, V.46-47.

15. "Nihil est enim tantum . . . multiforme, tot ac tam variis adfectibus concisum atque laceratum quam mala mens." Quintilian, *Institutiones* XII, i, 7.

16. "Nihil certum sequentis vaga et inconstans et sibi displicens levitas per nova consilia iactavit." Seneca, *De brevitate vitae* ii, 2.

17. See J. M. Rist, *Stoic Philosophy* (Cambridge: Cambridge University Press, 1969), 173-218, for a description of the Posidonian innovations. By the time Justus Lipsius writes in the sixteenth century, he can begin a discussion of Stoicism by making a fundamental distinction between the body and the soul (*De constantia* I, i-iii) and insist to a friend that "homo es, e duplici materie, caelesti et terrana; ad duo etiam natus caelam et terram" (*Epistularum selectarum . . . miscellanea* II, xxxiv).

18. "Animorum nulla in terris origo inveniri potest; nihil enim est in animis mixtum atque concretum aut quod ex terra natum atque fictum esse videatur, nihil ne aut humidum quidem aut flabile aut igneum. . . . Singularis est igitur quaedam natura atque vis animi, seiuncta ab his usitatis notisque naturis." Cicero, *Tusculan Disputations* I, xxvii, 66. Cicero is here quoting his own remarks from a *Consolatio*, now lost, which he wrote himself upon the death of his beloved daughter, Tullia. Cicero would rather dispense with materialism than with his belief in free will and the immortality of the soul, which he believes is incompatible with it.

19. "Quid enim est aliud animus quam quodam modo se habens spiritus?" Seneca, *Epistulae morales* L, 6.

20. "Potest ex casa vir magnus exire, potest et ex deformi humilique corpusculo formosus animus ac magnus . . . Claranus mihi videtur in exemplar editus, ut scire possemus non deformitate corporis foedari animum, sed pulchritudine animi corpus ornari." Seneca, *Epistulae morales* LXVI, 3-4.

21. "Atqui cum voles veram hominis aestimationem inire et scire, qualis sit, nudum inspice; ponat patrimonium, ponat honores et alia fortunae mendacia, corpus ipsum exuat." Seneca, *Epistulae morales* LXXVI, 32.

22. See, e.g., Robert Knoll, *Ben Jonson's Plays: An Introduction* (Lincoln: University of Nebraska Press, 1964), 45: "The first two of the comical satires stand as far apart from the indigenous drama as any of Jonson's plays. In them Jonson tries to turn London into Augustan Rome. He pontificates from a classical podium but . . . he is more ridiculous than persuasive. By the time of *Poetaster* he has begun to return to his native haunts; and his subsequent great plays . . . are back in the native tradition."

23. *Every Man Out of His Humour*, induction, 231-232. Jonson's change of artistic direction may seem misguided, since *Every Man In* is easier to enjoy than the comical satires that follow. But even in 1616, when his dramatic technique seems to have changed drastically in many respects, Jonson remains fiercely proud of the comical satires. Perhaps his affection for such controversial work is partly defensive. But since the experience of writing and staging the comical satires permanently alters Jonson's sense of his artistic endeavor, his intransigence may make sense.

24. O. J. Campbell, *Comicall Satyre in Shakespeare's Troilus and Cressida* (San Marino, Calif.: Huntington Library, 1938), and Alvin

Kernan, *The Cankered Muse* (New Haven: Yale University Press, 1959), relate Jonson's comical satires to late Elizabethan verse satire. Kernan treats Jonson's innovations at length; see esp. pp. 54-140.

25. "Quid est boni viri? Praebere se fato. Grande solacium est cum universo rapi." Seneca, *De providentia* v, 8.

26. "Ex superiore loco homines videntem." Seneca, *Epistulae morales* XLI, 4. This trope is also important in Epistle LXXV, in *Ad Marciam de consolatione*, and in *De vita beata*. Cicero uses it repeatedly in the *Tusculan Disputations* and of course in the *Somnium Scipionis*. In *The Antitheatrical Prejudice* (Berkeley: University of California Press, 1981), 38-42, Jonas Barish describes the cultural factors that help create the ambivalence or hostility many of the Roman moralists display toward acting and the theater.

27. Ben Jonson, rarely one to tout the superiority of Judeo-Christian civilization to classical civilization, here modifies his source, John of Salisbury's *Policraticus*. What is in the *Policraticus* a distinction between godly and pagan becomes in Jonson a standard Roman-Stoic distinction between the morally good minority and the bad, "sensuall" majority. Margaret Clayton identifies Jonson's source for this passage in "Ben Jonson, 'In Travaile with Expression of Another': His Use of John of Salisbury's *Policraticus* in *Timber*," *Review of English Studies* 30 (1981), 397-408.

28. Cf. Thomas Greene's remark about Jonson's poetry: "The . . . values of virtue tend in their constancy to be transcribed by nouns and adjectives . . . the hideous antics of vice, because variable, must depend on a livelier poetry of verbs." "Ben Jonson and the Centered Self," *Studies in English Literature* 10 (1970), 331-332.

29. For the former line of argument, see Gabriele Jackson, *Vision and Judgment in Ben Jonson's Drama* (New Haven: Yale University Press, 1968), 54-57, 69-76; for the latter line of argument, see Jonas Barish, *Ben Jonson and the Language of Prose Comedy* (Cambridge: Harvard University Press, 1960), 78-81.

30. Dryden broaches the issue in *Of Dramatick Poesie, An Essay* (1668): "The unity of design seems not exactly observ'd in it [*The Fox*]; for there appear two actions in the Play; the first naturally ending with the fourth Act; the second forc'd from it in the fifth: which yet is the less to be condemn'd in him, because the disguise of *Volpone*, though it suited not with his character as a crafty or covetous person, agreed well enough with that of a voluptuary: and by it the Poet gain'd the end at which he aym'd, the punishment of

Vice, and the reward of Virtue, both which that disguise produc'd. So that to judge equally of it, it was an excellent fifth Act, but not so naturally proceeding from the former." *The Works of John Dryden*, ed. Samuel Holt Monk et al. (Berkeley: University of California Press, 1971), XVII, 49-50. Dryden's comments on *Volpone*, as well as those cited in the next note, are conveniently available in *Jonson: Volpone: A Casebook*, ed. Jonas Barish (London: Macmillan, 1972).

31. See, e.g., comments by John Dennis (p. 30), Richard Cumberland (p. 41), and C. H. Herford (pp. 70-71) in *Volpone: A Casebook*. John Creasar's introduction to his edition of the play contains a careful discussion of the transition between the fourth and fifth acts, and what it implies about Volpone's character.

32. "Praecipuum munus annalium reor ne virtutes sileantur utque pravis dictis factisque ex posteritate et infamia metus sit." Tacitus, *Annals* III, lxv.

33. "Invenies sub Tyrannide adulationes, delationes, non ignota huic saeculo mala; nihil sincerum, nihil simplex, et nec apud amicos tutam fidem; frequentatas accusationes maiestatis, unicum crimen eorum qui crimine vacabant; cumulatas illustrium virorum neces, et pacem quovis bello saeviorem." Justus Lipsius, Dedicatory Letter to Emperor Maximilian II, *C. Cornelii Taciti opera omnia quae exstant* (Antwerp, 1581), 4r. Jonson relied upon Lipsius' great edition of Tacitus' works in writing *Sejanus*.

34. "Auctoritatem Stoicae sectae praeferebat, habitu et ore ad exprimendam imaginem honesti exercitus, ceterum animo perfidiosus, subdolus, avaritiam ac libidinem occultans." Tacitus, *Annals* XVI, xxxii.

35. "Specie bonarum artium falsos." Tacitus, *Annals* XIV, xxxii.

36. When Jonson maintains that "the good poet must of necessity be a good man," he is perhaps remembering Quintilian—"qui sit orator, virum bonum esse oportere, sed ne futurum quidem oratorem nisi virum bonum" (*Institutiones* XII, i, 3)—though he could have gotten the same idea from Cicero, Horace, Strabo, or any number of other writers. See esp. Cicero, *De oratore* III, xvi, 60-61; *De partitiones oratoria* XL; *Orator* iv, 14-17 and xxxiii, 118-xxxiv, 119; Quintilian, *Institutiones* II, xx, and XII, ii, 1-31; Horace, *Ars poetica*, 309ff.

37. I believe I got this idea about *Epicene* from a conversation with Anne Barton.

38. Of course this all requires quite a bit of fudging; the complete power over circumstances granted the king in the masque is itself a myth. See Stephen Orgel, *The Illusion of Power* (Berkeley: University of California Press, 1975), 87-88. Roman as well as Tudor moralists are fond of dwelling upon the real powerlessness of even the most absolute rulers.

39. "Numquam enim recta mens vertitur nec sibi odio est nec quicquam mutavit a vita optima." Seneca, *De vita beata* vii, 4.

40. "Sic maxime coarguitur animus inprudens; alius prodit atque alius et, quo turpius nihil iudico, impar sibi est." Seneca, *Epistulae morales* CXX, 22.

41. Seneca, *Epistulae morales* XII.

42.
> "Laudas
> fortunam et mores antiquae plebis, et idcm,
> si quis ad illa deus subito te agat, usque recuses,
> aut quia non sentis quod clamas rectius esse,
> aut quia non firmus rectum defendis, et haeres
> nequiquam caeno cupiens evellere plantam.
> Romae rus optas; absentem rusticus urbem
> tollis ad astra levis."
>
> (Horace, *Satires* II, vii, 23-29)

43.
> "Me pinguem et nitidum bene curata cute vises
> cum ridere voles, Epicuri de grege porcum."
>
> (Horace, *Epistles* I, iv, 15-16)

44. "Non sum sapiens et, ut malivolentiam tuam pascam, nec ero. . . . De virtute, non de me loquor." Seneca, *De vita beata* xvii, 3; xviii, 1.

45. Cicero and Seneca are criticized both in their own times and in the Renaissance for their failure to practice what they preach. Seneca himself complains, in *De brevitate vitae* v, 1, that Cicero is "neither content in good times nor patient in adversity" (nec secundis rebus quietus nec adversarum patiens). Petrarch, disturbed by the contrast between Cicero's philosophical ideas and the unsettled character he displays in his *Epistles*, addresses him two frank letters on the subject—*Familiarum rerum* 24, 2 and 3. In his *Roman History*, Dio similarly exploits a perceived gap between Seneca's life and teaching when he accuses him of the very sycophancy and extravagance that Seneca condemns in *Epistulae morales* and *Moral Essays* (LXI, Epitome, 10, 2-3).

46. The characterization of Jonson is Drummond's in *Conversations*, 687. Dekker's complaint comes from "To the World" (preface to *Satiro-Mastix*) in *Thomas Dekker: Dramatic Works*, ed. Fredson Bowers (Cambridge: Cambridge University Press, 1962), I, 309. The modern critic is Arthur Marotti, "All About Jonson's Poetry," *ELH* 39 (1972), 20.

47. "Non . . . singulis vocibus philosophi spectandi sunt, sed ex perpetuitate atque constantia."
"Sed tua quoque vide ne desideretur constantia."
"Cum aliis isto modo, qui legibus impositis disputant: nos in diem vivimus; quodcumque nostros animos probabilitate percussit, id dicimus, itaque soli sumus liberi." Cicero, *Tusculan Disputations* V, x-xi, 31-33.

48.   "Beatus ille qui procul negotiis
           ut prisca gens mortalium
           paternam rura bobus exercet suis
           solutus omni faenore."
                (Horace, *Epodes* ii, 1-4)

49.   "Haec ubi locutus faenorator Alfius
           iam iam futurus rusticus,
           omnem redegit Idibus pecuniam
           quaerit Kalendis ponere."
                (Horace, *Epodes* ii, 66-70)

50. "Neque enim me cuiusdam sectae velut quadam superstitione imbutus addixi." Quintilian, *Institutiones* III, i, 22; for the role of philosophy in the orator's education, see XII, ii, 26-27.

51.   "Nullius addictus iurare in verba magistri,
           quo me cumque rapit tempestas, deferor hospes."
                (Horace, *Epistles* I, i, 14-15)

52.   ". . . Nec cynicos nec stoica dogmata legit
           a cynicis tunica distantia, non Epicurum
           suspicit exigui laetum plantaribus horti."
                (Juvenal, *Satires* XIII, 121-123)
Cynics did not wear shirts; Stoics thought one should wear not only what was strictly necessary, but whatever was customary in one's locale. Cicero castigates the Cynics for ignoring decorum, a part of virtue, in *De officiis* I.

53. "Soleo enim et in aliena castra transire, non tamquam trans-
fuga, sed tamquam explorator." Seneca, *Epistulae morales* II, 6.

54. *Discoveries*, 154. Jonson wrote "tanquam explorator" in the
corner of the title page of every book he acquired. For a photo-
graphed title page of one of Jonson's books, see Herford and Simpson I, plate between pp. 264 and 265. Jonson uses the variant spell-
ing "tanquam" instead of the more usual "tamquam."

55. Jonas Barish, "Jonson and the Loathed Stage," *A Celebration
of Ben Jonson* (Toronto: University of Toronto Press, 1973), 27-53.

Chapter III. Profit, Delight, and Imitation

1. Cicero's definition of comedy, "the imitation of life, the mir-
ror of manners, the image of truth," is quoted by Donatus in *Ex-
cerpta de comoedia* IV, 1. See *Aeli Donati commentum Terenti*, ed. Paul
Wessner (Stuttgart: Teubner, 1962), I, 22. The reference is to Cicero, *De republica* IV, 13; in book IV, most of which is no longer
extant, Cicero discussed the role of drama and poetry in society.

2.   "Aut prodesse volunt aut delectare poetae
        aut simul et iucunda et idonea dicere vitae.

        . . . .

        ficta voluptatis causa sint proxima veris,
        ne quodcumque velit poscat sibi fabula credi."
                                (Horace, *Ars poetica*, 333-339)

3. For an account of Donatus' effect upon the way Renaissance
editors and literary theorists think about comedy, see Marvin Herrick, *Comic Theory in the Sixteenth Century* (Urbana: University of
Illinois Press, 1950).

4. "An Execration upon Vulcan," 90. Jonson's commentary was
lost in the fire that consumed his library in 1623. For sixteenth-
century attempts to reconcile Horace and Aristotle, see Marvin
Herrick, *The Fusion of Horatian and Aristotelian Literary Criticism,
1531-1555* (Urbana: University of Illinois Press, 1946), and Bernard
Weinberg, *A History of Literary Criticism in the Italian Renaissance*
(Chicago: University of Chicago Press, 1961), 111-155. The most
important of these critics for Jonson was probably Bernardino Parthenio, the editor of his text of Horace. Modern literary historians
still emphasize the connection: "The Horatian view . . . can scarcely
be separated . . . from the realist theory of comedy coming down

from Aristotle and expressed for Augustan Rome in the Ciceronian phrase (preserved by Donatus) *comoedia . . . imitatio vitae, speculum consuetudinis, imago veritatis.*" William K. Wimsatt and Cleanth Brooks, *Literary Criticism: A Short History* (New York: Knopf, 1957), 89.

5. Jonson's debt in this instance to Minturno's *De poeta* IV was first noticed by Henry Snuggs, "The Source of Jonson's Definition of Comedy," *MLN* 65 (1950), 543-544.

6. Philip Sidney, *A Defense of Poetry* in *Miscellaneous Prose of Sir Philip Sidney*, ed. K. Duncan-Jones and J. Van Dorsten (Oxford: Clarendon, 1973), 79-80.

7. *Discoveries*, 2394.

8. Many critics agree with Ian Donaldson that there is a "curious disjunction between commentary and work, a sense that Jonson's critical genius and Jonson's creative genius are at a loss to know what to do with one another." "Jonson and the Moralists," *Two Renaissance Mythmakers*, ed. Alvin Kernan (Baltimore: Johns Hopkins University Press, 1977), 146. Harry Levin argues that a "formidable misconception" can arise if one takes "the author's rationalizations about his own work too seriously." "An Introduction to Ben Jonson," *Ben Jonson: A Collection of Critical Essays*, ed. Jonas Barish (Englewood Cliffs, N.J.: Prentice-Hall, 1963), 41. Gabriele Jackson claims that "Jonson, in his numerous manifesto-like utterances, has himself been the most diligent obfuscator of his own creation." Preface to *Every Man in His Humour* (New Haven: Yale University Press, 1969), 19. Arthur Marotti hopes to avoid suggesting "an illusion of harmony between [Jonson's] criticism and his art." "All About Jonson's Poetry," *ELH* 39 (1972), 209. John Creasar complains about the "curious disjunction between critical theory and literary sensibility . . . often discernible in Jonson." He argues that Jonson's "prescriptive critical vocabulary, dominated as it was by rules and universal standards of decorum, simply could not give him the appropriate language" in which to discuss his own art. Introduction to *Volpone, or, the Fox* (New York: New York University Press, 1978), 9.

9. I will discuss the Roman social ideals *Volpone* caricatures in Chapter V.

10. Cf. Cicero, *De officiis* I, xlii, 150-151, or Seneca, *Epistulae morales* LXXXVIII, 1-2.

11. "Ista res maior est altiorque quam ut credi similis huic, in

quo est, corpusculo possit? Vis isto divina descendit." Seneca, *Epistulae morales* XLI, 4-5.

12. *Volpone*, II.ii.44-45, 49. For a more extended discussion of the parallels between "Scoto's" situation and Jonson's, see the notes to the scene in Alvin Kernan and J. Dennis Huston, *Classics of the Renaissance Theater* (New York: Harcourt, Brace, and World, 1969), 254-255.

13. See, e.g., T. S. Eliot, "Ben Jonson," in *Ben Jonson: A Collection of Critical Essays*, 19; Harry Levin, "An Introduction to Ben Jonson," 45-46; Edward Partridge, *The Broken Compass* (New York: Columbia University Press, 1958), 77; L. A. Beaurline, "Volpone and the Power of Gorgeous Speech," *Studies in the Literary Imagination* 6 (1973), 68-72; John Creasar, introduction to *Volpone*, 22, 24.

14. Richard Levin, "No Laughing Matter: Some New Readings of *The Alchemist*," *Studies in the Literary Imagination* 6 (1973), 85-99.

15. Jonas Barish argues for this interpretation in *Ben Jonson and the Language of Prose Comedy* (Cambridge: Harvard University Press, 1960), 213.

16. Douglas Duncan, for example, who stresses Jonson's debt in the middle plays to the moral irony of Erasmus and More, writes that "farce is a weapon which can be moral in that it tests the audience's powers of discrimination." *Ben Jonson and the Lucianic Tradition* (Cambridge: Cambridge University Press, 1979), 146.

17. "Non delectent verba nostra, sed prosint. . . . Quid aures meas scabis? Quid oblectas? Aliud agitur; urendus, secandus, abstinendus sum." Seneca, *Epistulae morales* LXXV, 5-7.

18. For early discussions of the morality of Jonsonian comedy, see the remarks by John Dryden and Jeremy Collier in C. H. Herford, Percy and Evelyn Simpson, *Ben Jonson* (Oxford, Clarendon, 1952), XI, 514, 521-522, and 549-552. Examples of more or less "moral" critics are L. C. Knights, *Drama and Society in the Age of Jonson* (London: Chatto and Windus, 1937); Helena Watts Baum, *The Satiric and the Didactic in Ben Jonson's Comedy* (Chapel Hill: University of North Carolina Press, 1947); George Parfitt, *Ben Jonson: Public Poet, Private Man* (London: Dent, 1976); and Gabriele Jackson, *Vision and Judgment in Ben Jonson's Drama* (New Haven: Yale University Press, 1968). For the reaction against "moral" criticism of Jonson, see, e.g., S. Schoenbaum, "The Humourous Jonson,"

in *The Elizabethan Theatre IV*, ed. G. Hibbard (Hamden, Conn.: Archon, 1974), 1-21; Richard Levin, "No Laughing Matter: Some New Readings of *The Alchemist*"; Ian Donaldson, "Jonson and the Moralists"; and John Creasar's introduction to *Volpone*. Others prefer an "evolutionary" view: e.g., Jonas Barish; John Enck; L. A. Beaurline, in *Jonson and Elizabethan Comedy: Essays in Dramatic Rhetoric* (San Marino, Calif.: Huntington Library, 1978); and Harry Levin, in "Jonson's Metempsychosis," *Philological Quarterly* 22 (1943), 231-239. They argue that Jonson takes a sternly moral line in early life but relaxes in later years. I agree that Jonson's attitude changes, but not precisely along the lines Barish and Beaurline suggest. Douglas Duncan's *Ben Jonson and the Lucianic Tradition*, at its best when it stops insisting that Jonson's irony is necessarily "Lucianic," makes a heroic attempt to bridge the gap between the "moralistic" and "nonmoralistic" readings of Jonson, by showing that wit and flexibility can themselves have moral uses. Though my approach and conclusions differ from Duncan's, my analysis of the way the audience is involved in the action of the middle comedies resembles his.

19. Wimsatt, *Literary Criticism: A Short History*, 72.

20. "Altum quiddam est virtus, excelsum et regale, invictum, indefatigabile; voluptas humile, servile, imbecillum, caducum." Seneca, *De vita beata* vii, 3.

21.   "Centuriae seniorum agitant expertia frugis,
        celsi praetereunt austera poemata Ramnes:
        omne tulit punctum qui miscuit utile dulci."
                        (Horace, *Ars poetica*, 341-343)

22. Barish, *Ben Jonson and the Language of Prose Comedy*, 112.

23. Prologue to *The Alchemist*, 11-14.

24. See, e.g., Barish, *Ben Jonson and the Language of Prose Comedy*, 195, or Beaurline, *Jonson and Elizabethan Comedy*, 14-24.

25. Jonson's elaboration of the metaphor may have something to do with his reading of Isaac Casaubon's *De satyrica graecorum poesi et romanorum satira libri duo* (Paris, 1605). Jonson makes extensive use of Casaubon's book in his notes to *Oberon*. Casaubon is the first to provide a correct etymology for the word "satire," deriving it not from "satyr" but from "satura," a varied feast.

26. Barish, *Ben Jonson and the Language of Prose Comedy*, 176.

27. Pepys, December 19, 1668, *The Diary of Samuel Pepys*, ed. Robert Latham and William Matthews (Berkeley: University of

California Press, 1970), IX, 395. Pepys enjoyed reading *Catiline*, remarking that it is "a play of much good sense and words to read." But at the theater he expected entertainment. Pepys loved Jonsonian comedy. He calls *Volpone* "a most excellent play—the best I think I ever saw" (January 14, 1665); upon seeing a performance of *Epicene* he writes, "I never was more taken with a play then I am with this *Silent Woman*. . . . There is more wit in it then goes to ten new plays" (April 16, 1667). He finds *The Alchemist* "a most incomparable play" (June 22, 1661). Though he objects to *Bartholomew Fair*'s profanity and anti-Puritanism, he still believes it a "most admirable play" (June 8, 1661) and "the best comedy in the world I believe" (August 2, 1664). So his reaction to *Catiline*, the performance of which he had eagerly anticipated, is interesting in its atypicality.

28. In his introduction to *Ben Jonson's Literary Criticism* (Lincoln: University of Nebraska Press, 1970), xv-xvi, James Redwine remarks: "One should probably be careful to distinguish between the pre-*Volpone* and the post-*Volpone* criticism. . . . Up to the time he wrote *Volpone*, his attitude toward the so-called laws would seem to be one of respectful independence . . . but his emphasis from *Volpone* on is on the necessity for laws."

29. Jonson's discussions of decorum in his prefaces and in *Discoveries* are variously indebted to Cicero, Horace, Seneca, and Quintilian. The important texts are Cicero, *De officiis* I, xxvii-xlii; *De oratore* III, x; Horace, *Ars poetica*; Seneca, *Epistulae morales* V, XIV, XVIII, XL, CIII, CXIV; Quintilian, *Institutiones* XI, i, 1-93.

30. "Illud est diligentius docendum, eum demum dicere apte, qui non solum quid expediat, sed etiam quid deceat inspexerit. Nec me fugit, plerumque haec esse coniuncta. . . . Aliquando tamen et haec dissentiunt. Quotiens autem pugnabunt, ipsam utilitatem vincet quod decet." Quintilian, *Institutiones* XI, i, 8-9.

31. In classical and Renaissance poetics, *imitatio* can mean either the imitation of life or the imitation of other poets. Jonson discusses this latter kind of imitation in the *Discoveries*, 883-885, 1697-1751, 2466-2522, and of course as a working artist he is constantly "convert[ing] the substance, or Riches of another *Poet*, to his own use" (2468-2469). Richard Peterson deals with "textual" *imitatio* in *Imitation and Praise in the Poems of Ben Jonson* (New Haven: Yale University Press, 1981). In the prologues and prefaces to the comedies, however, Jonson uses imitation to mean the representation of fa-

miliar characters, events, etc. in fictional form: "things (like truths) well faign'd."

32. Aristotle, *Poetics*, trans. Ingram Bywater, 1448 [b]4-13 (from *The Basic Works of Aristotle*, ed. Richard McKeon [New York: Random House, 1941], 1457).

33. See, e.g., Vincentius Madius (Vincenzo Maggi), *In Q. Horatii Flacci de arte poetica librum ad Pisones, interpretatio* (Venice, 1550), 361.

34. "Causa difficilis laudare pueros; non enim res laudanda, sed spes est." Quoted by Servius in his commentary upon the *Aeneid*, VI, 87.

35. "Non praestant philosophi quae loquuntur." "Multum tamen praestant quod loquuntur, quod honesta mente concipiunt; namque idem si et paria dictis agerent, quid esset illis beatius? Interim non est quod contemnas bona verba et bonis cogitationibus plena praecordia. . . . Quid mirum, si non escendunt in altum ardua adgressi? Sed si vir es, suspice, etiam si decidunt, magna conantis. Generosa res est respicientem non ad suas sed ad naturae suae vires conari, alta temptare et mente maiora concipere, quam quae etiam ingenti animo adornatis effici possunt . . . —qui haec facere proponet, volet, temptabit, ad deos iter faciet, ne ille, etiam si non tenuerit, 'Magnis tamen excidit ausis.' " Seneca, *De vita beata* xx, 1-5. Seneca quotes from Ovid, *Metamorphoses* II, 328, at the end of the passage.

36. In the preface to *Love's Triumph Through Callipolis*, line 3.

37. See, e.g., Alan Dessen, *Jonson's Moral Comedy* (Evanston, Ill.: Northwestern University Press, 1971), 107. Following Herford, Dessen reads *Epicene* as an unexpected revival of the cheerful comic technique Jonson had employed in *The Case Is Altered* and *Every Man in His Humour*. He believes that Dauphine, Clerimont, and Truewit occupy "a comfortable vantage point . . . apparently not to be questioned or endangered (perhaps analogous to the roles of Cynthia and Augustus Caesar)" in the comical satires.

38. See, e.g., Edmund Wilson, who finds "the story of *The Silent Woman* revolting in its forced barbarity" and who recoils from Jonson's "group of ferocious young men" ("Morose Ben Jonson," in *Ben Jonson: A Collection of Critical Essays*, 62, 66). Wilson argues that the plot of *Epicene* reveals Jonson's neurotic desire to torment the regressive aspects of his own nature, as embodied in Morose. Similarly L. A. Beaurline, in his introduction to *Epicene, or, the Silent Woman* (Lincoln: University of Nebraska Press, 1966), xix, believes that "the net effect of [the play] is to leave us troubled.

Some deep cynicism, some reserve of self-mockery, of loathing and contempt, seem to lurk beneath the dazzling surface of the play."

39. See, e.g., Edward Partridge's introduction to *Ben Jonson: Epicoene* (New Haven: Yale University Press, 1971), 19: "That Jonson sees [the friends'] plots against Daw, La Foole, and Morose as at least partly judicial, does not mean that he places himself on their side. . . . The play's ironic exposure extends to the young gentlemen as well as the old."

40. See, e.g., John Enck, *Ben Jonson and the Comic Truth* (Madison: University of Wisconsin Press, 1957), 147, who argues that "the ambivalence [about the status of Dauphine, Clerimont, and Truewit] rests upon, chiefly, [Jonson's] indecisiveness about official spokesmen at this point in his career." Likewise Jonas Barish, in *Ben Jonson and the Language of Prose Comedy*, 148, writes that "while Truewit, with the flag of Ovid nailed to his mast, sails grandly to victory, the tides and crosscurrents of the language are setting up a counterdrift that almost carries the ship into the wrong port. The result is a stalemate; what Jonson affirms on one level he denies on another." This view of *Epicene* can be compatible with the psychoanalytic one; Barish's reading in particular often approximates Wilson's, though it is far more sympathetic to Jonson.

41. Duncan, *Ben Jonson and the Lucianic Tradition*, 187.

42. "Defence of the Epilogue; or, An Essay on the Dramatic Poetry of the Last Age," in *Essays of John Dryden*, ed. W. P. Ker (Oxford: Clarendon, 1926), 174.

43. Jonas Barish, "Ovid, Juvenal, and The Silent Woman," *PMLA* 71 (1956), 213.

44. Ibid., 213-224.

45. Duncan, *Ben Jonson and the Lucianic Tradition*, 181-182.

46. Jackson, *Vision and Judgment in Ben Jonson's Drama*, 68.

47. Richard Levin, "No Laughing Matter: Some New Readings of *The Alchemist*," 99.

48. Richard Levin tends to ascribe the existence of critical positions with which he does not agree to the overingenuity of modern academic criticism. But the moral significance of *The Alchemist's* finale was debated in the Restoration.

49. Ian Donaldson, *The World Upside Down* (Clarendon: Oxford, 1970), 48.

50. In their edition of *Ben Jonson: Catiline* (Lincoln: University of Nebraska Press, 1973), 180-183, W. F. Bolton and Jane F. Gardner

show how Jonson systematically strips Cato's language even of the sparse ornamentation and simple rhetorical devices Sallust allows him.

51. Joseph Bryant, "*Catiline* and the Nature of Jonson's Tragic Fable," *PMLA* 69 (1954), 265-277. The rest of the paragraph summarizes Bryant's argument in this seminal article.

52. Jonson has not, however—as Bryant implies—invented Caesar's involvement out of whole cloth. Though Sallust, a former Caesarian supporter, is silent on the issue, Plutarch, in his life of Cicero, recounts rumors implicating Caesar in the Catilinarian conspiracy; he suggests that long before his open declaration of war on the Republic, Caesar secretly lent aid to causes which would undermine it. Moreover, the edition of Sallust that Jonson owned included in its supplementary material a reputable contemporary work, Constantius Felicius Durantinus' *Historia Coniurationis Catilinariae*, which Ellen Duffy has shown that Jonson consulted when writing *Catiline*. ("Ben Jonson's Debt to Renaissance Scholarship in 'Sejanus' and 'Catiline,' " *Modern Language Review* 42 [1947], 24-30). Durantinus supports Plutarch's account of Caesar's role in the conspiracy.

Chapter IV. Roman Moral Psychology and Jonson's Dramatic Forms

1. *Every Man Out of His Humour*, III.vi.195-199.

2. Northrop Frye, *Anatomy of Criticism: Four Essays* (Princeton: Princeton University Press, 1957), 43-44, 163-171.

3. For a concise discussion of the similarities between Freudian and Platonic psychology, see Bennett Simon, *Mind and Madness in Ancient Greece: The Classical Roots of Modern Psychiatry* (Ithaca: Cornell University Press, 1975), 200-212.

4. "Denique in disciplina nostra non tam quaeritur utrum pius animus irascatur, sed quare irascitur, nec utrum sit tristis, sed unde sit tristis, nec utrum timeat, sed quid timeat." Augustine, *City of God* IX, 5. However, the split between the Christians and the Stoically oriented Roman moralists is by no means as clear as Augustine makes it sound. Though really extreme Stoicism must be considerably modified to be wholly acceptable in a Christian framework, Roman moral psychology as well as Platonism get incorporated

into Christianity, and the two alternative models exist side by side through the Middle Ages and the Renaissance. Nor are the Roman moralists totally unreceptive to Platonism. They reject the psychology of sublimation and Plato's idealist ontology, but they greatly admire Socrates' personal example, and they like both Plato's doctrine of immortality and his identification of the true, the beautiful, and the good. They also find appealing the kinds of psychological theories that Plato proposes in the *Phaedo* and *The Republic*, which separate the reasoning part of the soul from the passions. Jonson's attraction to the Roman moralists, therefore, even encourages the rather special use of neo-Platonic imagery that D. J. Gordon and John Meagher find so important in the masques. Likewise Jonson adapts from the native, Christian dramatic tradition the conventions of the morality plays and estates satires which most closely approximate the ethical intuitions of the Roman moralists. He is consistently hostile to left-wing Protestantism, on the other hand, which tends to be aggressively Augustinian in its emphasis on conversion experience, on the centrality of faith rather than works, and on the unworthiness of mankind in general. See my remarks in Chapter 6, however, on Jonson's changing sense of these issues in later life.

5. "Commotam, inpotentem, alteri emancupatam, vilem sibi." Seneca, *Epistulae morales* CXVI, 5.

6.   "Hi mores, haec duri inmota Catonis
            Secta fuit, servare modum finemque tenere
            Naturamque sequi patriaeque inpendere vitam
            Nec sibi sed toti genitum se credere mundo.

            . . . Venerisque hic unicus usus,
         Progenies; urbi pater est urbique maritus,
         Iustitiae cultor, rigidi servator honesti,
         In commune bonus; nullosque Catonis in actus
         Subrepsit partemque tulit sibi nata voluptas."
                        (Lucan, *Pharsalia* II, 380-391)

7. "Patriae proditiones . . . rerum publicarum eversiones . . . cum hostibus clandestina colloquia." Cicero, *De senectute* xii, 40.

8. "Totus vero iste, qui vulgo appellatur amor—nec hercule invenio quo nomine alio possit appellari—, tantae levitatis est, ut nihil videam quod putem conferendum."

189

"Comoedia . . . si haec flagitia non probaremus, nulla esset omnino." Cicero, *Tusculan Disputations* IV, xxxii, 68.

9. Edmund Wilson, "Morose Ben Jonson," in *Ben Jonson: A Collection of Critical Essays*, ed. Jonas Barish (Englewood Cliffs, N.J.: Prentice-Hall, 1963), 66-68.

10. "Her Triumph," 21-24.

11. *Conversations*, 43-44.

12. Harry Levin, "An Introduction to Ben Jonson," *Ben Jonson: A Collection of Critical Essays*, 48.

13. "Shakespeare and Ben Jonson," *The Collected Works of William Hazlitt*, ed. P. P. Howe (London: Dent, 1930), VIII, 40.

14. Edward Walford, *Juvenal* (London: Blackwood and Sons, 1872), 29.

15. *The Alchemist*, II.ii.37-39.

16. *Volpone*, III.vii.202-203.

17. For examples of Freudian readings see Wilson, "Morose Ben Jonson"; and E. Pearlman, "Ben Jonson: An Anatomy," *English Literary Renaissance* 9 (1979), 364-394.

18. Cicero, *De officiis* I, xxvii-xxviii; xxxv.

19. See, e.g., Seneca, *De brevitate vitae* xvi, 5; or *De vita beata* xxvi, 6.

20. "Non enim ambrosia deos aut nectare aut Iuventate pocula ministrante laetari arbitror, nec Homerum audio, qui Ganymeden ab dis raptum ait propter formam, ut Iovi bibere ministraret: non iusta causa cur Laomedonti tanta fieret iniuria. Fingebat haec Homerus et humana ad deos transferebat: divina mallem ad nos." Cicero, *Tusculan Disputations* I, xxvi, 65. See also the discussions in *De natura deorum*, particularly in books III and IV.

21. Quintilian, *Institutiones* X, i, 88.

22. Horace, *Odes* III, xxvii.

23. A. C. Swinburne, *A Study of Ben Jonson* (London: Chatto and Windus, 1889), 25.

24. "An potest cupiditas finiri? Tollenda est atque extrahenda radicitus." Cicero, *De finibus* II, ix, 27. Here Cicero is arguing with the Epicureans; in *Tusculan Disputations* he repeats this remark against the Peripatetics: "Nos autem audeamus non solum ramos amputare miseriarum, sed omnes radicum fibras evellere" (III, vi, 13); "Sunt enim omnia ista ex errorum orta radicibus, quae evellenda et extrahenda penitus, non circumcidenda nec amputanda sunt" (IV, xxvi, 57).

25. "Facilius est excludere perniciosa quam regere et non admittere quam admissa moderari." Seneca, *De ira* I, vii, 2.

26. "Memini ex duabus illum partibus esse compositum; altera est inrationalis, haec mordetur, uritur, dolet; altera rationalis, haec inconcussas opiniones habet, intrepida est et indomita." Seneca, *Epistulae morales* LXXI, 27. See also Cicero, *Tusculan Disputations* IV, v, 10-11.

27. "Nullo interposito velamento quasi nudam." Augustine, *Soliloquies* I, iii, 22.

28. "Quid? vos studia libidinem vocatis?" Cicero, *Tusculan Disputations* IV, xxv, 55.

29. Cicero, *De fato* v, 11; see also his *Tusculan Disputations* IV, xxxvii, 80. Seneca, *Epistulae morales* CIV, 28, see also LXX and LXXI.

30. Horace, *Odes* II, xv; III, vi. Juvenal, *Satires* XI, 90-135; XIV, 138-172. Cicero, *De finibus* II, viii, 24; II, xx, 63-64.

31. "Duo tibi ponam ante oculos maxima et sexus et saeculi tui exempla: alterius feminae, quae se tradidit ferendam dolori, alterius, quae pari adfecta casu, maiore damno, non tamen dedit longum in se malis suis dominium, sed cito animum in sedem suam reposuit. . . . Elige itaque, utrum exemplum putes probabilius." Seneca, *Ad Marciam de consolatione* ii, 2-iii, 3.

32. *Discoveries*, 1039-1041.

33. "Virtutem in templo convenies, in foro, in curia, pro muris stantem . . . voluptatem latitantem saepius ac tenebras captantem circa balinea ac sudatoria ac loca aedilem metuentia." Seneca, *De vita beata* vii, 3. Ediles were the officials elected to uphold public morals.

34. Horace, *Ars poetica* 119-127.

35. John Creasar, introduction to *Volpone, or, The Fox* (New York: New York University Press, 1978), 10-34.

36. John Meagher, *Method and Meaning in Jonson's Masques* (London: University of Notre Dame Press, 1966), 125-143.

37. "Non nascitur itaque ex malo bonum, non magis quam ficus ex olea." *Epistulae morales* LXXXVII, 25.

38. "Virtus est vitium fugere et sapientia prima / stultitia caruisse." Horace, *Epistles* I, i, 41-42.

39. "In eodem pectore nullum est honestorum turpiumque consortium." Quintilian, *Institutiones* XII, i, 4.

40. *Discoveries*, 10.

41. "Una ratio est medendi, ut nihil quale sit illud, quod pertur-
bet animum, sed de ipsa sit perturbatione dicendum. Itaque primum
in ipsa cupiditate, cum id solum agitur, ut ea tollatur, non est quae-
rendum, bonum illud necne sit, quod libidinem moveat, sed libido
ipsa tollenda est . . . etiam si virtutis ipsius vehementior appetitus
sit." Cicero, *Tusculan Disputations* IV, xxix, 62. Augustine may have
this specific passage in mind when he explains his differences with
the Stoics; see note 4 above.

42. "Cum videantur dissidere, coniuncta sunt . . . ista, quae tam
dissimilia sunt, pariter incedunt." Seneca, *Epistulae morales* V, 7.

43. Cicero, *Tusculan Disputations* III, ix, 20-x, 21; IV, xxvi, 56.

44. Pearlman, "Ben Jonson: An Anatomy," 385-386.

45. Cicero, *Tusculan Disputations* IV, vi, 13-14.

46. "Est praeterea quaedam virtutum vitiorumque vicinia, qua
maledicus pro libero, temerarius pro forti, effusus pro copioso accipitur." Quintilian, *Institutiones* II, xii, 4.

47. "Pro bonis mala amplectimur. . . . Vitia nobis sub virtutum
nomine obrepunt, temeritas sub titulo fortitudinis latet, moderatio
vocatur ignavia, pro cauto timidus accipitur; in his magno periculo
erramus." Seneca, *Epistulae morales* XLV, 6-7.

48. Most of Jonson's erotic verse dates from after 1615, when his
sense of the issues I have discussed in this chapter begins to alter.
This poetry—mostly in *The Underwood*—is best understood, I believe, in conjunction with Jonson's other late work. I will ignore it
here and treat it in my final chapter.

49. For the relations between Jonson's masques and contemporary political conditions see Stephen Orgel, *The Illusion of Power*
(Berkeley: University of California Press, 1975). My discussion in
the following pages of the structural development of the Jonsonian
masque between 1605 and 1620, and my sense of the way Jonson
understands his responsibilities as a masque-writer, are indebted to
Orgel's *The Jonsonian Masque* (Cambridge: Harvard University Press,
1964) and to his introduction to *The Complete Masques* (New Haven:
Yale University Press, 1969).

50. In the preface to *Hymenaei*, Jonson rebukes "some [who] may
squemishly crie out, that all endevour of *learning*, and *sharpnesse* in
these transitorie *devices* . . . is superfluous." Jonson is no more prone
to squander erudition and creative energy upon a "transitory device" than his critics are. Rather, he writes masques "grounded
upon *antiquitie*, and solide *learnings*" in order to refute the charge

that they are empty and frivolous. By publishing the masques with prefaces, commentary, and Latin footnotes, he relocates the masque in the dignified and eternal category of great literature.

51. Seneca, *Epistulae morales* LI.

52. It is interesting, though I am not sure it is relevant, that James I and Jonson himself shared both Silenus' physical grossness and his intellectual acumen. Jonson conceives of himself as a Silenus-figure in his nondramatic poetry, but only much later in his career. See my discussion of *The Underwood* in Chapter VI.

53. In *The Irish Masque at Court*, for example, Dennis, Donnell, Dermock, and Patrick gawkily but sincerely express their loyalty to the king; nonetheless, the "civill gentleman of the nation" who arrives after their little dance banishes them with surprising severity. Likewise, the Shepherd in *Pan's Anniversary* roundly scolds the heedless but entertaining Fencer, who has tactlessly performed before the pacifist king: "Behold where they are, that have now forgiven you, whom should you provoke againe with the like, they will justly punish that with anger, which they now dismisse with contempt" (155-158).

54. "Vivere, Lucili, militare est." Seneca, *Epistulae morales* XCVI, 5. "Excutienda vitae cupido est discendumque nihil interesse, quando patiaris, quod quando patiendum est." *Epistulae morales* CI, 15.

55. "Marcet sine adversario virtus; tunc apparet quanta sit quantumque polleat, cum quid possit patientia ostendit. . . . [Fortuna] fortissimos sibi pares quaerit, quosdam fastidio transit. Contumacissimum quemque et rectissimum aggreditur, adversus quem vim suam intendat: ignem experitur in Mucio, paupertatam in Fabricio, exilium in Rutilio, tormenta in Regulo, venenum in Socrate, mortem in Catone. Magnum exemplum nisi mala fortuna non invenit." Seneca, *De providentia* II, 4-III, 4.

Chapter V. Jonson and the Roman Social Ethos

1. For remarks on the social implications of the plays and masques see, e.g., L. C. Knights, *Drama and Society in the Age of Jonson* (London: Chatto and Windus, 1937), 179-227; Stephen Orgel, *The Illusion of Power* (Berkeley: University of California Press, 1975); Leah Marcus, "Present Occasions and the Shaping of Ben Jonson's Masques," *ELH* 45 (1978), 201-225. On the poems, see Geoffrey Walton, "The Tone of Ben Jonson's Poetry," in *Seventeenth Century*

English Poetry: Modern Essays in Criticism, ed. William Keast (New York: Oxford University Press, 1971), 152-173; Hugh Maclean, "Ben Jonson's Poems: Notes on the Ordered Society" in ibid., 177-200; Earl Miner, *The Cavalier Mode from Jonson to Cotton* (Princeton: Princeton University Press, 1971); Ian Donaldson's introduction to *Ben Jonson: Poems* (London: Oxford University Press, 1975), xiii-xix.

2. Walton, "The Tone of Ben Jonson's Poetry," 152.

3. "To the Reader," *Poetaster*, 113-114. Such similarities seem to add credence to Edmund Wilson's contention that Morose represents a repressed phase of Jonson's personality. "Morose Ben Jonson," *Ben Jonson: A Collection of Critical Essays*, ed. Jonas Barish (Englewood Cliffs, N.J.: Prentice-Hall, 1963), 60-74. Geoffrey Walton notices, but does not attempt to account for, the coexistence of urbanity and incivility in Jonson's poetry. For more extended discussions of Jonson's misanthropy as expressed in the poetry, see Richard Newton, "Goe, quit 'hem all: Ben Jonson and Formal Verse Satire," *Studies in English Literature* 16 (1976), 105-116; he discusses the way Jonson is torn between a need to communicate and a fundamental yearning for "complete isolation . . . complete disengagement from the offending world." Robert C. Jones discusses similar issues in "The Satirist's Retreat in Jonson's 'Apologetical Dialogue,' " *ELH* 34 (1967), 447-467.

4. Walton, Maclean, and Miner (see note 1 above) all adduce a Roman source for Jonson's strong sense of social commitment.

5. Seneca, *Epistulae morales* CX, 14-19. The passage in *Discoveries*, which is more extended than Penyboy Senior's speech, is closer to Seneca.

6. Marx is an example of a political theorist who holds to the first view; Hobbes exemplifies the second approach; some modern sociobiologists exemplify the third. The Roman moralists are heavily dependent upon Stoic, Peripatetic, and Academic ideas for their social theory; since all three schools derive from Aristotle, it is not surprising that their views (and Jonson's after them) seem more akin to those of *The Politics* or *The Nicomachean Ethics* than to any other major political-philosophical texts.

7. "Natura bonum omne carum est bono et sic quisque conciliatur bono quemadmodum sibi." Seneca, *Epistulae morales* CIX, 13. For the Stoic theory of *oikeiosis*, or affinity, which lies behind Seneca's statement here and Cicero's extended discussion of social re-

lations in *De officiis*, see S. G. Pembroke, *"Oikeiosis,"* in *Problems in Stoicism*, ed. A. A. Long (London: Athlone, 1971), 114-149.

8. Cicero, *Tusculan Disputations* IV, xxvi, 56.

9. Kant, for instance, argues for the sufficiency of reason alone as a motive for altruistic behavior; Hume believes, on the contrary, that altruism arises out of an instinctive or emotive "general benevolence." For a discussion of the postclassical treatment of the issue, see Thomas Nagel, *The Possibility of Altruism* (Princeton: Princeton University Press, 1970).

10. Seneca sets forth the Stoic position in *Epistulae morales* XC (which deals with primitive man) and CXXI (on animal behavior). Cicero and Cato debate the tenability of the doctrine in *De finibus* III and IV. The *precise* relationship between instinct and reason is one of the thorniest issues in Stoic ethics, and of no consequence here. What is important is the general Stoic tendency, inherited by the Roman moralists, to consider instinct and reason as related phenomena, a tendency that often results in a certain carelessness about distinguishing between instinctive and reasonable forms of motivation.

11. "Ut enim quisque sibi plurimum confidit et ut quisque maxime virtute et sapientia sic munitus est, ut nullo egeat suaque omnia in se ipso posita iudicet, ita in amicitiis expetendis colendisque maxime excellit." Cicero, *De amicitia* ix, 30.

12. "Communitas cum hominum genere, caritas amicitia iustitia, reliquae virtutes . . . esse nulla potest nisi erit gratuita." Cicero, *Academica* II, xlvi, 140.

13. "Faciendarum amicitiarum artifex." Seneca, *Epistulae morales* IX, 5.

14. Cicero writes a *Consolatio*, now lost, as a remedy for his despair upon the death of his beloved daughter Tullia. Seneca composes *Ad Marciam* for a bereaved mother, *Ad Polybium* for a bereaved brother, and in *Epistulae morales* XCIX repeats to Lucilius the advice he once gave a grieving father. Tacitus' *Agricola* commemorates his father-in-law.

15. "Tum aetate tam puellari, praesertim meae comparata, potest et ipsa numerari inter vulnera orbitatis" (lit.: "that [her death] can be reckoned among the wounds of childlessness)." Quintilian, *Institutiones* VI, proemium, 5-6.

16. "Elegy on My Muse, the Truly Honoured Lady, the Lady Venetia Digby," 115-118. Jonson may delete mention of marriage

because of the scriptural pronouncement that in heaven there is neither marriage nor giving in marriage. But there is certainly no mention either of the family reunions which Jonson so fondly imagines
here.

17. Juvenal's *Satires* XIV treats of the responsibility of parents to
children. Quintilian writes his *Institutiones* for fathers anxious to
educate their sons in the best possible manner; initially, in fact, he
designs the work as an inheritance for his own son, and confesses
in book VI that the boy's death has deprived him of a personal stake
in it. Horace commemorates his father's care in *Satires* I, iv and vi.
And one of Jonson's most moving poems, discussed later in this
chapter, deals with the loss of his firstborn son.

18. "Verum etiam amicum qui intuetur, tamquam exemplar ali-
quod intuetur sui." Cicero, *De amicitia* vii, 23.

19. The Roman moralists, except for Horace, neither approve of
homosexuality nor admit to homosexual practices. Their objections
to Platonic friendship, however, are based on more than mere ho-
mophobia. It is easy enough to "save" the doctrines of the *Phaedrus*
and the *Symposium*, if one thinks they are worth saving, by recast-
ing them in a heterosexual form. Plutarch does just that in his dialogue *Erotikos*, a revisionary-Platonist celebration of marriage.

20. "Nihil autem est amabilius nec copulatius quam morum si-
militudo bonorum; in quibus enim eadem studia sunt, eaedem vo-
luntates, in iis fit ut aeque quisque altero delectetur ac se ipso, effi-
citurque id, quod Pythagoras vult in amicitia, ut unus fiat ex
pluribus." Cicero, *De officiis* I, xvii, 56.

21. "Cum iudicaris, diligere oportet; non, cum dilexeris, iudi-
care." Cicero, *De amicitia* xxii, 85; cf. Seneca, *Epistulae morales* III.

22. "Iustitia dicitur, cui sunt adiunctae pietas, bonitas, liberalitas,
benignitas, comitas, quaeque sunt generis eiusdem." Cicero, *De finibus* V, xxiii, 65.

23. This is a standard nineteenth-century complaint. See, e.g.,
William Hazlitt, "Shakespeare and Ben Jonson," *The Collected Works
of William Hazlitt*, ed. P. P. Howe (London: Dent, 1930), VIII, 38-
40; and A. C. Swinburne, *A Study of Ben Jonson* (London: Chatto
and Windus, 1889), 29. It finds its way into more recent discussions
of Jonson too—Wilson's "Morose Ben Jonson" and C. H. Herford's "Final Appreciation" (*Ben Jonson* [Oxford: Clarendon, 1925], I,
119-127). The intuition upon which the criticism is based is a sound
one. It is indeed true that Jonson often treats his characters with

unusual detachment. But his distinctive attitude toward them is the consequence of the social consciousness Jonson inherits from the Roman moralists, not of some emotional or imaginative impediment. I shall discuss the issue at length later in this chapter.

24. For example, in *The Cavalier Mode from Jonson to Cotton*, Earl Miner remarks: "Although the Stoics emphasized self-sufficiency, Lucius Annaeus Seneca and the other Roman Stoics revealed considerable capacity for friendship and affection" (p. 258). Seneca and Cicero, like Jonson, would delete the "although" at the beginning of Miner's sentence and replace it with "because."

25. Cicero, *De amicitia* x, 34-xiii, 44; xvi, 56-xvii, 61; xx, 75-xxvi, 100.

26. Walton, "The Tone of Ben Jonson's Poetry," 155-156.

27. "Ego cum genui, tum moriturum scivi." Seneca, *Ad Polybium de consolatione* xi, 2-3. Seneca is quoting from Ennius' *Telamo*. Cicero quotes the same remark and also credits Anaxagoras with an identical sentiment, in *Tusculan Disputations* III, xiv, 30; and III, xiii, 28: "Sciebam me genuisse mortalem." For Cicero especially, who suffered greatly when his daughter Tullia died, this kind of resignation becomes almost emblematic of the wise man, so that Laelius in *De amicitia* exclaims of Cato, "Si quisquam, ille sapiens fuit. Quo modo, ut alia omittam, mortem fili tulit!" (ii, 9). And Cato himself, in *De senectute*, praises Fabius in almost exactly the same terms: "Multa in eo viro praeclara cognovi, sed nihil admirabilius quam quo modo ille mortem fili tulit, clari viri et consularis" (iv, 12).

28. Tacitus, *Agricola* 29.

29. The idea of life as a loan, to be paid back on "the just day," comes up sooner or later in nearly every Roman moralist consolation. See, e.g., Cicero, *Tusculan Disputations* I, xxix, 93; Seneca, *Ad Polybium* x, 4-5; *Ad Marciam de consolatione* x, 1.

30. "Nihil mali accidisse Scipioni puto; mihi accidit, si quid accidit; suis autem incommodis graviter angi non amicum, sed se ipsum amantis est." Cicero, *De amicitia* ii, 10. For a virtually identical argument see Seneca, *Ad Polybium de consolatione* ix, 1-3.

31. *Epigrams* VI, xxix, 8.

32. "Non facit nobilem atrium plenum fumosis imaginibus." Seneca, *Epistulae morales* XLIV, 5.

33.   "Tota licet veteres exornent undique cerae
         atria, nobilitas sola est atque unica virtus.

. . . .

sanctus haberi
iustitiaeque tenax factis dictisque mereris?
agnosco procerem."
(Juvenal, *Satires* VIII, 19-26)

34. *Conversations*, 337; "To Sir William Jephson," 7, 12.

35. *The Underwood* 84, viii, 20-24.

36. "Sustines enim non parvam exspectationem imitandae indus-
triae nostrae, magnam honorum, non nullam fortasse nominis."
Cicero, *De officiis* III, ii, 6.

37. "Ode to Sir William Sidney, on His Birthday," 32-42.

38. "Never in my right mind could I regret this kind of father,"
writes Horace: "Nil me paeniteat sanum patris huius." *Satires* I, vi,
89.

39. "Solemus dicere non fuisse in nostra potestate, quos sortire-
mur parentes, forte hominibus datos; nobis vero ad nostrum arbi-
trium nasci licet. Nobilissimorum ingeniorum familiae sunt; elige
in quam adscisci velis." Seneca, *De brevitate vitae* xv, 3.

40. "Hos ante effigies maiorum pone tuorum." Juvenal, *Satires*
VIII, 23.

41. "id unum interim moneo, ut praeceptores suos non minus
quam ipsa studia ament, et parentes esse non quidem corporum sed
mentium credant." Quintilian, *Institutiones* II, ix, 1-2.

42. "Epitaph on Master Vincent Corbett," 5.

43. "As regards this matter, they believe that nature arranges for
children to be loved by their parents; from this source we derive
the association of the human race into communities" ("Pertinere
autem ad rem arbitrantur intellegi natura fieri ut liberi a parentibus
amentur; a quo initio profectam communem humani generis socie-
tatem persequimur"). Cicero, *De finibus* III, xix, 62. Cf. Piso's
statement two chapters later: "In omni autem honesto de quo lo-
quimur nihil est tam illustre nec quod latius pateat quam coniunctio
inter homines hominum et quasi quaedam societas et communicatio
utilitatum et ipsa caritas generis humani, quae nata a primo satu,
quod a procreatoribus nati diliguntur." *De finibus* V, xxiii, 65.

44. Miner, *The Cavalier Mode from Jonson to Cotton*, 259.

45. Maclean, "Ben Jonson's Poems: Notes on the Ordered Society," 175.

46. "Jonsonian comedy invariably tends in the direction of an
arraignment," Harry Levin claims in "An Introduction to Ben Jon-

son," in *Ben Jonson: A Collection of Critical Essays*, ed. Jonas Barish (Englewood Cliffs, N.J.: Prentice-Hall, 1963), 48. He could have made the same observation about Jonsonian tragedy, since both *Sejanus* and *Catiline* have as their climax a trial before the Roman Senate. Critics have given a fair amount of attention to Jonson's concern with "justice" and "judgment." John Enck, in *Ben Jonson and the Comic Truth* (Madison: University of Wisconsin Press, 1957), notes Jonson's lifelong engagement with these issues and interprets it as a function of his anxiety about the sources of authority. In *Vision and Judgment in Ben Jonson's Drama* (New Haven: Yale University Press, 1968), Gabriele Jackson describes Jonsonian "justice" in terms of what she sees as his absolutist ethical and metaphysical stance. Jonas Barish treats the steadily more ironic treatment of the trial in mature Jonsonian comedy as symptomatic of what he claims to be a progressive relaxation of Jonson's youthful censoriousness. ("Feasting and Judgment in Jonsonian Comedy," *Renaissance Drama*, n.s. 5 [1972], 3-51.) My debt to these critics will be obvious. I want to explain, in fact, why both Barish's and Jackson's accounts seem accurate even though they appear to contradict one another.

47. Northrop Frye, *Anatomy of Criticism: Four Essays* (Princeton: Princeton University Press, 1957), 163-164.

48. "Natura propensi sumus ad diligendos homines, quod fundamentum iuris est." Cicero, *De legibus* I, xv, 43.

49. Cicero, *De legibus* I, xvi-xviii.

50. Gabriele Jackson discusses the solipsism of the typical Jonsonian character in her introduction to *Every Man in His Humour*, 7-8.

51. "Homines autem hominum causa esse generatos." Cicero, *De officiis* I, vii, 22.

52. "Intellegitur studiis officiisque scientiae praeponenda esse officia iustitiae, quae pertinent ad hominum utilitatem, qua nihil homini esse debet antiquius." Cicero, *De officiis* I, xliii, 155.

53. See, e.g., Lucan, *Pharsalia*, passim; Cicero, *De officiis* III, 99-115; Horace, *Odes* III, v, 13-56. In this respect the Roman moralists, whatever their precise philosophical persuasion, usually differ from the Epicureans, who recommend a life of pleasant retirement over a strenuous and painful public career.

54. "In qua virtutis est splendor maximus, ex qua viri boni nominantur." Cicero, *De officiis*, I, vii, 20.

55. "Conversatio enim dissimilium bene composita disturbat et

renovat adfectus et quicquid imbecillum in animo nec percuratum est exulcerat." Seneca, *De tranquillitate animi* xvii, 3.

56. "Itaque quemadmodum in pestilentia curandum est, ne correptis iam corporibus et morbo flagrantibus adsideamus, quia pericula trahemus adflatuque ipso laborabimus, ita in amicorum legendis ingeniis dabimus operam, ut quam minime inquinatos adsumamus; initium morbi est aegris sana miscere." Seneca, *De tranquillitate animi* vii, 4.

57.   "Insuevit pater optimus hoc me,
ut fugerem exemplis vitiorum quaeque notando.
Cum me hortaretur, parce frugaliter atque
viverem uti contentus eo, quod mi ipse parasset:
'Nonne vides, Albi ut male vivat filius, utque
Baius inops? magnum documentum, ne patriam rem
perdere quis velit.' A turpi meretricis amore
cum deterreret: 'Scetani dissimilis sis.'
. . . .
               Avidos vicinum funus ut aegros
exanimat mortisque metu sibi parcere cogit,
sic teneros animos aliena opprobria saepe
absterrent vitiis."
                            (Horace, *Satires* I, iv, 105-129.

58. "To William Earl of Pembroke," 1-3.

59. "Odi profanum vulgus et arceo." Horace, *Odes* III, i, 1.

60. "Alienis perimus exemplis; sanabimur, separemur modo a coetu." Seneca, *De vita beata* i, 4-5.

61. *Discoveries*, 1497-1501.

62. Juvenal, *Satires* I; Quintilian, *Institutiones* II, xi-xii. Seneca, *Epistulae morales* XL, XLV, XLVIII, LII, LXXXVIII, CXI, CXVII. Jonson adapts Quintilian's passage in his preface to *The Alchemist*.

63. C. H. Herford and Percy Simpson, *Ben Jonson*, II, 80.

64. "The rod of correction is set aside," Robert Ornstein writes, "not because compassion triumphs, but because one cannot scratch a whore without discovering a wife." "Shakespearean and Jonsonian Comedy," *Shakespeare Survey* 22 (1969), 46.

65. "By Criticus he understandeth Dr. Done" (*Conversations*, 417). Jonson's judicial emphasis, and the connection he makes between judgment and creativity, seems to have impressed itself strongly upon his contemporaries. John Selden praises Jonson's "accurat

Judgment, and Performance" in his preface to *Titles of Honor*, 1614; reprinted in Herford and Simpson, XI, 383. The title page of *Ionsonus Virbius*, a memorial volume, identifies its subject as "most learned and judicious Poet" (ibid., 420). George Donne agrees that "Pure *Judgement*, JONSON, 'tis an *excellence* / Suted to [thy] *Pen* alone" (ibid., 462-463). Humphrey Moseley seems to be repeating a universally accepted formula when he casually calls Jonson "our ablest Judge and Professor of *Poesie*" (ibid., 459).

66. *Discoveries*, 2578-2593.

67. *Every Man Out of His Humour*, "The Characters," 111-113.

68. "Nullam enim virtus aliam mercedem laborum periculorumque desiderat praeter hanc laudis et gloriae: qua quidem detracta . . . quid est quod in hoc tam exiguo vitae curriculo et tam brevi tantis nos in laboribus exerceamus? . . . Nunc insidet quaedam in optimo quoque virtus, quae . . . admonet non cum vitae tempore esse dimetiendam commemorationem nominis nostri, sed cum omni posteritate adaequandam." Cicero, *Pro Archia* xi, 28-29.

69. *Discoveries*, 786-787.

70. *Discoveries*, 2532-2533.

71. "Quis enim placere populo potest, cui placet virtus?" Seneca, *Epistulae morales* XXIX, 11.

72. Cicero treats propriety as a species of virtue in *De officiis* I, xxvii, 93-xliii, 152. Seneca insists that philosophers avoid any eccentricity in *Epistulae morales* V, 4. One consequence of the Roman moralist emphasis on decorum is the tendency, shared by Jonson, to put what seem harmless eccentricities in the same category with serious failings. Thus Juvenal "fails to separate crimes from ordinary faux pas," as Richard Braun claims in his introduction to *Juvenal: Satires*, trans. Jerome Mazzaro (Ann Arbor: University of Michigan, 1965), 1. Tacitus lists among Nero's other outrages his insistence upon driving a four-horse chariot in a race, an occupation generally considered fit only for slaves (*Annals* xiv). Cf. Alexander Leggatt's comment in *Ben Jonson: His Vision and His Art* (London: Methuen, 1981), 80: "Jonson belongs to the long satiric tradition that regards bad manners and bad taste not simply as things to be shrugged off but as offenses that deserve the lash."

73. Horace, *Odes* III, i, 1-4; Juvenal, *Satires* II, 149-170; and XI, 77-127.

74. "Seseque non omnis circumdatum moenibus popularem alicuius definiti loci, set civem totius mundi quasi unius urbis agno-

verit . . . quam contemnet, quam despiciet, quam pro nihilo putabit ea, quae volgo dicuntur amplissima!" Cicero, *De legibus* I, xxiii, 61-62.

75. *Volpone*, prefatory epistle, 27-29.

76. *Every Man Out of His Humour*, revised conclusion (quarto), 10-12.

77. Induction to *The Magnetic Lady*, 122-124.

78. Critics who discuss Jonson's ambivalence to his audience include Douglas Duncan, *Ben Jonson and the Lucianic Tradition* (Cambridge: Cambridge University Press, 1979); and L. A. Beaurline, *Jonson and Elizabethan Comedy: Essays in Dramatic Rhetoric* (San Marino, Calif.: Huntington Library, 1978), 1-65.

79. "Scribendi recte sapere est et principium et fons.
Rem tibi Socraticae poterunt ostendere chartae,
verbaque provisam rem non invita sequentur.
Qui didicit patriae quid debeat et quid amicis,
quo sit amore parens, quo frater amandus et hospes,
quod sit conscripti, quod iudicis officium, quae
partes in bellum missi ducis, ille profecto
reddere personae scit convenientia cuique."

(Horace, *Ars poetica* 309-316)

80. Cicero, *Orator* iv, 14; *De oratore* III, 15. Quintilian, *Institutiones* I, proemium, 2. See also Seneca, *Epistulae morales* XL, CXIV; and Cicero, *Tusculan Disputations* I, ii, 6-iv, 8; *De officiis* I, i, 2-4.

81. *Discoveries*, 2394-2400. For the humanist understanding of the relation between rhetoric and philosophy, see Hanna Gray, "The Pursuit of Eloquence," in *Renaissance Essays*, ed. P. O. Kristeller and P. P. Weiner (New York: Harper, 1968), 199-216; and Jerrold Seigel, *Rhetoric and Philosophy in Renaissance Humanisim: Petrarch to Valla* (Princeton: Princeton University Press, 1968).

82. Cicero informs Atticus, for example, that "qualis vero sit orator ex eo quod is dicendo efficiet poterit intellegi. . . . Efficiatur autem ab oratore necne ut ei qui audiunt ita afficiantur ut orator velit, vulgi assensu et populari approbatione iudicari solet." Cicero, *Brutus* xlix, 184-185.

83. "Ipsi illi philosophi etiam illis libellis, quos de contemnenda gloria scribunt, nomen suum inscribunt: in eo ipso, in quo praedicationem nobilitatemque despiciunt, praedicari de se ac nominari volunt." Cicero, *Pro Archia* xi, 26-27.

84. *Conversations*, 631–632.

85. Creasar, Introduction to *Volpone, or, the Fox* (New York: New York University Press, 1978), 2.

86. "Satis sunt . . . mihi pauci, satis est unus, satis est nullus." Seneca, *Epistulae morales* VII, 10–11.

87. Cicero, *De legibus* I, vi–xix; II, iv–v.

88. "To the Reader," *Poetaster*, 212–213.

89. *Poetaster*, 226–228. Cf. Seneca's admiration of Democritus' remark: "Unus mihi pro populo est, et populo pro uno." *Epistulae morales* VII, 11.

90. *Discoveries*, 2331–2341.

91. *A Midsummer Night's Dream*, V.i.426.

92. Jonson's precedents for the implicit alliance of reader and satiric persona include Horace, Juvenal, and Persius; writers outside the Roman moral tradition, like Petronius or Apuleius, differ from Jonson's models when they make the persona itself a primary object of satiric attack.

93. Herford and Simpson, II, 80.

94. *Discoveries*, 2661–2668.

Chapter VI. The Late Jonson

1. Anne Barton, "*The New Inn* and the Problem of Jonson's Late Style," *English Literary Renaissance* 9 (1980), 399–400.

2. See, e.g., Edward Partridge, *The Broken Compass* (New York: Columbia University Press, 1958), 180–205; Robert Knoll, *Ben Jonson's Plays: An Introduction* (Lincoln: University of Nebraska Press, 1964), 183–190; Larry Champion, *Ben Jonson's Dotages: A Reconsideration of the Late Plays* (Lexington: University of Kentucky Press, 1967), 76–103. "Straight" readings of *The New Inn* include Anne Barton, "*The New Inn* and the Problem of Jonson's Late Style," and L. A. Beaurline, *Jonson and Elizabethan Comedy: Essays in Dramatic Rhetoric* (San Marino, Calif.: Huntington Library, 1978), 256–274.

3. Jonas Barish, *Ben Jonson and the Language of Prose Comedy* (Cambridge: Harvard University Press, 1960), 237.

4. For an extended discussion of this point, see Edward Partridge, "The Symbolism of Clothes in Jonson's Last Plays," *Journal of English and Germanic Philology* 56 (1957), 396–409.

5. "Inclusi in his compagibus corporis." Cicero, *De senectute* xxi, 77.

6. John Lemly, "Masks and Self-Portraits in Jonson's Late Poetry," *ELH* 44 (1977), 248.

7. See, e.g., *The Underwood* 52, 77, 84, iv; *Ungathered Verse* 25, 34.

8. "An Expostulation with Inigo Jones," 39-41. The mounting hostility between Jonson and Inigo Jones in these years ranges poet against architect, champion of words against purveyor of spectacle. For a discussion of the issues behind this quarrel, see D. J. Gordon, "Poet and Architect: The Intellectual Setting of the Quarrel Between Ben Jonson and Inigo Jones," in *The Renaissance Imagination*, ed. Stephen Orgel (Berkeley: University of California Press, 1975), 77-101.

9. Alan Dessen, in *Jonson's Moral Comedy* (Evanston, Ill.: Northwestern University Press, 1971), discusses Jonson's use of morality-play conventions in *The Staple of News* and other plays.

10. C. G. Thayer, *Ben Jonson: A Study in the Plays* (Norman: University of Oklahoma Press, 1963), 207.

11. See, e.g., C. H. Herford and Percy Simpson, *Ben Jonson* (Oxford: Clarendon, 1925), II, 197; Thayer, *Ben Jonson*, 216, 221-222; Champion, *Ben Jonson's Dotages*, 84-85, 95-103.

INDEX

Adoption, 124-125

Apuleius, 203

Aristophanes, 150

Aristotle, 15, 48, 64, 111, 126, 152, 181-182, 194

Aubigny, Esme Stuart, 6, 141

Audience, 33-34, 58-59, 98; expectations of, 71, 77, 91-92; Jonson's relations with, 12, 21, 32, 49-54, 58-59, 61-67, 74, 76, 105, 112, 134-150, 156-160, 202, 203; nature of, 134-139, 149-150, 159-160; sympathies of, 43, 68-72, 133, 143-150, 184

Augustine, 78-80, 89, 92-94, 98, 113, 115, 188-189, 192

Augustus Caesar, 9, 141; Jonson's character in *Poetaster*, 38, 91, 106, 109, 147

Bacon, Francis, 19

Baldwin, T. W., 169

Barish, Jonas, 46, 55, 69-70, 153-154, 177, 181, 183, 184, 187, 199

Barton, Anne, 151, 178, 203

Baum, Helena Watts, 183

Beaurline, L. A., 183, 184, 186, 202, 203

Bedford, Lucy Harington, Countess of, 6

Bolton, W. F., and Gardner, Jane F., 187-188

Braun, Richard, 201

Bryant, Joseph, 75, 188

Camden, William, 3, 117, 125

Campbell, O. J., 176-177

Career, ideas of, 10-11, 94-95, 105-106, 164, 172; Jonson's, 6-11, 17,
18-20, 29-30, 38, 44-45, 48-49, 57-59, 62-63, 67-68, 123, 132-134, 147-150, 151-167, 171, 176; Roman, 6, 9-11, 16, 112-113, 123-125, 179

Casaubon, Isaac, 3, 184

Catullus, 103, 117, 144

Champion, Larry, 203

Chapman, George, 4, 33

Characters, 21, 128, 175; and audience, 61, 146-150; Jonson's involvement with, 7, 11, 32, 67-68, 74, 76, 147-149, 163-164, 196-197; and psychology, 22-46, 77-87, 94-102, 114-115, 151, 153, 161-167, 199; servants, 7-8; women, 82-84

Charles I, 143

Christianity, 20, 177; Augustinian, 78-80, 94, 115; and fortune, 14, 142; and Roman philosophy, 129-130, 188-189

Cicero, 3, 19, 30, 169, 178; on comedy, 47-48, 62, 82, 181-182; on community life and public service, 10, 11, 82, 113-114, 115, 126, 127, 128, 129, 136-138, 141, 194-195; on death and immortality, 27, 119, 121, 136, 170, 176, 195, 197; on decorum, 65, 88, 180, 185, 201; on fame, 136, 140; on fortune, 14, 16; and friendship, 115, 116, 117, 118, 119, 121, 126, 127, 138-139, 197; life of, 9, 10-11, 42, 75, 123, 172, 179; on myths, 89-90, 91; on passion, 82, 92-94, 98-99, 190; on philosophy, 5, 42-43, 139, 170, 173, 190, 195; on psychol-

INDEX

Metamorphosis, 77, 88-92, 96, 107-
109, 156
Middleton, Thomas, 83
Milton, John, 4, 79, 80
Mimesis. *See* Imitation
Miner, Earl, 126, 169, 194, 197
Minturno, Antonio, 48, 182
Morality, and Jonson's art, 29-35,
37-40, 45-46, 47-62, 65-76, 82-
88, 95-102, 107-110, 127-128,
132-135, 139-141, 144-150, 177-
178, 183-184, 187
More, Thomas, 19, 171, 183
Moseley, Humphrey, 201

Nagel, Thomas, 195
Nero, 10, 37, 141, 201
Newton, Richard, 194
Nondramatic poetry: Jonson's, 19,
67, 100-101, 103-104, 111, 117,
131-132, 141, 143-146, 169, 193-
194; late poetry, 151-152, 157-
158, 192, 204

Oikeiosis, 194-195
Oldham, John, 22
Opportunism, 37-39, 44-46, 60-62,
67-68, 73-76
Orgel, Stephen, 179, 192, 193
Ornstein, Robert, 200
Ovid, 4, 70, 71, 89-91, 116, 117,
165, 186; and exile, 10; Jonson's
portrayal of, 91-92

Panegyric, 43, 65-66, 100-101, 103,
144
Parfitt, George, 183
Parody, 36, 49-52, 101, 128, 151-
152, 182, 203
Parthenio, Bernardino, 181
Partridge, E., 183, 187, 203
Patronage, 6-11, 57-58, 66, 141,
143, 172
Patterson, Annabel, 170

Peacham, Henry, 10
Pearlman, E., 99, 190
Pembroke, S. G., 194-195
Pembroke, William Herbert, Earl
of, 6, 141
Pepys, Samuel, 57, 184-185
Peripatetics, 5, 15, 53, 190, 194
Persius, 85, 86, 88, 169, 203
Peterson, Richard, 19, 169, 170,
185
Petrarch, 3, 79, 80, 179
Petronius, 203
Philosophy: Christian use of Ro-
man, 188-189; and medicine, 23-
24, 130; and poetry, 139-140,
192-193; and oratory, 180, 202;
Roman moralists and, 5-6, 11,
15-16, 42-46, 78-82, 114-115,
126, 170-171, 173, 179, 189, 194,
199. *See also* Epicureans; Peripatetics; Stoicism
Plato, 4, 48, 78-80, 89, 92, 93, 115,
116-117, 166, 167, 188-189, 196;
Apology, 62; *Phaedrus,* 196; *Symposium,* 78, 80, 94, 97, 113, 165,
196
Plautus, 30, 150
Pleasure: and poetry, 47-49, 52-59,
62-64, 66, 70-73, 132, 176; and
virtue, 16, 25, 27-28, 37, 45-46,
52-57
Pliny the Younger, 136, 169
Plot, 21, 23, 34-38, 45, 54-57, 77-
78, 88, 91-92, 100-101, 112, 151-
153, 161-162, 164; denouements,
37-38, 96, 126-129, 132-134, 147-
149, 154, 177-178, 187, 198-199
Plutarch, 188, 196
Poetry: and judgment, 134-135,
200-201; and kings, 40; and philosophy, 139-140, 192-193; process of composition, 11-14, 142,
172; and society, 105-106, 111-
113, 134-150; and the visual arts,

210

LIBRARY OF CONGRESS CATALOGING IN PUBLICATION DATA

Maus, Katharine Eisaman, 1955-
Ben Jonson and the Roman frame of mind.

Includes index.
1. Jonson, Ben, 1573?-1637—Knowledge—Rome.
2. Jonson, Ben, 1573?-1637—Knowledge—Literature.
3. English literature—Roman influences. 4. Neoclassicism.
5. Latin literature—History and criticism.
6. Literature, Comparative—English and Latin.
7. Literature, Comparative—Latin and English. I. Title.
PR2642.R65M37 1985   822'.3   84-17691
ISBN 0-691-06629-9 (alk. paper)